Practical Guide to Software Quality Management

Second Edition

For a listing of recent titles in the *Artech House Computing Library,* turn to the back of this book.

Practical Guide to Software Quality Management

Second Edition

John W. Horch

Artech House
Boston • London
www.artechhouse.com

Library of Congress Cataloging-in-Publication Data

A catalog record of this book is available from the Library of Congress.

British Library Cataloguing in Publication Data
Horch, John W.
   Practical guide to software quality management.—2nd ed.—(Artech House computing library)
   1. Software engineering—Quality control
   I. Title
   005.1'0685

   ISBN   1-58053-527-5

Cover design by Igor Valdman

International Standard Book Number: 1-58053-527-5

10 9 8 7 6 5 4 3 2 1

Contents

Preface

This book is intended to suggest and explore the various aspects of a total software quality system. It identifies the 10 basic elements of the software quality system and shows how each fits into the total picture of software quality management.

The subject matter is presented at a high level and is suitable for managers and engineers as an introduction to a software quality program. The audience for this book includes those who have been charged with the responsibility of creating and implementing a total software quality system in their organization. It also will be of use to those who need an overview of a total software quality framework. Individuals who have some parts of a system in place, such as a configuration management system or a standards program, and want to go forth with a full software quality effort also will find this text of interest.

The book delineates the elements of a total software quality system, explains briefly what comprises each element, and discusses the role of the software quality practitioner with respect to each element. It shows how the full set of elements interacts and how to integrate the elements to form the whole software quality system.

Introduction

This book is intended as a primer for those who need to understand the concepts and value of software quality management. It is not intended to be the "cutting edge of technology" reference for the experienced software quality practitioner. It is a description of what the 10 major software quality elements are and how they combine to form a solid software quality program. It is not the definitive text on how to accomplish all the software quality tasks available today.

The implementation of a software quality system is heavily dependent on the organization and its software work. The sample software quality system plan provided in Appendix B covers all 10 of the basic elements and should prove sufficient for most organizations. Those being audited for compliance with an ISO 9000 standard, or one of the several process maturity or process improvement models, may need to augment the sample plan to address organization-specific issues.

The basic elements of the quality system apply to any software development or maintenance. Small organizations will use these elements but, to a degree, commensurate them with their needs. Large organizations will also use these elements but will find that their application is more sophisticated and elaborate. Further, organizations, large or small, that are involved in the most current techniques and applications such as client-server, graphical user interfaces (GUIs), distributed processing, and the like will find the need to extend these elements beyond the basics given here. Similarly, organizations using advanced development methodologies such as information engineering, object-oriented techniques, mathematical proofs of correctness, and so on will use these quality system elements, but, again, will implement them in more sophisticated ways than organizations that are more traditionally oriented.

So, then, why should you read this book? Well, perhaps your situati parallels one of the following scenarios:

- You have done a good job testing the last few projects and your b promotes you to software quality manager. Corporate headquarte has decided that all software projects will be subject to quality ma agement and, as the director of information services, you are implement a software quality program.

- The chair of the ISO 9000 certification project has informed you th you are to bring the software area into line with the quality manag ment precepts of ISO 9001.

- An assessment of the software development organization, against t Software Engineering Institute's (SEI) Capability Maturity Model Int grated (CMMI), shows your organization to be at level one, and as vi president of management information systems, you are to take acti to raise that level.

- You are a senior systems analyst, and the head of software quali wants you to learn more about software quality and how you c effect and affect it.

All of these, and many others, are good reasons to start your quality sy tem understanding with this book. There are no magic solutions in th book. As previously stated, its goal is to provide insight into software quali systems. There are many other books available that will assist you in th application of each specific element in this text. If you are a tester, there a excellent texts on all sorts of testing concerns and applications. As a disast recovery manager, you can find much material that will tell you how to pr pare for and recover from disasters.

Each chapter contains two final sections, "The next step" and "Add tional reading." "The next step" includes one or two texts that I believe to sources of material for the where-do-we-go-from-here question. "Add tional reading" includes texts generally applicable to the software quali elements discussed in each section. The inclusion of these titles does n infer an endorsement of them nor a negative endorsement of those n included. As everyone knows who has ever visited the computer section of leading bookseller, there are far too many books to list in an introducto volume such as this one. The reader will note that a few of the "Addition reading" texts are from outside the United States. This may constitute a endorsement of sorts. I believe these to be of sufficient value as to warra the extra effort it may take to acquire them. The rest of the books listed are those that I have found beneficial.

The order of the chapters in this volume is, perhaps, an indication of the relative importance I attach to the 10 elements of a software quality program. It must be stated, though, that I recognize that this is almost certainly not the order in which you will implement, or have implemented, whatever software quality activities you are undertaking. I suspect that virtually all organizations do some sort of testing, conduct reviews, have some standards in place, and so on.

I would like you to use the order of the chapters as an agenda for your evaluation of your software quality program and its improvement.

Chapter 1 introduces my view of the content of a beneficial, and intentional, software quality system. Chapters 2 through 9 present discussions of each of the elements of the quality system, their areas of interest or application, and why they are important in a software quality system.

Chapter 10 could have been the first as well as the tenth. No project is complete without the documentation that defines its purpose and direction and describes its approach and progress. The documentation itself may be considered to be outside the purview of a quality system. It is, however, the basis for the vast majority of the quality system. A popular misconception is that the product of software development is the code, the whole code, and nothing but the code. Code is merely one of the documents that are the ongoing and sequential set of software development products. As anyone involved in a dispute over the terms of an agreement will tell you, if it isn't written, it isn't! The importance of documentation cannot be overemphasized. Its inclusion in a book on quality is part of that emphasis.

Chapter 11 considers the implications and concerns surrounding the actual implementation of the software quality system. Again, this text is not a step-by-step, how-to-implement-quality-management cookbook. This chapter, then, presents a discussion of things to remember when planning the introduction or improvement of the quality system.

As an added emphasis of the importance of documentation, a set of appendixes is included. These appendixes contain examples or starting-point outlines for some of the documentation discussed in the rest of the text. Many of the outlines are taken from, or based on, IEEE standards that address the specific topic. (Appendixes A, D, G, and H have been reprinted with permission from applicable IEEE standards. Full citations accompany each appendix.)

Appendix J, "Sample software quality charter," was contributed by an organization that requested anonymity. The charter is, though, the charter in place in that organization.

Contents

The Elements of a Complete Software Quality System

Starting a software quality program from scratch is time consuming and a task often doomed to failure before it is begun. Inadequate preparation, misused terms, lack of planning, and failure to recognize the roles of all individuals in the organization are only a few of the pitfalls waiting for the overanxious practitioner.

As stated in the Introduction, this is a what-to book. It is intended to serve as an introduction to the concepts involved in software quality systems and to suggest how the system's parts may be implemented. This chapter introduces some software quality terms, the basic elements of the software quality system, and a few important additional concerns. The balance of the book elaborates on each of the elements and concerns and discusses implementation of the overall software quality system.

1.1 Definitions

This text uses several terms that are granted many meanings throughout the computing and, in particular, the software industry. In this text, certain of these variably defined terms are used as defined in this section. Where available and appropriate, previously published definitions are used and their sources identified.

1

Activity: A task or body of effort directed at the accomplishment of a objective or the production of all or part of a product.

Anomaly: Any deviation from expected results or behavior.

Arithmetic defect: A software flaw in a mathematical computation.

Audit: "An activity to determine through investigation the adequacy o and adherence to, established procedures, instructions, specifications, code and standards or other applicable contractual and licensing requirement and the effectiveness of implementation" (ANSI N45.2.10-1973).

Client: That person or organization that causes the product to be deve oped or maintained. The client is often the customer.

Component: A general term for a portion of a product. A componer could be a chapter of a document or a unit or module of software. A compc nent may include the entire product.

Consumer: That person or organization that acquires a software proc uct. The consumer may be either the customer or the user.

Control Defect: A software flaw in a decision process.

Customer: That person or organization that pays for the product.

Defect: A flaw in the product resulting from the commission of an error

Element: *See* Unit.

Entity: Part of the overall company organization (e.g., software qualit group, development group).

Error: A mistake made by a person resulting in a defect in the produc

Failure: The experienced manifestation of a defect being encountered i the product.

Fault: *See* Defect.

Guideline: A preferred practice or procedure that is encouraged, but nc enforced, throughout the organization.

Input/Output defect: A software flaw in the process of passing infor mation into or out of the software element.

Inspection: "A formal evaluation technique in which software require ments, design, or code is examined in detail by a person or group other tha the author to detect faults, violations of development standards, and other problems" (IEEE Standard 100–1996).

ISO 9000, et al.:   International quality system standards published by the International Organization for Standardization (ISO). Intended to be used as the international definition of quality systems to be applied by producers or suppliers. Certification of an organization to ISO 9001 attests that the organization has a documented quality system and has evidence of its application.

Item: *See* Component.

Module: A group of units that together perform some convenient individual function or subfunction within the software system.

One-on-one review: The most informal examination, by a coworker of the producer, usually of a small portion of a product.

Peer review: A review of a product by peers of the producer. In some literature, the term *peer review* is used to mean any of the informal reviews.

Phase: Any of several convenient divisions of the software life cycle. These may typically include: concept development, requirements, design, coding, test, installation and acceptance, operation and maintenance, and retirement. Phases may or may not be sequential.

Process: The group of activities and procedures by which a producer develops or maintains a product.

Producer: The person or organization that, following a process, develops or maintains a product.

Product(s):   The final, or intermediate, output(s) from any given phase of the software life cycle. These usually include specifications, code, test results, and so on.

Program: "A schedule or plan that specifies actions to be taken" (IEEE Standard 100–1992).

Quality: Compliance of a product with the expectations of the user, based on the product's requirements.

Quality assurance: The set of activities intended to detect, document, analyze, and correct process defects and to manage process changes.

Quality assurance practitioner: A person whose task is to perform one or more of the quality assurance functions or activities comprising the quality system.

Quality control: The set of activities intended to detect, document, analyze, and correct product defects and to manage product changes.

Quality control practitioner: A person whose task is to perform one or more of the quality control functions or activities comprising the quality system.

(Software) quality groups: The organizational entity responsible for monitoring and reporting the performance of the (software) product development functions and activities.

Quality management: The empowering, and encouraging, of the producer to identify and submit improvements to the product development process.

Quality practitioner: A person whose task is to perform one or more of the functions or activities comprising the quality system. The quality practitioner may or may not be assigned to a (software) quality group. This includes both quality assurance and quality control practitioners.

(Software) quality systems: The total set of quality control, quality assurance, and quality management activities dedicated to the provision of quality products.

Requirement: "A condition of capability that must be met or possessed by a system or system component to satisfy a contract, standard, specification, or other formally imposed documents" (IEEE Standard 100–1996).

Review: A formal or informal meeting at which an output (product or component) of the software development life cycle is presented to the customer, user, or other interested parties for examination, evaluation, and approval.

SEI CMM: A five-level model of an organization's software process maturity, called the Capability Maturity Model (CMM), developed by the Software Engineering Institute (SEI).

Software: Computer programs, procedures, and possibly associated documentation and data pertaining to the operation of a computer system.

Software development life cycle: The portion of the software life cycle devoted to the actual creation of the software system, generally beginning with the requirements generation and ending with the installation of the software system into active production.

Software life cycle: The entire period during which a software system is active, beginning with its initial conceptual development and ending with its removal from active use and its archiving.

Software system: A total, integrated aggregation of software components that performs the set of specific functions as defined by its approved requirements.

Standard: A practice or procedure that is imposed and enforced throughout the organization.

Subsystem: A group of modules that together perform one of the major functions of the software system.

Supplier: The person or organization that provides the product.

Total quality: The culture that maximizes the likelihood that a product conforms to its requirements on an ongoing basis.

Total quality system: The set of activities required to provide decision-making, action-capable management with the information it needs to affect the product development process beneficially.

Unit: "A software component that is not subdivided into other components" (IEEE Standard 610.12–1990). This is also known as the "smallest replaceable component" and sometimes called an element.

Unit development folder: The "diary" of the development of a software component. It usually contains the portion of the approved requirements being addressed by the component, the design and test information that applies, and any additional information applicable to the understanding of the development approach used for the component.

User: That person who actually performs his or her job functions with the assistance of the product.

Vendor: A person or organization that sells part or all of a product, usually for inclusion in a larger product being developed by a producer.

Walk-through: A review method in which a producer leads one or more other members of the development team through a product, or portion thereof, that he or she has developed, while the other members ask questions and make comments about technique, style, possible errors, violations of development standards, and other problems.

1.2   The elements of a software quality system

There are two goals of the software quality system (SQS). The first goal is build quality into the software from the beginning. This means assuring th the problem or need to be addressed is clearly and accurately stated, ar that the requirements for the solution are properly defined, expressed, ar understood. Nearly all the elements of the SQS are oriented toward requir ments validity and satisfaction.

In order for quality to be built into the software system from its ince tion, the software requirements must be clearly understood and doc mented. Until the actual requirements, and the needs of the user that th fulfill, are known and understood, there is little likelihood that the user w be satisfied with the software system that is delivered. Whether we kno them all before we start, or learn some of them as we go, all requiremen must be known and satisfied before we are through. Further discussion requirements is provided in Chapters 6 and 10.

The second goal of the SQS is to keep that quality in the softwa throughout the software life cycle (SLC). In this chapter, the 10 elements the SQS are introduced and their contributions to the two goals indicate

The 10 elements of the SQS are as follows:

1. Standards;
2. Reviewing;
3. Testing;
4. Defect analysis;
5. Configuration management (CM);
6. Security;
7. Education;
8. Vendor management;
9. Safety;
10. Risk management.

While each element can be shown to contribute to both goals, there a heavier relationships between some elements and one or the other of th two goals. These particular relationships will become obvious as each ele ment is discussed in the chapters that follow.

Every SLC model has divisions, or periods of effort, into which the wor of developing and using the software is divided. These divisions or perioc are given various names depending on the particular life-cycle paradign being applied. For this discussion, the following periods of effort, together with their common names, are defined:

- Recognition of a need or problem (e.g., concept definition);
- Definition of the software solution to be applied (e.g., requirements definition);
- Development of the software that solves the problem or satisfies the need (e.g., design and coding);
- Proving that the solution is correct (e.g., testing);
- Implementing the solution (e.g., installation and acceptance);
- Using the solution (e.g., operation);
- Improving the solution (e.g., maintenance);

Regardless of their names, each division represents a period of effort directed at a particular part of the overall life cycle. They may be of various lengths and be applied in various sequences, but they will all exist in successful projects. Some newer life-cycle models or approaches for small to medium-sized projects (e.g., extreme programming, the rational unified process, and agile development) appear to circumvent some of these efforts. In reality, they merely reorder, reiterate, or resequence them.

There are also associations between certain elements and the various divisions or periods of the SLC. Again, most of the elements support most of the SLC, but certain elements are more closely associated with particular periods than with others.

Figure 1.1 displays the 10 elements as a cube supporting the goals of software quality and the periods of the SLC with which each element is most closely associated.

1.2.1 Standards

Software is becoming a science. The old days of free-form creativity in the development of software are gradually giving way to more controlled and scientific approaches. As some writers have said, "Software is moving from an arcane art to a visible science."

As implied by Figure 1.2, the standards manual can have inputs from many sources. Standards are intended to provide consistent, rigorous, uniform, and enforceable methods for software development and operation activities. The development of standards, whether by professional societies such as the Institute of Electrical and Electronics Engineers (IEEE), international groups such as International Organization for Standardization/

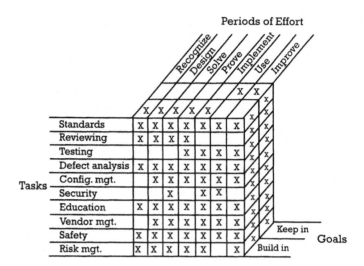

Figure 1.1 Quality tasks, life-cycle periods, and goals.

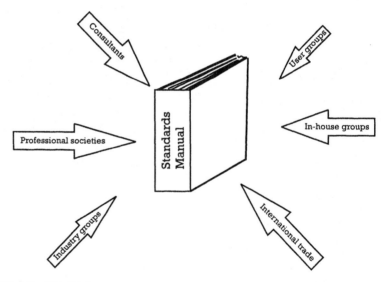

Figure 1.2 Standards sources.

International Electrotechnical Commission Joint Technical Committee On
(ISO/IEC JTC1), industry groups, or software development organizations fo
themselves, is recognizing and furthering that movement.

Standards cover all aspects of the SLC, including the very definition c
the SLC itself. More, probably, than any of the other elements, standard

can govern every phase of the life cycle. Standards can describe considerations to be covered during the concept exploration phase. They can also specify the format of the final report describing the retirement of a software system that is no longer in use.

Standards come into being for many reasons. They might document experience gained in the day-to-day running of a computer center, and the most efficient methods to be used. Laws and government regulations often impose standard procedures on business and industry. Industries can band together to standardize interfaces between their products such as in the communications areas. Contracts often specify standard methods of performance. And, in many cases, standards arise out of good common sense.

Whether a standard comes from within a company, is imposed by government, or is adopted from an industry source, it must have several characteristics. These include the following:

- *Necessity.* No standard will be observed for long if there is no real reason for its existence.
- *Feasibility.* Common sense tells us that if it is not possible to comply with the tenets of a standard, then it will be ignored.
- *Measurability.* It must be possible to demonstrate that the standard is being followed.

Each of these characteristics supports the total enforceability of the standard. An unenforceable standard is of no use to anyone.

Software standards should be imposed so that the producer of a software product or component can pay attention to the technical aspects of the task, rather than to the routine aspects that may be the same for every task. Standards, such as those for document formats, permit the producer to concentrate on technical issues and content rather than format or layout details.

Standards, while worthwhile, are less than fully effective if they are not supported by policies that clearly indicate their imposition. It should be the intent of responsible management to see that they are followed and enforced. Specific practices for standard implementation are often useful. In this way, adherence to the standard may be more uniform.

Lastly, not everything must be standardized. Guidelines that call out the preferred methods or approaches to many things are fully adequate. A set of standards that covers every minute aspect of an organization's activity can lose respect simply from its own magnitude. Competent and comprehensive guidelines give each person some degree of freedom in those areas where specific methods or approaches are not absolutely necessary. This leaves the

standards to govern those areas where a single, particular way of doing bu
ness is required.

1.2.2 Reviewing

Reviews permit ongoing visibility into the software development and inst
lation activities.

Product reviews, also called technical reviews, are formal or inform
examinations of products and components throughout the developme
phases of the life cycle. They are conducted throughout the softwa
development life cycle (SDLC). Informal reviews generally occur duri
SDLC phases, while formal reviews usually mark the ends of the phase
Figure 1.3 illustrates this point.

Informal reviews include walk-throughs and inspections. Wal
throughs are informal, but scheduled, reviews, usually conducted in and
peer groups. The author of the subject component—a design specificatio
test procedure, coded unit, or the like—walks through his or her comp
nent, explaining it to a small group of peers. The role of the peers is to lo
for defects in or problems with the component. These are then correcte
before the component becomes the basis for further development.

Inspections are a more structured type of walk-through. Though t
basic goal of an inspection—removal of defects—is the same as that of t

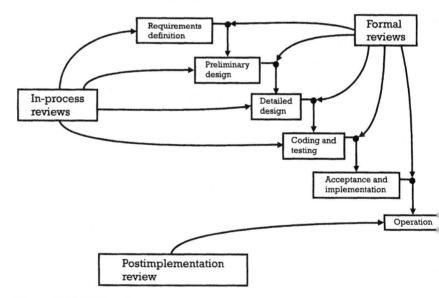

Figure 1.3 SDLC reviews.

walk-through, the format of the meeting and the roles of the participants are more strictly defined, and more formal records of the proceedings are prepared.

Process reviews may be held at any time. The purpose of a process review is to examine the success of the software process in effect. Data for the review is collected in the technical reviews and is usually based on defects identified by the technical reviews. Opportunities for improvements to the current process are sought. Management reviews are specialized process reviews, done on behalf of senior management, to examine project status and effective use of resources based on the current process.

Also included within the quality control activity of reviewing are audits. Audits are examinations of components for compliance with a content and format specification or for consistency with or comparison to a predecessor. An in-process audit of the unit development folder (UDF)—also called the software development file in some organizations—is usually informal. It compares the content and status of the UDF against standards governing the preparation and maintenance of the UDF. Its goal is to ascertain the UDFs are being used as required.

The physical audit (PA), often included as a part of the CM process, is an example of a formal audit. It compares the final form of the code against the final documentation for that code. The goal of the physical audit is to assure that the two products, documentation and code, are in agreement before being released to the user or customer. Another formal audit is the functional audit. The functional audit (FA), again often a CM responsibility, compares the test results with the currently approved requirements to assure that all requirements have been satisfied.

1.2.3 Testing

Tests provide increasing confidence and, ultimately, a demonstration that the software requirements are being satisfied. Test activities include planning, design, execution, and reporting. Figure 1.4 presents a simple conceptual view of the testing process. The basic test process is the same, whether it is applied to system testing or to the earliest module testing.

Test planning begins during the requirements phase and parallels the requirements development. As each requirement is generated, the corresponding method of test for that requirement should be a consideration. A requirement is faulty if it is not testable. By starting test planning with the requirements, nontestability is often avoided. In the same manner that requirements evolve and change throughout the software development, so,

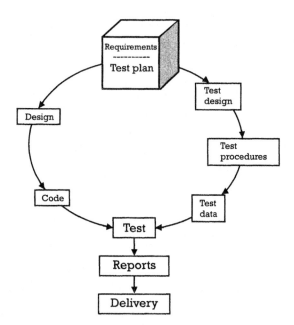

Figure 1.4   Simplified test process.

too, do the test plans evolve and change. This emphasizes the need for earl
and continuing, CM of the requirements and test plans.

Test design begins as the software design begins. Here, as before, a para
lel effort with the software development is appropriate. As the design of th
software takes form, the test cases, scenarios, and data are developed th.
will exercise the designed software. Each test case also will include speci
expected results so that a pass-fail criterion is established. As each requir
ment must be measurable and testable, so must each test be measurable.
test whose completion is not definitive tells little about the subject of th
test. Expected results give the basis against which the success or failure
the test is measured.

Actual testing begins with the debugging and early unit and module tes
conducted by the programmer. These tests are usually informally docu
mented (perhaps by notations in the UDF) and are not closely monitored b
the software quality practitioner since they are frequently experimental an
meant to help the programmer in his or her day-to-day software generatio
Formal test execution generally begins with integration tests in which mo
ules are combined into subsystems for functional testing. In larger system
it is frequently advisable to begin formal testing at the module level after th

programmer has completed his or her testing and is satisfied that the module is ready for formal testing.

An important aspect of complete testing is user acceptance testing. In these, usually last, tests, the concentration is on actual, delivered functionality and usability in the user's environment.

Test execution requires the use of detailed test procedures. These are step-by-step directions that tell the test conductor exactly what to do as the test is run. Every action, input, expected output, and response should be documented so that the test conductor is not put into the position of making test design decisions while the test is being run. Preparation of the test procedures is begun during the design phase and completed during the coding and debugging activities. By the time the coding phase is complete, all preparations for the formal testing activities should also be in place. Test cases, scenarios, data, and procedures, together with expected results and completion criteria, should be ready to be applied from module testing (if included on the particular project) through qualification and acceptance tests.

Test reports document the actual results of the testing effort as it progresses. For each test that is run, a report of the expected results, actual results, and the conclusions of the test conductor concerning success of the test should be prepared. Included in the report are the anomalies that were found and recommended action with respect to them. Errors, defects, faults, questionable or unexpected results, and any other nonpredicted outcomes are recorded and assigned for action. Once the anomaly has been addressed, the test, or an appropriate portion thereof, will be rerun to show that the defect has been corrected. As the tests progress, so do the levels of detail of the test reports, until the final acceptance test report is prepared that documents the fitness of the software system for use in its intended environment.

1.2.4 Defect analysis

Defect analysis is the combination of defect detection and correction, and defect trend analysis. Defect detection and correction, together with change control, presents a record of all discrepancies found in each software component. It also records the disposition of each discrepancy, perhaps in the form of a software problem report or software change request.

As shown in Figure 1.5, each needed modification to a software component, whether found through a walk-through, review, test, audit, operation, or other means is reported, corrected, and formally closed. A problem or requested change may be submitted by anyone with an interest in the

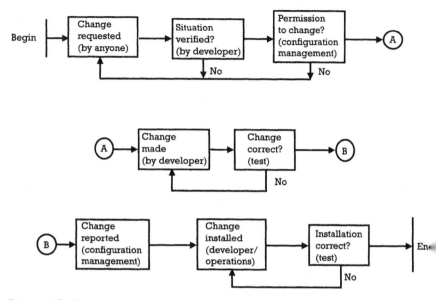

Figure 1.5 Typical change procedure.

software. The situation will be verified by the developers, and the CM activ
ity will agree to the change. Verification of the situation is to assure that th
problem or need for the change actually exists. CM may wish to withhol
permission for the change or delay it until a later time; perhaps because c
concerns such as interference with other software, schedule and budge
considerations, the customer's desires, and so on. Once the change is com
pleted and tested, it will be reported by CM to all concerned parties, installe
into the operational software by the developers or operations staff, an
tested for functionality and compatibility in the full environment.

This procedure is required for the ongoing project to make sure that a
defects found are properly fixed and closed. It also serves future projects b
providing a means for feeding defect information back into the developmen
life cycle and modifying the software development process so that futur
occurrences of certain defects are reduced. Figure 1.6 places the chang
procedure into the larger picture of development process analysis an
improvement.

A running record of defects, their solutions, and status is provided by th
defect trend analysis effort. (The actual changes are made according to th
configuration control process.) As previously mentioned, the record o
defects and their solutions can serve to do the following:

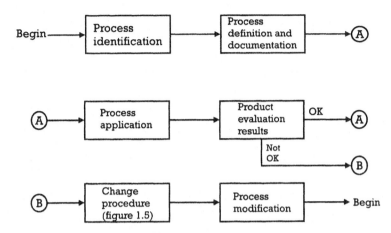

Figure 1.6 Development process improvement.

- Prevent defects from remaining unsolved for inappropriate lengths of time;
- Prevent unwarranted changes;
- Point out inherently weak areas in the software;
- Provide analysis data for development process evaluation and correction;
- Provide warnings of potential defects through analysis of defect trends.

Formal recording and closure procedures applied to defects are insufficient if corresponding reports are not generated so that project management has visibility into the progress and status of the project. Regular reports of defect detection and correction activity keep management apprised of current defect areas and can warn of potential future trouble spots. Further, analysis of ongoing defect and change reports and activities provide valuable insight into the software development process and enhance the software quality practitioner's ability to suggest error-avoidance and software development process modification.

1.2.5 Configuration management

CM is a three-fold discipline. Its intent is to maintain control of the software, both during development and after it is put into use and changes begin.

As shown in Figure 1.7, CM is, in fact, three related activities: identific
tion, control, and accounting. If the physical and functional audits a
included as CM responsibilities, there are four activities. Each of the acti
ties has a distinct role to play. As system size grows, so does the scope a
importance of each of the activities. In very small, or one-time use, system
CM may be minimal. As systems grow and become more complex, or
changes to the system become more important, each activity takes on
more definite role in the overall management of the software and its inte
rity. Further, some CM may be informal for the organization itself, to ke
track of how the development is proceeding and to maintain control
changes, while others will be more formal and be reported to the custom
or user.

Configuration identification is, as its name implies, the naming, a
documentation, of each component (document, unit, module, subsyste
and system) so that at any given time, the particular component of intere
can be uniquely identified. This is important when documenting, testin
changing, or delivering software to the customer; in other words, throug
out the entire SLC. Unless it is known which specific version or compone
of the software is being affected, (i.e., coded, changed, tested) the software
out of control. Tests may be run on the wrong version of the code, chang
may be made to an obsolete version of a document, or a system composed
the wrong versions of the various components may be delivered to the us
or customer.

Configuration control is that activity that prevents unauthorized chang
to any software product. Early in the SLC, documentation is the prima
product. Configuration control takes on an increasingly formal role as th
documents move from draft to final form. Once published, any changes
the documents are formally processed so that capricious, unnecessary,
unapproved changes are not made. As the life cycle moves into the co
ing, testing, and operation and maintenance phases, changes to eith

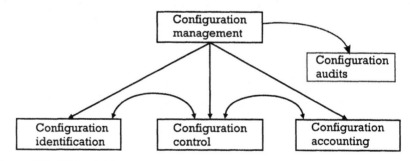

Figure 1.7 CM activities.

documents or code are closely controlled. Each change is verified for necessity and correctness before approval for insertion, so that control of the software can be maintained.

Configuration accounting keeps track of the status of each component. The latest version or update of each software component is recorded. Thus, when changes or other activities are necessary with respect to the component, the correct version of the component can be located and used. Each new edition of a document, each new assembly or compilation of the code, each new build of the software system is given a new specific identifier (through configuration identification) and recorded. All changes to that version or edition of a component are also referenced to it so that, if necessary, the history of activity with respect to any component can be recreated. This might be necessary in the loss of the current version or to return to a previous version for analysis or other purposes. Ultimately, the deliverable version, or build, of the software is created. Configuration accounting helps manage the builds and make the build process repeatable.

One last point should be made. That is, for very long term or long-lived systems, the development environment itself may need to be configuration managed. As operating systems, platforms, languages, and processes evolve over time, it may not be possible to recreate a given system without the original development environment and its components.

1.2.6 Security

Security activities are applied both to data and to the physical data center itself. These activities are intended to protect the usefulness of the software and its environment.

The highest quality software system is of no use if the data center in which it is to be used is damaged or destroyed. Such events as broken water pipes, fire, malicious damage by a disgruntled employee, and storm damage are among the most common causes of data center inoperability. Even more ominous is the rising incidence of terrorist attacks on certain industries and in various countries, including our own, around the world.

Another frequent damager of the quality of output of an otherwise high-quality software system is data that has been unknowingly modified. If the data on which the system is operating has been made inaccurate, whether intentionally or by accident, the results of the software will not be correct. To the user or customer, this appears to be inadequate software.

Additionally, though not really a software quality issue per se, is the question of theft of data. The security of stored or transmitted data is of paramount concern in most organizations. From the theft of millions of

dollars by interception of electronic funds transfers to an employee who ju
changes personnel or payroll records, data security is a major concern.

Finally, the recent onslaught of hackers and software attackers and tl
burgeoning occurrences of viruses also need to be considered. These threa
to software quality must be recognized and countered.

The role of the software quality practitioner is, again, not to be tl
policeperson of the data or to provide the data or data center security. Tl
software quality practitioner is responsible for alerting management to tl
absence, or apparent inadequacy, of security provisions in the software.
addition, the software quality practitioner must raise the issue of data cent
security and disaster recovery to management's attention.

1.2.7 Education

Education assures that the people involved with software development, ar
those people using the software once it is developed, are able to do their jol
correctly.

It is important to the quality of the software that the producers be edi
cated in the use of the various development tools at his or her disposal.
programmer charged with writing object-oriented software in C++ canno
perform well if the only language he or she knows is Visual Basic. It
necessary that the programmer be taught to use C++ before beginning tl
programming assignment. Likewise, the use of operating systems, da
modeling techniques, debugging tools, special workstations, and test too
must be taught before they can be applied beneficially.

The proper use of the software once it has been developed and put in
operation is another area requiring education. It this case, the actual sof
ware user must be taught proper operating procedures, data entry, repo
generation, and whatever else is involved in the effective use of the softwa
system's capabilities.

The data center personnel must be taught the proper operating proce
dures before the system is put into full operation. Loading and initializing
large system may not be a trivial task. Procedures for recovering fro
abnormal situations may be the responsibility of data center personnel. Eac
of the many facets of operating a software system must be clear so that tl
quality software system that has been developed may continue to provic
quality results.

The software quality practitioner is not usually the trainer or educato
These functions are normally filled by some other group or means. The rol
of the software quality practitioner is, as always, to keep management atter
tion focused on the needs surrounding the development and use of a qualit

software system. In this case, the software quality practitioner is expected to monitor the requirements for, and the provision of, the education of the personnel involved in the SLC.

Lastly, the support personnel surrounding software development must know their jobs. The educators, CM and software quality practitioners, security and database administrators, and so on must be competent to maintain an environment in which quality software can be built, used, and maintained.

1.2.8 Vendor management

When software is purchased, the buyer must be aware of, and take action to gain confidence in, its quality. Not all purchased software can be treated in the same way, as will be demonstrated here. Each type of purchased software will have its own software quality system approach, and each must be handled in a manner appropriate to the degree of control the purchaser has over the development process used by producer. The following are three basic types of purchased software: •

1. Off-the-shelf;
2. Tailored shell;
3. Contracted.

Off-the-shelf software is the package we buy at the store. Microsoft Office, Adobe Photoshop, virus checkers, and the like are examples. These packages come as they are with no warrantee that they will do what you need to have done. They are also almost totally outside the buyer's influence with respect to quality.

The second category may be called the tailored shell. In this case, a basic, existing framework is purchased and the vendor then adds specific capabilities as required by the contract. This is somewhat like buying a stripped version of a new car and then having the dealer add a stereo, sunroof, and other extras. The only real quality influence is over the custom-tailored portions.

The third category is contracted software. This is software that is contractually specified and provided by a third-party developer. In this case, the contract can also specify the software quality activities that the vendor must perform and which the buyer will audit. The software quality practitioner has the responsibility in each case to determine the optimum level of influence to be applied, and how that influence can be most effectively applied.

The purchaser's quality practitioners must work closely with the vendor quality practitioners to assure that all required steps are being taken.

Attention to vendor quality practices becomes extremely important when the developer is off-shore or remote, such as in India, Nepal, or another country.

1.2.9 Safety

As computers and software grow in importance and impact more and more of our lives, the safety of the devices becomes a major concern. The literature records overdoses of medicines, lethal doses of radiation, space flights gone astray, and other catastrophic and near-catastrophic events. Every software project must consciously consider the safety implications of the software and the system of which it is a part. The project management plan should include a paragraph describing the safety issues to be considered. appropriate, a software safety plan should be prepared.

1.2.10 Risk management

There are several types of risk associated with any software project. Risks range from the simple, such as the availability of trained personnel to undertake the project, to more threatening, such as improper implementation of complicated algorithms, to the deadly, such as failure to detect an alarm in a nuclear plant. Risk management includes identification of the risk; determining the probability, cost, or threat of the risk; and taking action to eliminate, reduce, or accept the risk. Risk and its treatment is necessary topic in the project plan and may deserve its own risk management plan.

1.3 Additional issues

Several other issues can, and will, impact the scope and authority of the software quality system. These include maintaining the software once it is in operation, documenting the software's development and configuration deciding where to place the software quality practitioners within the overall organization, and the concerns of implementing the quality system.

1.3.1 Maintenance

Software maintenance can best be viewed and treated as an extension or repetition of the development process.

Software maintenance includes two primary activities: correction of defects that were not found during development and testing, and enhancement of the software to meet new or changed requirements after installation. As suggested in Figure 1.8, each maintenance action or project is treated in much the same way as original development, and the parallels with the SDLC can be seen. The maintenance process begins with identifying the need for a change. The occurrence of a failure due to a previously unencountered defect will trigger a change. New requirements may come from user requests; the need for increased throughput in the data center; a change in processing technology, such as moving from mainframes to a client-server approach; or just the desire to reengineer old legacy code.

Whatever the reason for the change, effort is expended to determine exactly what will be needed (concept definition and requirements specification); how the change will be affected (design); the actual creation of the new or modified software (code and unit test); and the testing, approval, and installation of the change (integration, testing, and installation). Thus, in almost all cases (there are exceptions to most rules), maintenance can be seen primarily as a return to the regular SDLC activities, though usually on a smaller scale.

It is important to note the need for rigorous CM during the maintenance phase. Especially during periods of rapid change, such as might be found during the modification of software to address new government regulations, or the introduction of a new weapon system in a combat vehicle, there is

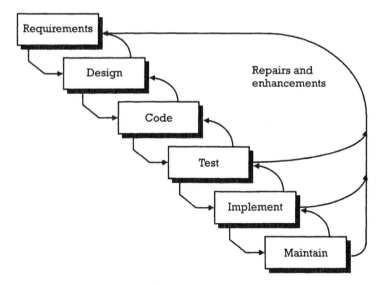

Figure 1.8 Recycling the life cycle.

significant danger of making changes to the wrong version of a module subsystem. If multiple changes are being made simultaneously, as is oft the case, one change may unknowingly affect another. In today's world the Internet, World Wide Web, and e-commerce, changes are not only ne essarily very rapid but also very visible. Errors may be seen or experienc by hundreds or even thousands of on-line users in the space of a short tim

CM must be part and parcel of changes in this environment, and t software quality practitioner must take an aggressive role in confirming th all CM procedures are being followed. This is in addition to the softwa quality practitioner's regular monitoring role in all software developme activities, whether original development or maintenance.

1.3.2 Documentation

The purpose of documentation is to record what is required of the softwar how it is to be accomplished, proof that it was provided, and how to use ar maintain it. The role of the software quality practitioner is to monitor th documentation activities and keep management apprised of their status ar quality.

It is like the old adage, if you don't know where you're going, any roa will take you there (but it doesn't matter, because you won't realize th you've arrived, anyway). Without adequate documentation, the task hand is never accurately specified. What is really wanted is not made clea The starting and ending points are poorly specified, and no one is sure whe the project is complete. Inadequate documentation is like not knowir where you are going. The system designers are not sure what the custome or user really wants, the programmer is not sure what the designer intend and the tester is not sure what to look for. Finally, the customer or user not sure that they got what they wanted in the first place.

The depth of the documentation depends on the scope of the specif project. Small projects can be successful with reduced documentatio requirements. But, as the size of the project increases, the need for mor complete documentation also increases. In the case of small or uncompl cated projects, the information contained in some documents can be pro vided in higher-level documents. As system size increases, addition documents may be needed to adequately cover such topics as interfaces an data design. More comprehensive test documentation will also be require such as specific test plans, cases, and reports.

Too much documentation can be as bad as too little. Overdocumentatio can induce a user to say, "I'm not going to read all that!" The time sper documenting a project is wasted if the documentation does not add to th required body of knowledge about the project. Overdocumentation can introduce inconsistencies, conflicting information, and other kinds of defects that detract from performance in the long run.

Documentation should be sufficient to accurately and completely tell what to do (concept and requirements), how to do it (plan and design), how to show that it was done (test), and how to use the system (user). The software quality practitioner monitors and reviews the documentation to see that it satisfies this need.

1.3.3 Organizational considerations

The placement of the software quality practitioner or group within the organization is a critical factor in its effectiveness.

While there are several acceptable structures, each dependent on the specific total business organization, there are certain conditions that must be observed to enable the SQS to be effective. Figure 1.9 depicts several possible organizational reporting arrangements. Each has its merits and faults, which will be explored in Chapter 11.

It is important to note that, in some companies, the SQS functions and activities may not be under the auspices of a formal software quality group at all. Remembering that the SQS functions are to be carried out by those parts of the organization best qualified to perform them, there are some companies that stop at that point and have various managers responsible for

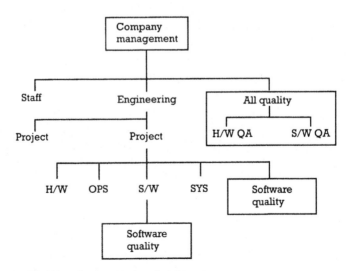

Figure 1.9 Traditional organizational styles.

individual SQS functions. This approach would seem to have some econ
mies connected with it, since there is not the cost of a dedicated staff just f
software quality. However, the coordination among the various responsit
managers may, in fact, be time-consuming enough to actually cost mo
than a software quality group. In addition, when a manager has an assig
ment such as the development of a new software system, and some ancilla
tasks such as documentation coordination, CM, training, security, or so
ware quality, the development task usually gets the bulk of the manage
attention, and other tasks may be given less attention or effort.

Software quality is, as has been said frequently, everyone's individu
responsibility. Each participant in the SLC is expected to do his or her j
correctly. Unfortunately, this is often an unachieved goal. Software quali
tasks, then, must be assigned to the group or individual who can, and w
be accountable for the assessment of, and reporting on, the quality of t
software throughout its life cycle.

1.3.4   Implementation of the total software quality system

Implementation of a software quality system requires a delegation
authority (a charter to perform the activities), cooperation of the organiz
tion (which is usually gained through demonstration of usefulness ov
time), and order (a logical progression of steps leading to the actual applic
tion and performance of the SQS activities).

No activity should be started until a formal charter of responsibilitie
accountabilities, and authority vested in the SQS is created and assigned
the software quality practitioner or group by management. This, howeve
only creates the SQS. It does not establish the set of functions and activiti
that must be performed, nor the order in which they will be inaugurate
The software quality practitioners themselves must plan, design, and imple
ment the overall SQS.

The four major elements in a successful software quality system are th
quality culture of "do it right the first time," a quality charter that specifi
the responsibilities and authorities of each person with respect to quality,
software quality manual that details the various components of the organ
zation's SQS, and the SQS standards and procedures themselves. Table 1
shows how the various affected parts of the organization must contribute
the elements for the institution of an effective and acceptable SQS.

One very important aspect of the whole process is the continue
involvement of the development group from the very beginning. As eac
part of the SQS is conceived and planned, the quality charter establishe
the quality manual prepared, and the SQS implemented, the involvement

Table 1.1 Key Software Quality Roles

Senior Management	SQS Program Element	Technical Personnel
Insist upon	Culture	Input to
Commit to	Charter	Input to
Input to	Manual	Input to
Fully support	Total SQS	Cooperate with

the producers will help to assure their acceptance and cooperation. Their participation, from the beginning, reduces the elements of surprise and, sometimes, distrust on the part of those whose work is the subject of the software quality activities.

Management, too, must be kept fully apprised of the activities and progress of the implementation of the SQS. They have provided the initial impetus for the SQS with their insistence on the concept of an organizational culture based on quality. Next, they have started the process through their demonstrated commitment to the quality charter. Continued support for the effort depends on their continued belief that an SQS will be beneficial in the long run. By maintaining close contact with management during the startup period, potential future pitfalls can be recognized and avoided.

Finally, a logical implementation plan must be worked out and accepted by all affected groups and by management. The needs of the various groups and their priorities must be reflected in the actual implementation schedule.

In the final analysis, the startup of the SQS closely resembles the creation of a software system. Each part of the SDLC is paralleled and each must be carefully addressed. Most of all, however, all affected organizations should be a party to the planning, design, and implementation of the SQS.

1.4 Summary

A total software quality system is more than reviews, testing, or standards. It is the comprehensive application of a 10-element discipline. The role of the software quality function is to review the state of the software development process and its products and report that state to decision-making, action-capable management. It is not the role of the software quality function to manage, direct, or control the software development process.

The ultimate objective of the software quality system is to provide, based on the results of the 10 elements, information that will permit decision-making, action-capable management to beneficially affect the software development process.

While it is not an absolute necessity that the SQS functions be under the cognizance of a software quality organization, the accountability for the SQS functions becomes more visible and addressable if a software quality group does, in fact, exist. This group is not necessarily responsible for the actual performance of the SQS functions, but rather is responsible to alert management to the need for, and the efficacy of, those functions. The functions themselves are to be performed by the organizational entities most qualified to perform them (e.g., training by the training department, CM by the CM department, and so forth).

The software quality practitioner must be administratively and financially independent of the parts of the organization that it will monitor. This means at least on the same organizational level within a project or in a matrix management situation in which the SQS is administered by an organizational element completely outside the project organization.

In order that the software quality practitioners have the authority commensurate with their responsibilities and accountabilities, there should be a written charter from senior management that specifies the roles, objectives, and authority of the SQS and software quality practitioners. The preparation and approval of the charter will serve to get the commitment of senior management to whatever software quality system is finally implemented. Senior management commitment is a key requisite to the success, both near and long term, of the SQS. An SQS, and the software quality practitioners who execute it, are at high risk from political and financial variations within the organization without the formal commitment of senior management.

1.5   The next step

To delve deeper into the topic of software quality management, the following two texts might be of interest:

Shari Lawrence Pfleeger et al. *Solid Software*, Upper Saddle River, NJ: Prentice Hall, 2002.

Roger S. Pressman. *Software Engineering: A Practitioner's Approach*, New York: McGraw-Hill, 2001.

Additional reading

Boehm, B. W., *Software Engineering Economics*, Englewood Cliffs, NJ: Prentice Hall, 1981.

Cai, Kai-Yuan, *Handbook of Software Quality Assurance*, Englewood Cliffs, NJ: Prentice Hall, 1999.

Crosby, P. B., *Quality Is Free*, New York: McGraw-Hill, 1979.

Ginac, Frank P., *Customer-Oriented Software Quality Assurance*, Englewood Cliffs, NJ: Prentice Hall, 2000.

Humphrey, Watts S., *Managing the Software Development Process*, Reading, MA: Addison-Wesley, 1989.

Mai, Masaaki, *Kaisen—The Key to Japan's Competitive Success*, New York: Random House, 1996.

Schulmeyer, G. Gordon, and James I. McManus (eds.), *Handbook of Software Quality Assurance, Third Edition*, Englewood Cliffs, NJ: Prentice Hall, 1999.

Walton, Mary, *The Deming Management Method*, New York: Putnam, 1986.

CHAPTER

2

Contents

Standards

Standards are the keystone of an SQS. They provide the basis against which activities can be measured and evaluated. Further, they provide common methods and practices so that the same task can be accomplished the same way each time it is done.

Standards applied to software development provide uniform direction on how the development is to be conducted. Standards also apply to the balance of the SLC. They may prescribe everything from the form on which an original system concept is submitted for consideration to the location in the computer center for four-ply printer paper storage. The degree of standardization is, of course, a company decision. It is important, however, that the development portion of the SLC be standardized as much as is practical. Through the use of intelligent standards, productivity increases can be had, since many mundane decisions need not be made every time a software system is undertaken.

Standards arise from many sources. They may come from the day-to-day activities within the organization, as a "best way to do it" surfaces in some area. An example of this might be the method by which access to the interactive software development facility is allocated. Companies within a given industry often band together to set standards so that their products can be used together or so that information passing between them means the same thing to everyone (e.g., the telephone industry standards for interconnection). Computer user groups and computer-industry associations often work on standards dealing with software development. A subgroup of

29

the IEEE, the Software Engineering Standards Committee, develops sta
dards dealing with software development. These standards deal with top
ranging from the SLC as a whole down through individual activities with
the life cycle, such as testing and documentation. Still another source
standards is outside consulting firms that can be retained to study an inc
vidual company's specific situation and develop a set of standards especia
tailored to that company's needs.

More and more organizations are recognizing the importance of stab
identified processes and their relationship to the overall direction of t
organization. Standards play an important role in the development, mai
tenance, and execution of organizational mission statements, policies, a
process procedures. External standards often define or limit the breadth
an organization's freedom in the conduct of its business. Internal standar
define the organization's own performance expectations and requiremen
Definition of processes is often in the context of standards. These are all su
ject to evaluation during process reviews.

Standards are one of the yardsticks against which the processes of so
ware development and usage can be evaluated. Deviation from the vario
applicable standards is an indication that the software development proce
is veering away from the production of quality software.

2.1   Areas of standardization

Standardization may be applied to any or all of the areas of software deve
opment and maintenance. Such broad use of standards is rarely the case ar
usually not appropriate. Areas that are usually involved in the standardiz
tion effort include, but are by no means limited, to the following:

- SLC;
- Documentation;
- Coding;
- Naming;
- Operating procedures and protocols;
- User development.

2.1.1   The software life cycle

The SLC describes the whole software process from conception throug
retirement of a given system. Two life cycles are used in discussing softwar

The overall SLC for a system, an example of which is shown in Figure 2.1, begins with the original idea for the software system, or its conception, and the evaluation of that concept for necessity and feasibility. The life cycle ends when the software system is retired from use and set aside. Figure 2.1 also shows that, within the full life cycle, there is the SDLC. This is the portion of the overall SLC that deals expressly with the development of the software system. It begins with the formation of the formal requirements documentation, which states specifically what the system will do, and ends with the implementation of the system into full use. Clearly, there are other software development paradigms; the example shown is only an example of one that is commonly used.

The SLC, and thus the SDLC, is usually divided into portions of work or effort called phases. In the life of a software system, many functions or activities are performed. These activities are grouped into phases so that they can be conveniently referenced, monitored, and managed. In Figure 2.1, the SLC is divided into six major phases, plus the effort required to retire a system at the end of its useful life. The SDLC is composed of the middle four major phases. In any particular organization, the various activities may be grouped differently, or the phases may be combined, further divided, or given different names.

It is appropriate at this point to recognize the methodology called prototyping. Prototyping, a simplified overview of which is presented in Figure 2.2, is an increasingly popular adjunct to the SDLC as we present it in this text. Prototyping has as its goal the quick analysis of the problem to be solved and experimentation with potential solutions. Used properly, it is a powerful requirements analysis and design tool. Used improperly, it can lead to undocumented and unmaintainable software.

A detailed discussion of prototyping is beyond the intent and scope of this text. It is the subject of much current literature and the interested reader is encouraged to pursue the topic. It is sufficient to observe that, while the development of a prototype system can support activities within the SDLC, the prototyping development itself is expected to follow a standard SDLC. Prototyping is often used when the requirements determination

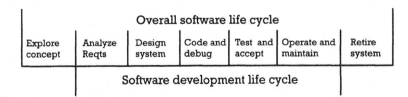

Overall software life cycle						
Explore concept	Analyze Reqts	Design system	Code and debug	Test and accept	Operate and maintain	Retire system
	Software development life cycle					

Figure 2.1 Two software life cycles.

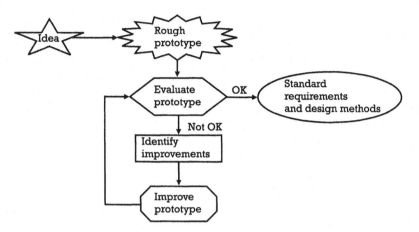

Figure 2.2   General prototyping approach.

and expression techniques include use cases. A use case is a description
what the software must do, or how it must behave, if the user is exercisin
some particular functionality. As discussed in Chapter 4, use cases are als
popular means of determining test cases for the software.

The SLC is the basis for many standards applicable to the developmer
and use of quality software. One of the first standards that should be pr
pared is the life-cycle description, sometimes called the software develo
ment methodology. Which phases comprise the SLC and the SDLC an
which activities comprise each of the phases must be clearly delineate
Once the life-cycle phases are defined, the process of determining prop
subjects for standardization within the life-cycle activities can begin.

Most standards will be applicable to activities during the SDLC, since th
is where the heaviest concentration of tasks is found. This in no way mean
that standards for the other phases should be ignored or not prepared. A
the SQS matures, it will determine, together with the rest of the softwai
organization, new areas to which standards can be usefully applied.

The arrival of computer-aided software engineering tools has opene
another opportunity and necessity for SLC standardization. Which tools t
use; how to specify, acquire and apply them; and the interfaces amon
them; may need to be addressed by standards.

2.1.2   Documentation

Comprehensive documentation standards are a basic necessity for thoroug
design, test, operation, and maintenance.

A major complaint against most software systems is that they are poorly documented. A generality is that documentation is done, if at all, after the software system is delivered. Thus, while in the best of worlds the documentation describes the delivered system, it often fails to describe what was originally requested by the customer. Further, there is often little documentation of the test program applied to the software system. This makes the software's ability to perform as desired suspect. Also, user documentation—how to use the software system—frequently is accused of being unusable itself.

Standards for documentation should address two fronts—the required documentation for each software system and the format and content requirements for that documentation. Documents prepared in nonstandard formats increase the likelihood of misunderstanding or incorrect interpretation.

A comprehensive set of documentation standards can help assure that the documentation of a software system is capable of the tasks for which it is intended. Without standards with regard to what to document and how to document it, the system may well go into production and fail for one of the following reasons:

▸ It is not what the customer really wanted.

▸ The users and operators do not know how it works.

The most important document, and frequently the least standardized and least well done, is the requirements document. The requirements document is intended to spell out specifically the problem of need to be addressed by the software. It must describe the intended software system from an external, operational point of view. Once the requirements have been determined and expressed, they must be managed. Every system being developed will undergo requirements changes. Some will be necessary, some just "nice to have"; others actually may be harmful or detrimental to the system as a whole. Without rigorous standards for the analysis, definition, expression, and control of the requirements, a software development project is in danger of failing to satisfy its users.

2.1.3 Coding

Coding standards can help reduce artistry and enhance clarity and maintainability.

Some coding standards take effect earlier than others, sometimes reaching back into the design phases. A standard that calls for structured coding

techniques will usually imply the imposition of a standard that calls
structured design techniques. Conversely, standards requiring obje
oriented development techniques will often lead to standards for coding
one or another of the newer languages that support object development

Standards such as these are intended to permit greater understandi
throughout the balance of the SLC. Peers who are involved in wa
throughs and inspections are better able to understand the code as th
prepare for the review. Maintainers have a much easier time of corre
ing and enhancing code that is well structured and follows adequa
standards.

Some coding standards deal with which specific language is to be use
Many shops relying on large mainframe-based systems still use Cobol
PL/I as their standard application language. Another, differently oriente
development organization may standardize on Visual Basic, C++, or Jav
Some organizations have several standard languages, depending on whi
type of application is being developed, or even specific characteristics of
given application.

Beyond standards specifying a given language, an organization may pr
pare standards for subroutine calls, reentrant or recursive coding tec
niques, reuse of existing code, or standards covering restrictions on verbs
coding constructs.

Most organizations have specific approaches that are preferred c
perhaps, prohibited. The coding standards will reflect the needs and perso
ality of the organization. A set of standards is useful in creating an enviror
ment in which all programmers know the rules that govern their work. If
coding convention is beneficial to the performance of the coding staff,
should be made a standard so that all coding can benefit from it. On th
other hand, if a particular coding technique is found to be detrimental,
standard prohibiting its use is appropriate so that all programmers kno
to avoid it.

2.1.4 Naming

Standard naming conventions assist in readability and CM. The standardiz
tion of naming conventions for system components (units, modules), dat
and even entry points within the code is both easy and beneficial. There
usually little resistance to a consistent naming or labeling scheme, and i
major benefit is the ease of identifying the object being named or labele
Beyond that, CM, especially configuration identification, is much mor
difficult if there are no consistent rules or standards for componer
identification.

Naming standards are based on consistent identifiers in specific locations within the name. As Figure 2.3 shows, identifiers may be assigned to decreasing hierarchical levels within a system; the first characters specifying the system itself and subsequent characters define lower levels within the system. Data can be similarly named, as can subroutines and even external interfaces.

The important point in naming conventions is that all components of a given software system can be identified as belonging to that system. This, in turn, can simplify the bookkeeping for testing, integrating, and delivering the system, since each component is uniquely identified. This, as will be discussed later, is also very important for managing the overall configuration or version of a product. To have the user or customer accept one version of the system and then mistakenly deliver a different version obviously is undesirable.

Configuration identification, while going beyond the basic naming standards and conventions, depends on unique identifiers for all components of a particular software system. It can perform its function with whatever naming standards, conventions, schemes, or methods are used. However, a standard naming convention greatly eases the configuration identification task.

The tasks of the software developer and tester are also simplified if standard naming conventions are used. Confusion and doubt as to exactly which interface is to be exercised or which module is to be tested are minimized. The developer can easily determine the subroutine to call or entry point to use if there are standard rules and formats for the names of those items.

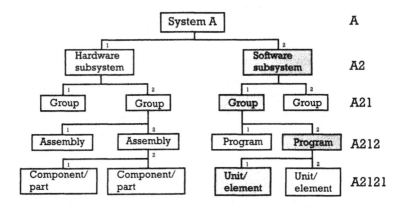

Each item is a named element of the system

Figure 2.3 Identification based on hierarchy.

2.1.5   Operating procedures and protocols

Operating procedures are standardized so that everyone does the same thi
the same way with a given software system.

Standardizing the operational environment is important to software sy
tem results. Correct data, entered in different ways, can give different, y
seemingly correct, results. Sequencing subsystem operations in nonstanda
ways may lead to varied results, all of which might be taken as correct. To
sure, much of the opportunity for variation in use or operation of a softwa
system can be eliminated by the software itself. On the other hand, softwa
cannot easily control procedures, so standards are used to govern tl
remaining variables.

Standard user procedures tend to reduce errors and defects, maximi
system response time, simplify user education, and increase understandir
of system outputs.

Standards applied to users may address time of day or cycle consider
tions with respect to the running of the system. A payroll system may
run on Friday as a standard to permit proper interface with the timeca
reporting system. A corresponding standard may call for running on Thur
day in holiday situations. By having standards for use, the user is not put
the position of making decisions that could conflict with those made l
someone else. Further, it reduces the likelihood that a person making tl
same decision will make it differently from time to time.

The standardization of operating procedures and protocols applies
large centralized data centers, client-server installations, standalone ar
networked workstations, and specific application systems. Specific applic
tion systems standards can regulate when the system is run, how to recove
from system crashes, and the like. Equally important, though, the overa
operation of the data center or network should have governing standard
Such things as scheduled maintenance time, job-entry rules, mass stora{
allocation, remote job-entry procedures, log-on and log-off procedure
password use, data access, and distributed computing are all subjects fc
appropriate standardization. Such standards have high payback in smooth(
operation, reduced errors and defects, and easier education of personnel.

2.1.6   User development

User development of software needs strict standards so that the actions (
one user do not affect other users or the data center itself.

The rapidly growing capability for user-developed software provides
fast, easy method of providing quick service for small tasks. Another, assoc
ated area is the availability of off-the-shelf software from both regul&

commercial suppliers and on-line bulletin boards. Software can be purchased or downloaded and made into an integral part of larger systems being developed. Users have the ability to buy a package, merge it with another package, write some special code for their own needs, and run this amalgam of software without the intervention of the regular software organization. While convenient and often productive, this has opened the door for uncontrolled software development, potentially damaging access to the organizational database, excessive loading of the data processing facilities, and wasteful duplication of effort and resources. Standards for user development of software are needed to address these potential conditions.

User development can take many forms. The development can be done by someone on behalf of the user (but not via the established software development processes). For example, some years ago, a company that made computer systems for restaurants and resorts had a salesman who fancied himself a wizard programmer and configured some function keys at the top of the keyboard to do specific tasks such as create an end-of-shift report. Customers were impressed by his programming prowess and his ability to take a simple request and automate it quickly.

The trouble came later when a customer called the company's customer support center after a power failure at the restaurant wiped out all the fancy function key programs created by the salesman. When the customer began complaining that the F8 function did not work anymore, customer support was baffled. It took some time, and the tracking down of that particular salesman, to figure out what had gone wrong.

This is a simple case of uncontrolled, undocumented, and unsupervised development. Instead of enhancing the customer relationship, as the salesman thought he was doing, this case of rogue programming actually put the account in peril and potentially cost the company thousands of dollars and a customer.

User understanding and observation of standards is required to avoid negative impact on the overall data processing facility. Uncontrolled purchase of small, local (departmental) computational facilities can be an unnecessary drain on a company's resources and can lead to incompatibilities between local facilities and the main data center or network. Further, as software is developed, it can, if unregulated, lead to data interface, integrity, and security problems. Acquisition of software from nonstandard sources or suppliers also increases the likelihood of virus infections and other security concerns.

User development of software can be a beneficial addition to the computational capabilities of an organization. However, standards are easier to develop and enforce in traditional mainframe environments, since all

processing is done under a central operating system. As control and processing move toward a decentralized environment, enforcement becomes mo
difficult. Not only are user development standards more necessary, b
increased surveillance of storage and files is appropriate to reduce th
chances of misuse of unauthorized or nonlicensed commercial softwar
Standards for user development, ranging from equipment and languag
selection to data security and networking, will permit maximum user flex
bility and still maintain central control for efficient overall data processing.

Changes to standards affecting user work flow and tasks may also b
impacted by new standards governing user development of software. Use
should have the opportunity to participate in the standardization activitie
They might even have a trial-use period. The quality practitioner will war
to assure that addressing the dangers inherent in uncontrolled user develo
ment are not creating unnecessary restrictions.

2.1.7 Emerging technologies

The software development and maintenance world is in a period of gre
expansion and change. While most of the new technologies can be trace
back to old methods and look more like changes than innovations, th
applications of the technologies are often new or at least different. Some
us see object-oriented design and development as little more than a refin
ment of subroutines and independent modules. Client-server technolo
probably really began when IBM introduced its CICS operating system; th
clients were terminals, and the *server* was a big mainframe. GUIs are n
longer new but necessary. Further, the proliferation of software fe
e-commerce has added a new dimension of technology.

In any event, developers are having a hard time finding standards
govern these technologies. That is not to say that there are no standard
available; some new concepts have gained wide industrial acceptance an
are more de facto standards than formal standards. This places the burde
on the users of these technologies to develop their own approaches an
standards. The alternative is to gamble on adopting one or another of the d
facto standards and hope that the industry as a whole goes in the sam
direction. The same is true for the burgeoning field of multimedia software.

2.2 Sources of standards

It was stated in Section 2.1 that standards should cover as much of the ove
all SLC as is practical and appropriate for a given organization. That is clear

a large, as well as important, task. Certainly, in an organization of more than minimum size, it will involve more than just one or two persons. Even then, to create all the standards needed can be an overwhelming task and one that cannot be accomplished in a timely manner. The goal should be to identify the minimum set of standards that will serve the organization's actual needs and then identify the sources for those standards.

Software standards can come from many sources. The standards coordinator (or whoever has the responsibility for standards) can make use of some or any of the standards-acquisition means and sources. The three main standards-acquisition methods are as follows:

1. Developing them in-house;

2. Buying them from consultants or other similar organizations;

3. Adapting industry prepared and consensus-approved standards.

The three main standards sources are as follows:

1. External standards developers;

2. Purchased standards;

3. In-house development.

2.2.1 External standards developers

Standards can be found in several locations and are available from several sources. Some externally available standards are useful as starting points for an in-house standards program. Some are likely to be imposed as a condition of commerce with a particular business field or with other countries.

One advantage to the standards developed by the various industry and other groups is that they reflect the consensus of the groups involved. Several industry-segment points of view are usually represented so that a wide range of applications is available. Table 2.1 presents some typical standards subjects and representative external standards and sources applicable to them. The list is certainly not all-inclusive, but it does indicate the breadth of standards available.

International standards   Of increasing interest is the activity within the international sector with respect to software standards. The ISO has published what is called the 9000 series of standards (ISO 9000, 9001, 9002, 9003, 9004) dealing with quality. Standard 9001, "Quality Systems—Model for Quality Assurance in Design, Development, Production, Installation and Servicing,"

Table 2.1 Representative Standards Sources

Major Subject	Specific Area	Standard Developer	Standard Number
Software life cycle	Life-cycle processes	IEEE ISO/IEC	1074, 1074.1 12207
	Project management	IEEE	1058
	Development	DoD IEEE ISO	498 1074 12207
	Reviews	IEEE NIST	1028, 1059 500-165
	Testing	IEEE NIST	829, 1008, 1012,1059 500-75, 500-165
	Quality program	IEEE AS ISO NRC	1298 3563.1, 3563.2 9000 et al NUREG/CR-4640
	Metrics	IEEE ISO/IEC	982.1, 982.2, 1044, 1044.1, 1045, 1061 9126
	Case tools	IEEE	1175, 1209, 1343
Documentation	Quality plans	IEEE IEEE/EIA	730, 730.1 1498/IS 640
	Requirements specifications	IEEE ISO/IEC	830 12207
	Design specifications	IEEE ISO/IEC	1016, 1016.1l 12207
	User documentation	IEEE	1063
Naming	CM	IEEE EIA	1042, 828 649
User development	Software packages	ISO/IEC	12119

is the one most often applied to software development since it includes a
aspects of product development from requirements control through mea
urements and metrics applied to the quality program and the control of th
products. (The 2000 edition merges 9002 and 9003 into 9001.)

Written from a primarily manufacturing point of view, ISO 9001 h
been difficult to relate to the software realm. Therefore, ISO subsequent
added an annex to ISO 9000, called Part 3. This annex explains how th
requirements of ISO 9001 can be applied to software. A working group
Standards Australia subsequently prepared AS 3563, which is a better inte
pretation of ISO 9001 for software.

More recently, the responsibility for 9000 Part 3 has been transferred to ISO/IEC JTC1/SC7 (JTC1), another international group dedicated to information technology standards. JTC1 includes several subcommittees that undertake the development of software standards. Organizations that do, or expect to do, business with countries other than their own, are well advised to seek out and comply with the tenets of the international standards. At the time of this writing, JTC1's subcommittee SC7 had published IS 12207 "Information Technology—Software Life Cycle Processes" and was working on several standards that will support 12207.

It is important to recognize that simply adhering to a process is no guarantee of quality if the process itself is flawed. For example, a concrete life preserver built to an established, fully ISO 9000–compliant and carefully followed process, would probably fail to garner customer kudos for its quality.

Industrial and professional groups   Several industry and professional societies are developing generic standards that can be used as is or tailored as appropriate.

A number of professional and technical societies are increasingly active in the preparation of software standards. The IEEE and the Electronic Industries Association (EIA) have ongoing working groups addressing standards and guidelines in the software engineering area. The American National Standards Institute (ANSI) is the coordinating body for standards of all types within the United States. Another group becoming active in the software area is the American Society for Quality.

These, and other, groups are preparing generic software engineering standards that can be adopted as they are written or adapted by an individual organization. Many of them are also suitable for inclusion in software acquisition contracts, as well as in-house use.

Government agencies   In addition to the previously mentioned groups, many software standards are available from various government agencies. In particular, the Department of Defense (DoD), the Nuclear Regulatory Agency, the National Institute of Standards and Technology (NIST), and various other governmental agencies are standards sources. As a large buyer of software, as well as a developer, the federal government has prepared and is still generating standards meant primarily for software acquisition contracts. These are frequently applicable, in whole or in part, to a specific organization's internal standards needs. The DoD recently declared its intention to cease active writing of its own standards and to adopt existing software standards.

Manufacturers' user groups   Another source of software standards can
found in computer user groups. GUIDE International and SHARE (IBN
DECUS (DEC), and other major user groups often address the question
software standards as a part of their activities. The standards generated
these user groups are usually generic in nature. They are sometimes stand
lone, but frequently benefit from adaptation.

2.2.2 Purchased standards

Standards can be purchased and then adapted to the needs of a speci
organization. Companies sometimes will provide their standards manuals
other, similar companies for a fee. This is especially true in industries
which there is a great deal of interaction or interfacing such as between tel
phone companies. Although there may be strong resistance to this in indu
tries in which competition is strong, in general, most organizations a
willing to share, even on an informal basis, their software standards in tl
interest of overall improvement in the software area. It must be remen
bered, though, that standards received from another company, no matt
how similar, are specific to that company's specific situation and need
Standards obtained in this way represent only a starting point for the sta
dards effort in the receiving company.

Another avenue for purchased standards is through a consultant or col
sulting company. Many consultants will prepare a full set of software sta
dards specific to a client company. This can be an easy way to get an initi
set of the most critical standards in place quickly. The consultant can the
continue the standards development effort or turn the rest of the task ov
to the client company. The advantage of this approach is rapid standarc
development, usually using the consultant's prior experience in the particu
lar industry and software area. The main disadvantage is the perception
the consultant as an outsider who "doesn't really understand the situation
Involvement of the affected departments, as "internal consultants" to,
joint participants with, the real consultant can usually diminish this percep
tion. In some cases, the consultant could even be used to gain acceptance
in-house-developed standards that were being resisted. However, paying a
outside consultant to deliver standards, regardless of the actual source
those standards, sometimes lends undeserved value to them.

2.2.3 In-house development

Standards, from whatever external source, usually need to be adapted to th
individual needs and environment of the specific organization or projec

In-house development is the only way to assure that each standard reflects the organization's actual needs and environment. There are at least three major approaches to in-house standards development, in addition to an enormous number of variations and combinations. The three major approaches are as follows:

1. Ad hoc standardization;

2. Standards groups;

3. Standards committees.

Ad hoc standardization   Any of the SLC staff may be assigned, as an additional but temporary part of their job, the responsibility and authority to create and institute software standards. Since the affected staff is involved with various parts of the entire life cycle of all projects, they have a high degree of insight into the SLC and its standardization needs. They can become aware of areas and tasks that need standardization, observe the various methods in use, and propose the most appropriate methods as candidates to be standards. As the monitor of SLC activities, the software quality practitioner is in the proper position to determine the appropriateness of the standard once it is in use.

An advantage of ad hoc standardization is that the experts in the area being standardized can be called on to write—and to follow—the standard. A disadvantage is that the writers may not be aware of side issues or potential conflicts with other standards. The "corporate memory" of the continuity and consistency of the standards program may also be lost.

In general, it is not recommended that the software quality practitioner write standards. That role could place practitioners in the position of imposing standards on tasks and activities that they themselves do not perform. For example, the software quality practitioner does little coding, rarely operates the data center, and usually does not perform data entry.

Standards groups   A second method of in-house development is through a separately chartered standards group (SG). Since the SG has, as its whole task, the management of the body of standards, it can often spend more time researching a standard or looking to outside sources for a particular standard. The advantage of having an SG is maintaining the continuity and corporate memory of the standards program.

The SG, however, suffers the same disadvantage as the software quality practitioner—standardizing from outside a task or activity. That is, the SG members usually are not in a position to follow the standards they create. In

addition, an SG usually does not have the insight available to the softwa
quality practitioner as to needed standards or standards appropriateness.

Standards committees   The third major approach to standards developme
is the chartering of a standards committee (SC). Usually the SC comprises t
managers of each department in the data processing organization: applic
tions development, operations, systems programming, and so on, as shown
Figure 2.4. The SC is responsible for identifying needed standards and tho
requiring modification or replacement. The specific generation of a standa
is assigned to the manager of that department that will be most affected by tl
standard—language standard to applications development, database defin
tion standard to database administration, and so on. The advantage of th
approach is that the most knowledgeable and affected department prepar
the standard with inputs from all other interested departments. The disadvar
tage is the usually difficult task of involving the actual department manage
so that full departmental visibility is ensured.

Standards coordinator   In any of the previously mentioned approaches, (
combinations thereof, a specific person should have the job of ensuring th
needed standards are identified, created, and followed. That person, the star
dards coordinator, may be a software quality practitioner, manager of the S(
or chairperson of the SC. The important matter is that he or she has the ear (
the software quality practitioner or upper management to ensure that star
dards receive the attention they merit and require.

It is the role of the standards coordinator to ascertain the standar
requirements for each installation and situation and then arrange for thos

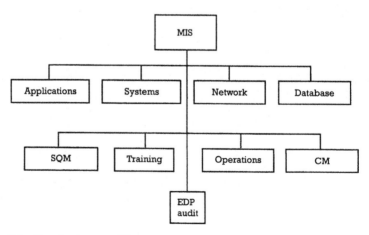

Figure 2.4   Standards committee.

needed standards to be available, invoked, and followed. As is the case with the software quality practitioner, the standards coordinator usually should not prepare the standards.

It is the responsibility of the standards coordinator to provide standards as needed and monitor compliance with them. It is the role and responsibility of everyone in the organization to identify potential standards needs and adhere to those standards that have been applied. It is the role of management to enforce the application of and compliance with the implemented standards.

.3 Selection of standards

Standards must be selected that apply to a company's specific needs, environment, and resources.

Standards for almost everything are available, often from several different sources. As described in Section 2.2, standards can be obtained from industry and professional groups, other companies, private consultants, or the government. They can also be prepared in-house. The major concern, then, is not where to find them, but to be sure that the ones being obtained are necessary and proper for the given organization. Even in a particular company, all the standards in use in one data center may not apply to a second data center. For example, the company's scientific data processing needs may call for different standards from its financial data processing center.

Many things can affect the need for standards and the standards needed. As stated, different data processing orientations may call for specific standards. Such things as runtimes, terminal response times, language selection, operating systems, and telecommunications protocols are all subject to standardization on different terms in different processing environments. Even such things as programmer workstation size and arrangement, data input and results output locations, training and educational needs, and data access rights often are determined on a basis that includes the type of processing as a consideration.

Not all standards available for a given subject or topic may apply in every situation. Language standards, particularly selecting the languages to be used, may have exceptions or not be applied at all. A particular standard life-cycle model may be inappropriate in a given instance or for a specific project. Data access or telecommunications standards may be modified or waived to fit a particular project or installation.

2.4   Promulgation of standards

Standards must be available to the intended users. They must also be f‌
lowed and kept up-to-date with the user environment.

2.4.1   Availability

Two common methods of providing standards to the standards user are cu‌
rently popular.

The foremost method of publishing standards is by way of a standar‌
manual. This is, usually, a large loose-leaf binder with the organizatio‌
standards filed in some logical order. It can also be a set of binders, each co‌
ering some subset of the total standards set. The loose-leaf binder approa‌
is a convenient and generally inexpensive way of keeping the standar‌
filed, up-to-date, and accessible.

This approach has some drawbacks, however. Unless some offic‌
updating method is used, the holders of the manuals may be careless abo‌
making changes to their copies as new, revised, or obsolete standards a‌
added, replaced, or removed. Using an incorrect standard is sometim‌
worse then using none at all. Loose-leaf pages, especially in a heavily us‌
book or section, frequently become torn out of the book and lost. A co‌
mon excuse for not following a standard is that the offender's standar‌
book has been misplaced, borrowed, or was never issued.

Finally, in a large organization, the cost of providing and maintaining‌
set of standards books may be significant. One way to cut this cost is‌
restrict the distribution of manuals to some subset of the using populatio‌
However, that solution has the usual effect of diminishing the use of t‌
standards because of the increased difficulty of access.

As more organizations adopt Internet and intranet technology, one w‌
to counter some of the more severe drawbacks of the book-style manual‌
to make the standards available on-line. In organizations with widesprea‌
use of terminals, there is an increasing trend to having the full set of sta‌
dards available for access through the terminal network. That way, emplo‌
ees who want to look up a standard need only call it up on their screen. ‌
addition, on-line access eliminates the problems associated with correcti‌
and updating the manual; the only copy of the standard that is affected‌
the one in the database. Once that is changed, everyone has access to t‌
new version without having to manually update his or her own book.

Like all methods, though, the on-line one has its drawbacks, not t‌
least of which is cost. In a large organization that already has widesprea‌
terminal usage and a large database capability, automating a standar‌

manual will be a relatively inexpensive situation. For organizations that do not have the facilities already in place, putting the standards on-line probably is not cost-justifiable, since there will be limited automated access and the book method will probably still have to be used as well.

2.4.2 Compliance

Standards that are not followed are frequently worse than no standards at all.

Standards are intended to improve the overall quality of software as it progresses through the life cycle. When a standard has been established and implemented for a particular subject, the organization as a whole expects the standard to be followed. If it is not followed, some things may be done incorrectly or lead to errors on the part of those who work in other portions of the life cycle.

The role of the software quality practitioner, and specifically the standards coordinator, is to monitor and report to management on the adherence of the entire computational organization to the standards that have been implemented. It is not the role of the software quality practitioner or the SC to enforce the standards. Enforcement is the responsibility of management.

Not every case of noncompliance with a standard represents disregard for, or lack of knowledge of, the standard. In some cases, lack of compliance may be a signal that the standard is no longer appropriate or applicable. While it is not practical to investigate every case of noncompliance with a standard, it is necessary to look for trends in noncompliance that may indicate missing, faulty, or even incorrect standards. Observation of noncompliance trends can give clues that may indicate the need for companion standards to those that already exist, additional standards that complement those in place, or modification or replacement of existing standards. The software quality practitioner or the standards coordinator is responsible for identifying such cases through an ongoing review of the standards and their continuing applicability.

2.4.3 Maintenance

Standards must be kept current with the changing computational environment.

No matter where the standards have come from or how they are made available, they will quickly fall into disuse if they do not continue to reflect the organization's needs. Standards become obsolete as mainframes,

operating systems, federal regulations, business emphases, and the li
change and evolve. Probably no installation is the same today as it was as l
tle as a year ago. Further, some of the subjects of standards have al
changed. Thus, some method of keeping standards up-to-date must be pr
vided. Clues that it is time to review a standard include increasing instanc
of noncompliance, installation of new equipment or support softwar
expansion into a new area of business emphasis, the advent of new gover.
ment regulations, and so on.

The standards coordinator is the person primarily responsible for sta
dard maintenance, but anyone in the organization can point out the pote
tial need for change. Just as in the sequence for requesting changes
software, there should be a formal standards change request and a standa
method for processing that change request. Once the request is received, t
standards coordinator can verify the need for the change, present it to t
standards generating group, and get the change made and distributed.

2.5   Nonstandard standards

It should be noted that not everything in the software arena must be sta
dardized. There may be preferred practices or suggested practices on whic
there is no agreement as to a single standard way to behave. In these case
recommended approaches or guidelines may be appropriate.

A recommended approach can be seen as the preferred, but n
required, situation. In that case, words such as should, ought to, or oth
similar, strongly suggestive phrases might be used. A guideline would l
even less restrictive and use verbs like could, might, or may. Use of recon
mended approaches and guidelines permits some control of activity pe
formance without unnecessarily restricting otherwise proper or benefici
behavior.

2.6   Summary

Standards are the keystone of the SQS. They provide the basis against whic
reviewing and monitoring are conducted. Areas of standardization cover th
entire SLC from the definition of the SLC itself through the methods t
which software is withdrawn from use. All aspects of the SLC are open 1
standardization, even the process by which the standards themselves a1
created. Standards may be purchased, obtained from professional and us
groups, and specifically developed for or by the organization.

No matter how standards come into being, however, they must be relevant to the organization and the software development process; that is, they must be reflective of the needs of the organization. Standards must be appropriate to the environment in which the software is to be developed and used.

Recommended approaches and guidelines are alternatives to standards in those situations in which some consistency is needed but absolute consistency may be inappropriate.

Finally, the application of standards must be uniform and enforced across the full organization, at least at the project level. While it is desirable from a consistency point of view to impose the same standards on all software development groups within an organization, it is not always feasible from a business standpoint. Within a single project, however, there must be standards uniformity.

‽.7 The next step

Two texts that can help the reader's standards development activities are as follows:

John T. Rabbitt and Peter A. Bergh. *The ISO 9000 Book: A Global Competitor's Guide to Compliance and Certification,* New York: Quality Resources, 1993.

Stan Magee and Leonard L. Tripp. *Guide to Software Engineering Standards,* Norwood, MA: Artech House, 1997.

Additional reading

Deming, W. Edwards, *Out of the Crisis,* Cambridge, MA: MIT Center for Advanced Engineering Study, 1986.

ISO/IEC JTC1/SC7, *Information Technology—Software Life Cycle Processes—ISO/IEC 12207,* ISO/IEC Copyright Office, Geneva, Switzerland, 2000.

Software Engineering Standards Committee, *IEEE Standards Collection—Software Engineering,* IEEE Press, (current edition).

CHAPTER

3

Contents

Reviews

Reviews are the first and primary form of quality control activity. Quality control is concerned with the search for faults or defects in the various products of software development. While testing of code, as will be discussed in Chapter 4, is also concerned with the search for faults, reviews are (as has been demonstrated in countless studies) far more effective because they look for faults sooner than testing. Reviews are also more cost-effective because they consume fewer resources than do tests. They are short, require small groups of reviewers, and can be scheduled and rescheduled with minimum impact. Reviews are conducted during the process of the development, not at the end, as is the case with testing. Quality control has as its mission the detection and elimination of defects in the product. Reviews are the front line in this mission.

Reviews take place throughout the SLC and verify that the products of each phase are correct with respect to phase inputs and activities. They are sometimes referred to as precode testing. In one sense, reviews really are testing, or challenging, the product against its requirements. The only difference between testing by means of reviewing and testing by executing code is the method.

Reviews take on many forms. They may be informal peer reviews, such as one-on-one, walk-throughs, inspections, or audits. They may also be formal reviews such as verification reviews, decision-point reviews, physical or functional audits, or post-implementation reviews. Regardless of their form, the primary purpose of a review is to identify defects in the product being considered.

Boehm (see 1.5) and others have developed graphs similar to that
Figure 3.1, which show that the costs of defects rise very steeply the lon
they remain in the products. Reviews are aimed at finding the defects
they are created, rather than depending on the test and operation phases
uncover them.

Each review has a specific purpose, objective, audience, and cast of p;
ticipants. Some reviews may be held multiple times during the develo
ment, such as design walk-throughs. Others, such as the functional aud
are of such magnitude that they normally are one-time events that form t
basis for major decisions about the product. In each case, however, a form
and procedure for the review should be reflected in the organizatio
standards.

A major role of the software quality practitioner is to confirm that t
reviews are scheduled as appropriate throughout the SLC and that they a
held as scheduled. In some organizations, a software quality practitioner
tasked to be the chair of the review. This is up to each individual organi
tion. It is imperative, however, that for all reviews, except perhaps ve
informal one-on-ones or early walk-throughs, the software quality prac
tioner is an active participant. The practitioner should also make sure tl
minutes and action items are recorded as necessary, and that any acti
items are suitably addressed and closed before approving and recording t
review as complete. Of course, keeping management informed of t
reviews and their results is imperative.

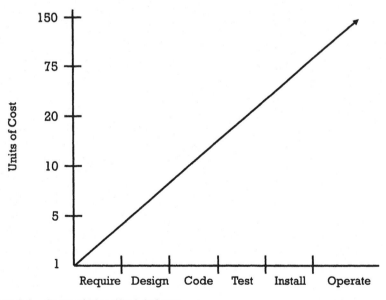

Figure 3.1 Costs of identified defects.

It must be noted that the entire goal of a SQS is to increase the quality of the delivered product. This, of course, entails the intentional seeking of faults and defects. It also entails an opportunity for the unskilled manager to make personnel decisions based on defects found. Some managers will be tempted to use the number of errors made by a developer as the basis for performance evaluation This is a self-defeating approach for two reasons. First, the employees may begin to react to the stress of reviews and try to minimize their defect-finding effectiveness so as to not look bad. Second, as the effectiveness of the reviews goes down, the defects being delivered to the customer will increase, which undermines the customer's confidence.

.1 Types of reviews

Reviews take on various aspects depending on their type. The two broad types of reviews are as follows:

1. In-process (generally considered informal) review;
2. Phase-end (generally considered formal) review.

3.1.1 In-process reviews

In-process reviews are informal reviews intended to be held during the conduct of each SDLC phase. Informal implies that there is little reporting to the customer on the results of the review. Further, they are often called peer reviews because they are usually conducted by the producer's peers. Peers may be coworkers or others who are involved at about the same level of product effort or detail.

Scheduling of the reviews, while intentional and a part of the overall project plan, is rather flexible. This allows for reviews to be conducted when necessary: earlier if the product is ready, later if the product is late. One scheduling rule of thumb is to review no more than the producer is willing to throw away. Another rule of thumb is to have an in-process review every two weeks. Figure 3.2 offers suggestions on the application of these two rules of thumb. Each project will determine the appropriate rules for its own in-process reviews.

There is a spectrum of rigor across the range of in-process reviews. The least rigorous of these reviews is the peer review. It is followed, in increasing rigor, by walk-throughs of the in-process product, such as a requirements document or a design specification. The most rigorous is the inspection.

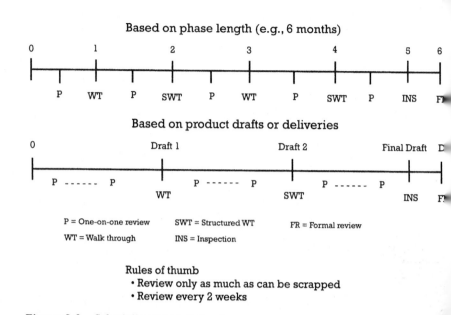

Based on phase length (e.g., 6 months)

Based on product drafts or deliveries

P = One-on-one review   SWT = Structured WT   FR = Formal review

WT = Walk through   INS = Inspection

Rules of thumb
• Review only as much as can be scrapped
• Review every 2 weeks

Figure 3.2   Scheduling rules of thumb.

These are discussed more completely next. Table 3.1 summarizes some of the characteristics of in-process reviews.

One-on-one reviews   The one-on-one review is the least rigorous of the reviews and, thus, usually the least stressful. In this review, the producer asks a coworker to check the product to make sure that it is basically correct. Questions like, "Did I get the right information in the right place?" and "Did I use the right formula?" are the main concerns of the one-on-one review. The results of the review are often verbal, or at the most, a red mark or two on the draft of the product.

Table 3.1   In-Process Review Characteristics

Review Type	Records	CM Level	Participants	Stress Level
One-on-one	None	None	Coworker	Very low
Walk-through	Marked-up copy or defect reports	Probably none	Interested project members	Low to medium
Structured walk-through	Defect reports	Informal	Selected project members	Medium
Inspection	Defect report database	Formal	Specific role players	High

One-on-one reviews are most often used during the drafting of the product, or the correcting of a defect, and cover small parts at a time. Since there is virtually no distribution of records of the defects found or corrections suggested, the producer feels little stress or threat that he or she will be seen as having done a poor job.

Walk-throughs   As the producer of a particular product gets to convenient points in his or her work, a group of peers should be requested to review the work as the producer describes, or walks through, the product with them. In this way, defects can be found and corrected immediately, before the product is used as the basis for the next-phase activities. Since it is usually informal and conducted by the producer's peers, there is less tendency on the part of the producer to be defensive and protective, leading to a more open exchange with correspondingly better results.

Participants in the walk-through are usually chosen for their perceived ability to find defects. The leader must make sure that the presence of a lead or senior person does not inhibit participation by others.

In a typical walk-through, the producer distributes the material to be reviewed at the meeting. While earlier distribution of the material would probably enhance the value of the walk-through, most describers of walk-throughs do not require prior distribution. The producer then walks the reviewers through the material, describing his or her thought processes, intentions, approaches, assumptions, and perceived constraints as they apply to the product. The author should not to justify or explain his or her work. If there is confusion about a paragraph or topic, the author may explain what he or she meant so that the review can continue. This, however, is a defect and will be recorded for the author to clarify in the correction process.

Reviewers are encouraged to comment on the producer's approach and results with the intent of exposing defects or shortcomings in the product. On the other hand, only deviations from the product's requirements are open to criticism. Comments, such as "I could do it faster or more elegantly," are out of order. Unless the product violates a requirement, standard, or constraint or produces the wrong result, improvements in style and so on are not to be offered in the walk-through meeting. Obviously, some suggestions are of value and should be followed through outside of the review.

It must be remembered that all reviews take resources and must be directed at the ultimate goal of reducing the number of defects delivered to the user or customer. Thus, it is not appropriate to try to correct defects that are identified. Correction is the task of the author after the review.

Results of the walk-through should be recorded on software defe reports such as those discussed in Chapter 6. This makes the defects found bit more public and can increase the stress and threat to the producer. It als helps ensure that all defects found in the walk-through are addressed an corrected.

Inspections   Another, more rigorous, in-process review is the inspection, a originally described by Fagan (see Additional reading). While its similariti with walk-throughs are great, the inspection requires a more specific cast participants and more elaborate minutes and action item reporting. Unlik the walk-through, which may be documented only within the UDF, th inspection requires a written report of its results and strict recording of troub reports.

Whether you use an inspection as specifically described by Fagan (some similar review, the best results are obtained when the formality an roles are retained. Having a reader who is charged with being sufficientl familiar with the product to be able to not read but paraphrase the doc mentation is a necessity. The best candidate for reader is likely the perso for whom the product being reviewed will be input. Who has more intere in having a quality product on which to base his or her efforts?

Fagan calls for a moderator who is charged with logistics preparatior inspection facilitation, and formal follow-up on implementing the inspec tion's findings. Fagan also defines the role of the recorder as the person wh creates the defect reports, maintains the defect database for the inspectior and prepares the required reports. Other participants have various levels (personal interest in the quality of the product.

Typically, an inspection has two meetings. The first is a mini walk through of the material by the producer. This is not on the scale of a regula walk-through but is intended to give an overview of the product and it place in the overall system. At this meeting, the moderator sees that th material to be inspected is distributed. Individual inspectors are then sched uled to review the material prior to the inspection itself. At the inspectior the reader leads the inspectors through the material and leads the search fc defects. At the inspection's conclusion, the recorder prepares the require reports and the moderator oversees the follow-up on the corrections an modifications found to be needed by the inspectors.

Because it is more rigorous, the inspection tends to be more costly i time and resources than the walk-through and is generally used on projec with higher risk or complexity. However, the inspection is usually mor successful at finding defects than the walk-through, and some companie use only the inspection as their in-process review.

It can also be seen that the inspection, with its regularized recording of defects, will be the most stressful and threatening of the in-process reviews. Skilled managers will remove the defect histories from their bases of performance evaluations. By doing so, and treating each discovered defect as one that didn't get to the customer, the manager can reduce the stress associated with the reviews and increase their effectiveness.

The software quality role with respect to inspections is also better defined. The software quality practitioner is a recommended member of the inspection team and may serve as the recorder. The resolution of action items is carefully monitored by the software quality practitioner, and the results are formally reported to project management.

In-process audits   Audits, too, can be informal as the SDLC progresses. Most software development methodologies impose documentation content and format requirements. Generally, informal audits are used to assess the product's compliance with those requirements for the various products.

While every document and interim development product is a candidate for an audit, one common informal audit is that applied to the UDF or software development notebook. The notebook or folder is the repository of the notes and other material that the producer has collected during the SDLC. Its required contents should be spelled out by a standard, along with its format or arrangement. Throughout the SDLC, the software quality practitioner should audit the UDFs to make sure that they are being maintained according to the standard.

3.1.2 Phase-end reviews

Phase-end reviews are formal reviews that usually occur at the end of the SDLC phase, or work period, and establish the baselines for work in succeeding phases. Unlike the in-process reviews, which deal with a single product, phase-end reviews include examination of all the work products that are to have been completed during that phase. A review of project management information, such as budget, schedule, and risk, is especially important.

For example, the software requirements review (SRR) is a formal examination of the requirements document and sets the baseline for the activities in the design phase to follow. It should also include a review of the system test plan, a draft of the user documentation, perhaps an interface requirements document, quality and CM plans, any safety and risk concerns or plans, and the actual status of the project with regard to budget and schedule plans. In general, anything expected to have been produced during that phase is to be reviewed. The participants include the producer and softwa quality practitioner as well as the user or customer. Phase-end reviews are primary means of keeping the user or customer aware of the progress a direction of the project. A phase-end review is not considered finished un the action items have been closed, software quality has approved the resul and the user or customer has approved going ahead with the next pha These reviews permit the user or customer to verify that the project is pr ceeding as intended or to give redirection as needed. They are also maj reporting points for software quality to indicate to management how t project is adhering to its standards, requirements, and resource budgets.

Phase-end reviews should be considered go-or-no-go decision points. each phase-end review, there should be sufficient status information ava able to examine the project's risk, including its viability, the likelihood th it will be completed on or near budget and schedule, its continued need, a the likelihood that it will meet its original goals and objectives. History h documented countless projects that have ended in failure or delivered pro ucts that were unusable. One glaring example is that of a bank finally ca celing a huge project. The bank publicly admitted to losing more than $1 million and laying off approximately 400 developers. The bank cited inad quate phase-end reviews as the primary reason for continuing the project long as it did. Properly conducted phase-end reviews can identify projects trouble and prompt the necessary action to recover. They can also identi projects that are no longer viable and should be cancelled.

Figure 3.3 shows various phase-end reviews throughout the SDLC. Fc mal reviews, such as the software requirements review, preliminary desi review (PDR), and the critical design review (CDR) are held at major mil stone points within the SDLC and create the baselines for subsequent SDl phases. The test readiness review (TRR) is completed prior to the onset acceptance or user testing.

Also shown are project completion audits conducted to determine rea ness for delivery and the post implementation review, which assesses prc ect success after a period of actual use.

Table 3.2 presents the typical subjects of each of the four major develo ment phase-end reviews. Those documents listed as required are considere the minimum acceptable set of documents required for successful softwa development and maintenance.

3.1.3 Project completion analyses

Two formal audits, the functional audit (FA) and the physical audit (PA are held as indicated in Figure 3.3. These two events, held at the end of tl

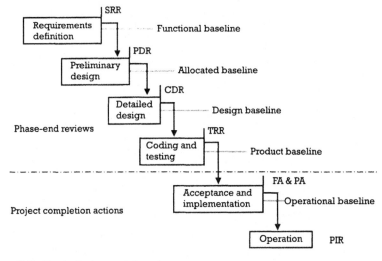

Figure 3.3   Typical phase-end reviews.

SDLC, are the final analyses of the software product to be delivered against its approved requirements and its current documentation, respectively.

The FA compares the software system being delivered against the currently approved requirements for the system. This is usually accomplished through an audit of the test records. The PA is intended to assure that the full set of deliverables is an internally consistent set (i.e., the user manual is the correct one for this particular version of the software). The PA relies on the CM records for the delivered products. The software quality practitioner frequently is charged with the responsibility of conducting these two audits. In any case, the software quality practitioner must be sure that the audits are conducted and report the finding of the audits to management.

The postimplementation review (PIR) is held once the software system is in production. The PIR usually is conducted 6 to 9 months after implementation. Its purpose is to determine whether the software has, in fact, met the user's expectations for it in actual operation. Data from the PIR is intended for use by the software quality practitioner to help improve the software development process. Table 3.3 presents some of the characteristics of the PIR.

The role of the software quality practitioner is often that of conducting the PIR. This review is best used as an examination of the results of the development process. Problems with the system as delivered can point to opportunities to improve the development process and verify the validity of previous process changes.

Table 3.2 Phase-End Review Subject Documents

Review	Required	Others
Software requirements	Software requirements specification	Interface requirements specification
	Software test plan	
	Software development plan	
	Quality system plan	
	CM plan	
	Standards and procedures	
	Cost/schedule status report	
Preliminary design	Software top-level design	Interface design
	Software test description	Database design
	Cost/schedule status report	
Critical design	Software detailed design	Interface design
	Cost/schedule status report	Database design
Test readiness	Software product specification	User's manual
	Software test procedures	Operator's manual
	Cost/schedule status report	

Table 3.3 PIR Characteristics

Timing	3 to 6 months after software system implementation
Software system goals versus experience	Return on investment Schedule results User response Defect history
Review results usage	Input to process analysis and improvement
	Too often ignored

3.2 Review subjects

Reviews are conducted throughout the SDLC with development review focusing on code and its related products.

Design and code reviews held during the course of the various phases are usually in the form of walk-throughs and inspections. These are held to get an early start on the elimination of defects in the products being examined. They are generally informal, which makes them more productive and less threatening to the egos and feelings of the producers of the products being reviewed.

Test reviews are much the same as code reviews, covering the test program products rather than the software products. They include the same types of formal and informal reviews and are held throughout the SDLC. Their function is to examine the test program as it is being developed and to make sure that the tests will exercise the software in such a manner as to find defects and to demonstrate that the software complies with the requirements.

3.3   Documentation reviews

One of the two goals of the SQS is to facilitate the building of quality into the software products as they are produced. Documentation reviews provide a great opportunity to realize this goal. By maintaining a high standard for conducting and completing these reviews and establishing the respective baselines, the software quality practitioner can make significant contributions to the attainment of a quality software product.

Software quality practitioners have much to do with the documentation reviews. They must make sure that the proper reviews are scheduled throughout the development life cycle. This includes determining the appropriate levels of formality, as well as the actual reviews to be conducted. The software quality practitioner also monitors the reviews to see that they are conducted and that defects in the documents are corrected before the next steps in publication or development are taken. In some cases, software quality itself is the reviewing agency, especially where there is not a requirement for in-depth technical analysis. In all cases, the software quality practitioner will report the results of the reviews to management.

There are a number of types of documentation reviews, both formal and informal, that are applicable to each of the software documents. The appendixes present suggested outlines for most of the development documents. These outlines can be used as they are or adapted to the specific needs of the organization or project.

The most basic of the reviews is the peer walk-through. As discussed in Section 3.1, this is a review of the document by a group of the author's peers

who look for defects and weaknesses in the document as it is being pr
pared. Finding defects as they are introduced avoids more expensive corre
tive action later in the SDLC, and the document is more correct when it
released.

Another basic document review is the format review or audit. This ca
be either formal or informal. When it is a part of a larger set of docume
reviews, the format audit is usually an informal examination of the over
format of the document to be sure that it adheres to the minimum standar
for layout and content. In its informal style, little attention is paid to tl
actual technical content of the document. The major concern is that a
required paragraphs are present and addressed. In some cases, this audit
held before or in conjunction with the document's technical peer wal
through.

A more formalized approach to the format audit is taken when there
no content review scheduled. In this case, the audit takes the form of
review and will also take the technical content into consideration. A form
format audit usually takes place after the peer walk-throughs and may be
part of the final review scheduled for shortly before delivery of the docu
ment. In that way, it serves as a quality-oriented audit and may lead to fo
mal approval for publication.

When the format audit is informal in nature, a companion conte
review should evaluate the actual technical content of the document. The
are a number of ways in which the content review can be conducted. First
a review by the author's supervisor, which generally is used when form
customer-oriented reviews, such as the PDR and CDR, are scheduled. Th
type of content review serves to give confidence to the producer that th
document is a quality product prior to review by the customer.

A second type of content review is one conducted by a person or grou
outside the producer's group but still familiar enough with the subject ma
ter to be able to critically evaluate the technical content. Also, there are th
customer-conducted reviews of the document. Often, these are performe
by the customer or an outside agency (such as an independent verificatio
and validation contractor) in preparation for an upcoming formal, phase
end review.

Still another type of review is the algorithm analysis. This examines th
specific approaches, called out in the document, that will be used in th
actual solutions of the problems being addressed by the software system
Algorithm analyses are usually restricted to very large or critical system
because of their cost in time and resources. Such things as missile guidance
electronic funds transfer, and security algorithms are candidates for this typ

of review. Payroll and inventory systems rarely warrant such in-depth study.

3.3.1 Requirements reviews

Requirements reviews are intended to show that the problem to be solved is completely spelled out. Informal reviews are held during the preparation of the document. A formal review is appropriate prior to delivery of the document.

The requirements specification (see Appendix D) is the keystone of the entire software system. Without firm, clear requirements, there will no way to determine if the software successfully performs its intended functions. For this reason, the informal requirements review looks not only at the problem to be solved, but also at the way in which the problem is stated. A requirement that says "compute the sine of x in real time" certainly states the problem to be solved—the computation of the sine of x. However, it leaves a great deal to the designer to determine, for instance, the range of x, the accuracy to which the value of sine x is to be computed, the dimension of x (radians or degrees), and the definition of real time.

Requirements statements must meet a series of criteria if they are to be considered adequate to be used as the basis of the design of the system. Included in these criteria are the following:

- Necessity;
- Feasibility;
- Traceability;
- Absence of ambiguity;
- Correctness;
- Completeness;
- Clarity;
- Measurability;
- Testability.

A requirement is sometimes included simply because it seems like a good idea; it may add nothing useful to the overall system. The requirements review will assess the necessity of each requirement. In conjunction with the necessity of the requirement is the feasibility of that requirement. A requirement may be thought to be necessary, but if it is not achievable, some other approach will have to be taken or some other method found to

address the requirement. The necessity of a requirement is most often de:
onstrated by its traceability back to the business problem or business ne
that initiated it.

Every requirement must be unambiguous. That is, every requireme
should be written in such a way that the designer or tester need not try
interpret or guess what the writer meant. Terms like *usually, sometimes, a*
under normal circumstances leave the door open to interpretation of what
do under unusual or abnormal circumstances. Failing to describe behavi
in all possible cases leads to guessing on the part of readers, and Murph
Law suggests that the guess will be wrong a good portion of the time.

Completeness, correctness, and clarity are all criteria that address t
way a given requirement is stated. A good requirement statement will pr
ent the requirement completely; that is, it will present all aspects of t
requirement. The sine of x example was shown to be lacking several nec
sary parts of the requirement. The statement also must be correct. If, in fa
the requirement should call for the cosine of x, a perfectly stated requir
ment for the sine of x is not useful. And, finally, the requirement must
stated clearly. A statement that correctly and completely states the requir
ment but cannot be understood by the designer is as useless as no stateme
at all. The language of the requirements should be simple, straightforwa
and use no jargon. That also means that somewhere in the requiremer
document the terms and acronyms used are clearly defined.

Measurability and testability also go together. Every requirement w
ultimately have to be demonstrated before the software can be consider
complete. Requirements that have no definite measure or attribute that c
be shown as present or absent cannot not be specifically tested. The sine o
example uses the term *real time*. This is hardly a measurable or testable qua
ity. A more acceptable statement would be "every 30 milliseconds, starti
at the receipt of the start pulse from the radar." In this way, the time interv
for real time is defined, as is the starting point for that interval. When th
test procedures are written, this interval can be measured, and the comp
ance or noncompliance of the software with this requirement can be show
exactly.

The formal SRR is held at the end of the requirements phase. It is a den
onstration that the requirements document is complete and meets the crit
ria previously stated. It also creates the first baseline for the software syster.
This is the approved basis for the commencement of the design efforts. A
design components will be tracked back to this baseline for assurance th
all requirements are addressed and that nothing not in the requiremen
appears in the design.

The purpose of the requirements review, then, is to examine the statements of the requirements and determine if they adhere to the criteria for requirements. For the software quality practitioner, it may not be possible to determine the technical accuracy or correctness of the requirements, and this task will be delegated to those who have the specific technical expertise needed for this assessment. Software quality or its agent (perhaps an outside contractor or another group within the organization) will review the documents for the balance of the criteria.

Each nonconformance to a criterion will be recorded along with a suggested correction. These will be returned to the authors of the documents, and the correction of the nonconformances tracked. The software quality practitioner also reports the results of the review and the status of the corrective actions to management.

3.3.2 Design reviews

Design reviews verify that the evolving design is both correct and traceable back to the approved requirements. Appendix E suggests an outline for the design documentation.

3.3.2.1 Informal reviews

Informal design reviews closely follow the style and execution of informal requirements reviews. Like the requirements, all aspects of the design must adhere to the criteria for good requirements statements. The design reviews go further, though, since there is more detail to be considered, as the requirements are broken down into smaller and smaller pieces in preparation for coding.

The topic of walk-throughs and inspections has already been addressed. These are in-process reviews that occur during the preparation of the design. They look at design components as they are completed.

Design documents describe how the requirements are apportioned to each subsystem and module of the software. As the apportionment proceeds, there is a tracing of the elements of the design back to the requirements. The reviews that are held determine if the design documentation describes each module according to the same criteria used for requirements.

3.3.2.2 Formal reviews

There are at least two formal design reviews, the PDR and the CDR. In addition, for larger or more complex systems, the organization standards may call for reviews with concentrations on interfaces or database concerns.

Finally, there may be multiple occurrences of these reviews if the system
very large, critical, or complex.

The number and degree of each review are governed by the standar
and needs of the specific organization.

The first formal design review is the PDR, which takes place at the end
the initial design phase and presents the functional or architectural brea
down of the requirements into executable modules. The PDR presents tl
design philosophy and approach to the solution of the problem as stated
the requirements. It is very important that the customer or user take ;
active role in this review. Defects in the requirements, misunderstandings
the problem to be solved, and needed redirections of effort can be resolv
in the course of a properly conducted PDR.

Defects found in the PDR are assigned for solution to the appropria
people or groups, and upon closure of the action items, the second baselir
of the software is established. Changes made to the preliminary design a
also reflected as appropriate in the requirements document, so that tl
requirements are kept up to date as the basis for acceptance of the softwa
later on. The new baseline is used as the foundation for the detailed desi
efforts that follow.

At the end of the detailed design, the CDR is held. This, too, is a time f
significant customer or user involvement. The result of the CDR is tl
code-to design that is the blueprint for the coding of the software. Mu
attention is given in the CDR to the adherence of the detailed design to tl
baseline established at PDR. The customer or user, too, must approve tl
final design as being acceptable for the solution of the problem presented
the requirements. As before, the criteria for requirements statements mu
be met in the statements of the detailed design.

So that there is assurance that nothing has been left out, each element
the detailed design is mapped back to the approved preliminary design ar
the requirements. The requirements are traced forward to the detaile
design, as well, to show that no additions have been made along the w;
that do not address the requirements as stated. As before, all defects foun
during CDR are assigned for solution and closure. Once the detailed desi
is approved, it becomes the baseline for the coding effort. A requiremen
traceability matrix is an important tool to monitor the flow of requiremen
into the preliminary and detailed design and on into the code. The matr
can also help show that the testing activities address all the requirement

3.3.2.3 Additional reviews

Another review that is sometimes held is the interface design review. Tl
purpose of this review is to assess the interface specification that will hav

been prepared if there are significant interface concerns on a particular project. The format and conduct of this review are similar to the PDR and CDR, but there is no formal baseline established as a result of the review. The interface design review will contribute to the design baseline.

The database design review also may be conducted on large or complex projects. Its intent is to ascertain that all data considerations have been made as the database for the software system has been prepared. This review will establish a baseline for the database, but it is an informal baseline, subordinate to the baseline from the CDR.

3.3.3   Test documentation reviews

Test documentation is reviewed to ensure that the test program will find defects and will test the software against its requirements.

The objective of the test program as a whole is to find defects in the software products as they are developed and to demonstrate that the software complies with its requirements. Test documentation is begun during the requirements phase with the preparation of the initial test plans. Test documentation reviews also begin at this time, as the test plans are examined for their comprehensiveness in addressing the requirements. See Appendix G for a suggested test plan outline.

The initial test plans are prepared with the final acceptance test in mind, as well as the intermediate tests that will examine the software during development. It is important, therefore, that each requirement be addressed in the overall test plan. By the same token, each portion of the test plan must specifically address some portion of the requirements. It is understood that the requirements, as they exist in the requirements phase, will certainly undergo some evolution as the software development process progresses. This does not negate the necessity for the test plans to track the requirements as the basis for the testing program. At each step further through the SDLC, the growing set of test documentation must be traceable back to the requirements. The test program documentation must also reflect the evolutionary changes in the requirements as they occur. Figure 3.4 shows how requirements may or may not be properly addressed by the tests. Some requirements may get lost, some tests may just appear. Proper review of the test plans will help identify these mismatches.

As the SDLC progresses, more of the test documentation is prepared. During each phase of the SDLC, additional parts of the test program are developed. Test cases (see Appendix H) with their accompanying test data are prepared, followed by test scenarios and specific test procedures to be executed. For each test, pass/fail criteria are determined, based on the

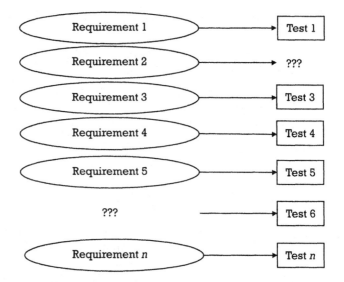

Figure 3.4 Matching tests to requirements.

expected results from each test case or scenario. Test reports (see Appendix I) are prepared to record the results of the testing effort.

In each instance, the test documentation is reviewed to ascertain that the test plans, cases, scenarios, data, procedures, reports, and so on are complete, necessary, correct, measurable, consistent, traceable, and unambiguous. In all, the most important criterion for the test documentation is that specifies a test program that will find defects and demonstrate that the software requirements have been satisfied.

Test documentation reviews take the same forms as the reviews of the software documentation itself. Walk-throughs of the test plans are conducted during their preparation, and they are formally reviewed as part of the SRR. Test cases, scenarios, and test data specifications are also subject to walk-throughs and sometimes inspections. At the PDR and CDR, these documents are formally reviewed.

During the development of test procedures, there is a heavy emphasis on walk-throughs, inspections, and even dry runs to show that the procedures are comprehensive and actually executable. By the end of the coding phase, the acceptance test should be ready to be performed, with all documentation in readiness.

The acceptance test is not the only test with which the test documentation is concerned, of course. All through the coding and testing phase, there have been unit, module, integration, and subsystem tests going on.

Each of these tests has also been planned and documented, and that documentation has been reviewed. These tests have been a part of the overall test planning and development process and the plans, cases, scenarios, data, and so on have been reviewed right along with the acceptance test documentation. Again, the objective of all of these tests is to find the defects that prevent the software from complying with its requirements.

3.3.4 User documentation reviews

User documentation must not only present information about the system, it must be meaningful to the reader.

The reviews of the user documentation are meant to determine that the documentation meets the criteria already discussed. Just as important, however, is the requirement that the documentation be meaningful to the user. The initial reviews will concentrate on completeness, correctness, and readability. The primary concern will be the needs of the user to understand how to make the system perform its function. Attention must be paid to starting the system, inputting data and interpreting or using output, and the meaning of error messages that tell the user something has been done incorrectly or is malfunctioning and what the user can do about it.

The layout of the user document (see Appendix K for an example) and the comprehensiveness of the table of contents and the index can enhance or impede the user in the use of the document. Clarity of terminology and avoiding system-peculiar jargon are important to understanding the document's content. Reviews of the document during its preparation help to uncover and eliminate errors and defects of this type before they are firmly imbedded in the text.

A critical step in the review of the user documentation is the actual trial use of the documentation, by one or more typical users, before the document is released. In this way, omissions, confusing terminology, inadequate index entries, unclear error messages, and so on can be found. Most of these defects are the result of the authors' close association with the system rather than outright mistakes. By having representatives of the actual using community try out the documentation, such defects are more easily identified and recommended corrections obtained.

Changes to user work flow and tasks may also be impacted by the new software system. To the extent that they are minor changes to input, control, or output actions using the system, they may be summarized in the user documentation. Major changes to behavior or responsibilities may require training or retraining.

Software products are often beta-tested. User documents should also tested. Hands-on trial use of the user documentation can point out the d ferences from old to new processes and highlight those that require mc complete coverage than will be available in the documentation itself.

3.3.5 Other documentation reviews

Other documents are often produced during the SDLC and must reviewed as they are prepared.

In addition to the normally required documentation, other documer are produced during the software system development. These include t software development plan, the software quality system plan, the CM pla and various others that may be contractually invoked or called for by t organization's standards. Many of these other documents are of an admin trative nature and are prepared prior to the start of software development.

The software development plan (see Appendix A), which has ma other names, lays out the plan for the overall software development effo It will discuss schedules, resources, perhaps work breakdown and ta assignment rules, and other details of the development process as they a to be followed for the particular system development.

The software quality system plan and the CM plan (see Appendixes and C, respectively) address the specifics of implementing these two dis plines for the project at hand. They, too, should include schedule ar resource requirements, as well as the actual procedures and practices to applied to the project. There may be additional documents called out by t contract or the organization's standards as well.

If present, the safety and risk management plans (see Appendixes L ar M) must undergo the same rigor of review as all the others. The softwa maintenance plan (see Appendix N), if prepared, is also to be reviewed.

Since these are the project management documents, it is important th they be reviewed at each of the formal reviews during the SLC, with modi cations made as necessary to the documents or overall development proce to keep the project within its schedule and resource limitations.

Reviews of all these documents concentrate on the basic criteria ar completeness of the discussions of the specific areas covered. Attention mu be paid to complying with the format and content standards imposed f each document.

Finally, the software quality practitioner must ascertain that all docu ments required by standards or the contract are prepared on the require schedule and are kept up to date as the SLC progresses. Too often, docu mentation that was appropriate at the time of delivery is not maintained the software is maintained in operation. This leads to increased difficulty and cost of later modification. It is very important to include resources for continued maintenance of the software documentation, especially the maintenance documentation discussed in Chapter 8. To ignore the maintenance of the documentation will result in time being spent reinventing or reengineering the documentation each time maintenance of the software is required.

.4 Summary

Reviews take on many forms. Each review has a specific purpose, objective, audience, and cast of participants.

Informal, in-process peer reviews generally occur during the execution of each SDLC phase. They concentrate on single products or even small parts of single products. It is the intention of in-process reviews to detect defects as quickly as possible after their insertion into the product.

Formal, phase-end reviews usually occur at the ends of the SDLC phases and establish the baselines for work in succeeding phases. They also serve as points in the development when the decision to continue (go) or terminate (no go) a project can be made. The phase-end reviews are much broader in scope than in-process reviews. They cover the entire family of products to be prepared in each major SDLC phase, as well as the various documented plans for the project.

Formal project completion audits include the FA and PA. These assess readiness to ship or deliver the software. The PIR assesses the success of the software in meeting its goals and objectives once the software is in place and has been used for a time.

Documentation reviews and audits, both formal and informal, are applicable to each of the software documents. The most basic of the reviews is the peer walk-through. Another basic document review is the format review. This can be either formal or informal. Requirements reviews are intended to show that the problem to be solved is completely spelled out. Design reviews verify that the evolving design is both correct and traceable back to the approved requirements. Test documentation is reviewed to assure that the test program will find defects and will test the software against its requirements. The reviews of the user documentation are meant to determine that the documentation meets the criteria that have been discussed.

Other documents are often produced during the SLC and must be reviewed as they are prepared. Reviews of all of these documents concentrate on the basic criteria and on the completeness of the discussio of the specific areas covered.

Design and code reviews held during the course of the various phases a usually in the form of walk-throughs and inspections. These generally infc mal reviews are held to get an early start on eliminating defects in the pro ucts being examined.

Test reviews are much the same as code reviews, covering the test pr gram products rather than the software products.

Implementation reviews are conducted just prior to implementing t software system into full use.

Reviews take place throughout the SLC and verify that the products each phase are correct with respect to its phase inputs and activities.

3.5   The next step

To find out how to start a review program, consult the following source:

Steve Rakitin, *Software Verification and Validation for Practitioners and Managers, Secor Edition*, Norwood, MA: Artech House, 2001.

Charles P. Hollocker, *Software Reviews and Audits Handbook*, New York: John Wiley Sons, 1990.

Additional reading

Dunn, Robert, *Software Defect Removal*, New York: McGraw-Hill, 1984.

Gilb, Tom, et al., *Software Inspections*, Reading, MA: Addison-Wesley, 1993.

Fagan, M. E., "Design and Code Inspections to Reduce Errors in Program Development," *IBM Systems Journal*, Vol. 15, No. 3, 1976.

Strauss, Susan H., and Robert G. Ebenau, *Software Inspection Process*, New York: McGraw-Hill, 1994.

Wheeler, David A., *Software Inspection: An Industry Best Practice*, Los Alamitos, CA: IEEE Computer Society Press, 1996.

Wiegers, Karl Eugene, *Peer Reviews in Software: A Practical Guide*, Reading, MA: Addison-Wesley, 2001.

Yourdon, Edward, *Structured Walk-throughs*, Englewood Cliffs, NJ: Prentice Hall, 1989.

Testing

The goals of testing are to find defects and verify that the software meets its requirements as perceived by the user. It is unfortunate that, in many cases, the testing program is actually aimed at showing that the software, as produced, runs as it is written. That is, the tests are aimed at showing that the software does not fail, rather than that it fulfills its requirements. This is far short of the real goal of a sound testing program. Testing that is not based on challenging requirements compliance is generally a waste of time.

It has been shown that the cost of finding and correcting a defect goes up dramatically with the length of time the defect is present. This is especially true in the case of design and requirements defects. When a test program merely shows that the software runs, the design and requirements defects are going to come up in the acceptance and operation phases of the SLC. The user or customer is going to discover that the system received is not the system desired or expected. The software will have to go back through large portions of the SDLC, and the costs will be significant.

Two alternatives are to accept the system as is and live with it or to modify it while it is being used. These, too, are expensive situations. The final alternatives are to throw it out and start over or just abandon the whole project altogether. None of these alternatives is especially attractive. The answer seems to be to generate a testing program that will exercise the software against its requirements in such a way as to uncover as many defects as possible as soon as possible in the SDLC.

The types of testing covered here are unit, module, integration, user acceptance, and regression. These tests follow the natural progression of t SLC and lead from one into the next. As the testing progresses, the empha shifts slightly from the pure defect search to a more sophisticated demo stration of the requirements. Early testing intends to exercise as many of t software paths as is practical in order to find mistakes in coding, errors design, and so on. As the SDLC matures, there is less opportunity to exerci all paths of the software, so the concentration is on integrating the modul and subsystems into the whole, and exercising the growing entity again the requirements. The basic goal of finding defects remains, but there is re ance on the earlier testing for the finer, internal details of each modul Later testing deals with the system itself and its interfaces with the outsid as defined in the requirements.

It must be remembered that all testing is designed to challenge the sof ware implementation of the approved requirements. In straightforward da processing applications, this is a straightforward task. In applications such client-server, GUIs, or distributed processing, the approach becomes muc more sophisticated. The underlying rule remains requirements-based tes ing. The quality control practitioner must be well versed in the types applications being tested. To expect a practitioner with specific experience testing traditional accounting systems to step in and immediately be succes ful at testing a distributed processing, embedded, real-time software syste is asking too much. The quality assurance practitioner will recognize this a training requirement and recommend that the tester be given the prop training before he or she is given the new testing task.

The testing program begins in the requirements phase and, effectivel never ends. Regression tests continue for as long as changes and enhanc ments are being made to the system. Figure 4.1 depicts this concept. Plar ning for such a long-lived effort must also begin in the requirements phas and be updated at each milestone step along the way. The planning wi include not only the tests to be run, but also the resources needed, includin people, hardware, support software, schedule, and so on.

4.1 Types of testing

The four most common types of testing are unit, module, integration, an user or acceptance testing. The tests may have different names in differer organizations, but the types are basically the same.

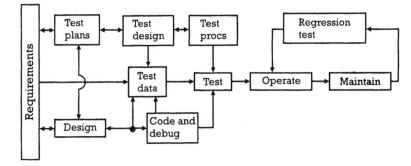

Figure 4.1 SLC testing.

4.1.1 Unit testing

Unit testing, the most basic type of software testing, ignores the concept that document reviews are really a type of testing. Unit testing is usually conducted by the individual producer.

Unit testing is primarily a debugging activity that concentrates on the removal of coding mistakes. It is part and parcel with the coding activity itself. Even though unit testing is conducted almost as a part of the day-to-day development activity, there must be some level of planning for it. The programmer should have documented at least the test data and cases he or she plans to use and the results expected from each test. Part of each walkthrough or inspection of the software should be dedicated to the review of the unit test plans so that peers can be sure that the programmer has given thought to the test needs at that level.

It is worth reiterating the tenet that the tests run must be oriented to the finding of defects in the software, not showing that the software runs as it is written. Further, the defects being found will include not only mistakes in the coding of the unit, but design and even requirements inadequacies or outright mistakes. Even though the unit is the smallest individually compilable portion of the software system, its interfaces and data manipulation can point out wide-reaching defects. Informal though it may be, the unit testing activity is the first chance to see some of the software in action.

It can be seen that the rule of finding defects, not showing that software runs, could be in jeopardy here. In fact, a tradeoff is in play with having programmers test their own software. The expense, in both time and personnel, to introduce an independent tester at this point usually offsets the danger of inadequate testing. With high-quality peer reviews and good, though informal, documentation of the tests and their results, the risk is reduced to a low level. Software quality practitioners, in their audits of the UDF and their

reviews of the testing program as a whole, will also give close attention
the unit test plans and results.

4.1.2 Module testing

Module testing is a combination of debugging and integration. It is som
times called glass box testing (or white box testing), because the tester h
good visibility into the structure of the software and frequently has access
the actual source code with which to develop the test strategies. As integr
tion proceeds, the visibility into the actual code is diminished and the ter
gray box is heard. This refers to the more limited visibility into the softwa
and its structure.

As units are integrated into their respective modules, the testing mov
appropriately from a unit testing—debugging—mode into the more rigoro
module testing mode. Module integration and testing examine the fur
tional entities of the system. Each module is assigned some specific functi
of the software system to perform. As the units that comprise the modu
are brought together into that functional unit, the module tests are run.

The testing program becomes somewhat more rigorous at the modu
level since the individual programmer is not now the primary tester. The
will be in place a more detailed test plan, sets of data and test cases, ar
expected results.

The recording of defects is also more comprehensive at this stage of t
test program. Defects are recorded in defect history logs and regularized te
reports are prepared. As they are found, the defects are fed back into t
code and unit test phase for correction. Each defect is tracked from its fin
ing and reporting through its correction and retest. The results of the corre
tion are monitored and controlled by the CM system that is begun at th
point in the SLC. This is important, since many of the errors that have bee
made, and defects that have been discovered, will affect the design ar
requirements documentation.

Most of the minor coding mistakes will have been caught and correct
in the unit testing process. The defects that are being found in the modu
tests are more global in nature, tending to affect multiple units and mo
ules. Defects in interfaces and data structures are common, but a significa
number of the defects will involve deficiencies in the design and requir
ments. As these deficiencies come to light and are corrected, the design ar
requirements baselines will change.

It is critical to the rest of the SLC that close control of the evolving docr
ments be maintained. If the corrections to the defects found in the test pr
gram are allowed to change the products of earlier SLC phases witho

proper control and documentation, the software system can quickly get out of control. When requirements or design change without commensurate modification to the rest of the system, there will come a time when the various pieces do not fit together, and it will not be clear which versions of the units and modules are correct.

Software quality practitioners will have reviewed the test plans, and the rest of the documentation, prior to the conduct of the module tests. Software quality practitioners are also expected to review the results of the testing. These reviews provide assurance that defects will be recorded, tracked, resolved, and configuration-managed.

4.1.3 Integration testing

Integration testing may be considered to have officially begun when the modules begin to be tested together. This type of testing, sometimes called gray box as discussed in Section 4.1.2, implies a limited visibility into the software and its structure. As integration proceeds, gray box testing approaches black box testing, which is more nearly pure function testing, with no reliance on knowledge of software structure or software itself. Integration testing is largely guided by the critical or detailed design and then the preliminary or architectural design.

As modules pass their individual tests, they are brought together into functional groups and tested. Testing of the integrated modules is designed to find latent defects, as well as interface and database defects. Because the testing up to this point has been of individual modules, several types of defects cannot be detected. Such things as database interference, timing conflicts, interface mismatches, memory overlaps, and so on are found only when modules are forced to work together in integrated packages.

Integration testing uses the same sorts of conditions and data as the individual module tests. Valid data and messages are input, as are invalid conditions and situations. The test designer must be very creative in seeking out valid combinations of circumstances that are possible, but may provide illegal or invalid conditions to the software. The response of the integrated software to these situations is determined, as well as the software performance with valid inputs.

Integration testing is the level at which the quality control practitioner or tester begins to see differences between traditional systems and client-server or distributed processing applications. The greatly increased sets of inputs and initial conditions require some of the more elaborate testing schemes such as record and playback, automated test generation, software characterization, data equivalence, sampling, and the like.

The reporting of test results is very important in the integration to period. How the software responds is recorded and analyzed so that corre tions can be made that fix the experienced defect but do not introduce ne defects somewhere else. Error and defect logs should be maintained f trend analysis that can point to particularly vulnerable portions of the so ware and its development. These portions can then receive additional tes ing to ferret out deep-seated anomalies and improper responses. Clo control must be maintained of the configuration of the software syste through this period so that all changes are properly documented ar tracked. It is in this time frame that many software systems get out of har and accounting is lost as to which version of which unit, module, or subsy tem are the proper one to use at any point.

It is the integration test phase that will uncover many hidden defec with the design and requirements. Formal reviews and less-formal wal throughs and inspections have been used to find many of the design ar requirements defects. But as the software is put into use in an increasing realistic manner, other defects may surface that were beyond the depth the earlier defect-finding efforts. As defects are found in design or requir ments, they must be corrected and the changes in the earlier documer made. This, in turn, may necessitate rework of design, code, and earlier tes ing. Finding such serious defects at this point is very expensive but less than finding the defects in the operations phase. Thus, every effort must I made to maximize the defect-finding capability of the integration tests.

An important role for the software quality practitioner in this effort the review of the integration test plans, cases, scenarios, and procedure Software quality practitioners should make every effort to assure that th integration tests cover the full range of capabilities of the integrated set modules. Review of the test results, and the decisions made on the basis those results, should also be reviewed and approved by the software quali practitioner before testing progresses beyond the integration phase.

4.1.4   User or acceptance testing

User testing is primarily intended to demonstrate that the software compli with its requirements. This type of testing is black box testing, which do not rely on knowledge of the software or the structure of the software. Th testing is intended to challenge the software in relation to its satisfaction the functional requirements.

These tests have been planned based on the requirements as approve by the user or customer. All testing up to this time has been oriented i finding defects in the software. The early tests were also based on th requirements but were designed to show that the software did not comply in one fashion or another to the requirements. By the time the acceptance-testing period is reached, the software should be in a sufficiently defect-free state to permit the emphasis to change.

One important aspect of the acceptance test is that, whenever possible, it is performed by actual intended users of the system. In that way, while it is being shown that the software complies with its requirements, there is still the opportunity to introduce anomalous user actions that have not as yet been encountered. Persons unfamiliar with the system may enter data in incorrect, though technically permitted, ways. They may push the wrong buttons or the correct buttons in an incorrect sequence. The response to these unexpected or incorrect situations is of great importance to users who do not want their system to collapse due to human mistakes. The overriding requirement for every system is that it perform its intended function. This means that if incorrect actions or data are presented, the system will not just abort but will tell the user what has been done wrong and will provide an opportunity for the user to retry the action or input. Invalid data received from outside sources should also be treated in such a manner as to prevent collapse of the system.

Another important consideration of an acceptance test is verification that the new software does not cause changes to workflow or user responsi-bilities that have been overlooked. While it may be shown that the software performs exactly as expected, the associated human-factor changes may make the system difficult to use or cause negative effects on the related work of the users.

The acceptance or user test is usually the last step before the user or cus-tomer takes possession of the software system. It is important that software quality and CM practitioners play very active roles in reviewing and execut-ing the tests, as well as in the change management of the system during this period. Software quality practitioners may even have performed the full execution of the acceptance test as a dry run prior to the system's release for the user operation of the test. CM of the system at this time is critical to the eventual delivery of the exact system that passes the acceptance test.

4.1.5 Special types of tests

Four types of tests may be considered to fall into the special category. These tests are planned and documented according to the same rules and stan-dards as the other types of tests, but they have specific applications. The four major special tests are as follows:

1. Regression;

2. Stress;

3. Recovery;

4. Back-out and restoration.

4.1.5.1 Regression tests

Regression tests show that modifications to one part of the system have n invalidated some other part. Regression tests are usually a subset of the us or acceptance test. They are maintained for the verification that chang made as a result of defects or enhancements during operation do not resu in failures in other parts of the system. Regression tests are an abbreviat revalidation of the entire system using generally valid data to show that tl parts that were operating correctly before the changes are still performing required.

A number of studies indicate that as many as 50% of all changes made a software system result in the introduction of new defects. This may be lo or high, but there is a significant risk involved in the introduction of corre tions. Some, of course, are errors in the change being made, such as codin errors, change design mistakes, and the like. Others, however, come fro unexpected interactions with subsystems other than the one being mod fied. A change to the way a database variable is updated in one module ma affect the time at which another module should read that variable in its ow computations.

Close CM control and analysis of changes, and their impact on the sy tem as a whole, is necessary. Software quality practitioners must be sur that a change control board or equivalent function is involved in all chang activity during both integration testing and the operation phases of the SL(This protects the integrity of the baseline system itself and helps ensure th changes are being made to the correct versions of the affected softwar Delivery of the proper versions of the modifications is also a function of CM which software quality practitioners must monitor.

4.1.5.2 Stress tests

Stress tests cover situations that occur when the software is pushed to, c beyond, its limits of required capability. Such situations as the end of th day, when 23:59:59 hours becomes 00:00:00 and the software is required t recognize that 00:00:00 is later that 23:59:59, must be challenged. The rollo ver of the year field is also a situation ripe for testing. The well-known Y2 situation was concerned with whether software would realize that the yea 00 or 000 was later than the year 99 or 999.

Other stress situations occur when the software is presented with the full number of transactions it is expected to handle plus one or two more. What happens when the transaction $n + 1$ is presented? Does one of the existing transactions get overwritten? Is there a weighting algorithm that selects some transaction for replacement? Is the new transaction merely ignored?

Still another test case is the situation in which the software is run for a long time without interruption. This could easily expose flaws in house-keeping or initialization routines.

Stress tests are an important part of any test program. The types of stress that might be exercised will become apparent as the software develops and the testers understand its construction more clearly. There should be a valid way of handling these and other situations spelled out in the requirements statement. The compliance of the software with the requirement is to be challenged.

4.1.5.3 Recovery tests

Most data centers have recovery procedures for the repair of data on a damaged disk or tape, and they also consider the case of operator errors that may invalidate some of the data being processed. Recovery from abnormal terminations or system crashes may also require recovery tests.

Recovery testing is conducted when a hardware fault or operating error damages the software or the data. This type of testing is critical to the confidence of the user when a data or software restoration has been conducted.

Often, restoration testing can be accomplished by using the regression test software. In other cases, the full acceptance test might be required to restore confidence in the software and its data.

4.1.5.4 Back-out and restoration tests

To back-out and restore is the decision to remove a new software system in favor of the older version that it replaced. Needless to say, developers are usually very embarrassed by such an action because it recognizes that the new system was insufficiently tested or was still so error-ridden that it was worse to use than the old system.

In the case of back-out and restore, the new system is removed from production, any new database conditions are restored to the way they would have been under the old system, and the old system itself is restarted. In the least critical case, the database used by the new system is the same as that of the old system. More often, though, the new system provides expanded database content as well as improved processing. When the contents of the new database must be condensed back into the form of the old

database, care must be taken to restore the data to the form in which the
system would have used it.

The testing required includes at least the acceptance test of the old s
tem, which often is augmented by the running of the most recent set
regression tests used for the old system. Clearly, there must have been so
planning for back-out and replacement when the new system was install
The old system would normally have been archived, but the saving of t
acceptance test and the regression tests must also have been part of t
archiving process.

Great care must be taken to see that the backing out and replacement a
well planned and carried out. Time-critical issues regarding the need for t
replaced system can add to the concerns and complexity of this action.

It is rare that a newly installed system is so badly flawed that it must
replaced. However, it is the responsibility of the quality practitioner to ma
management aware of the threat, no matter how remote.

4.2 Test planning and conduct

Testing is like any other project. It must be planned, designed, documente
reviewed, and conducted.

4.2.1 Test plans

Because proper testing is based on the software requirements, test planni
starts during the requirements phase and continues throughout the SDL
As the requirements for the software system are prepared, the original pla
ning for the test program also gets under way. Each requirement will eve
tually have to be validated during the acceptance testing. The plans for ho
that requirement will be demonstrated are laid right at the start. In fact, or
of the ways that the measurable and testable criteria for the requiremen
are determined is by having to plan for the test of each requirement. Th
test planning at this point is necessarily high level, but the general thrust
the acceptance demonstration can be laid out along with the approaches
be used for the intermediate testing.

Requirements traceability matrices (RTM), which track the requiremen
through design and down to the code that implements them, are used
prepare test traceability matrices (TTM). These matrices track the requir
ments to the tests that demonstrate software compliance with the requir
ments. Figure 4.2 is an example of what a test traceability matrix mig
look like. Each requirement, both functional and interface, is traced to th
primary (P) test that demonstrates its correct implementation. In an ide

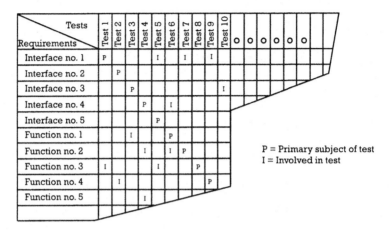

Figure 4.2   Test traceability matrix.

test situation, each requirement will be challenged by one specific test. This is rarely the case, but redundant testing of some requirements and the failure to test others is quickly apparent in the TTM. Also in Figure 4.2, other tests in which the requirements are involved (I) are indicated. In this way, there is some indication of the interrelationships between the various requirements. As the software matures, and requirements are modified, this matrix can offer clues as to unexpected, and usually undesirable, results if a requirement is changed or eliminated.

Conflicts between requirements can sometimes be indicated in the TTM, as the I fields are completed. A common example of requirements conflict is the situation that calls for high-speed processing and efficient use of memory, as in the case of real-time, embedded software. The fastest software is written in highly linear style with little looping or calling of subroutines. Efficient use of memory calls for tight loops, subroutine calls, and other practices that tend to consume more processing time.

Figure 4.2 is an example of a TTM at the system or black box testing level, since the requirements are noted as functions. As the SDLC progresses, so does the planning for the testing, and the TTM becomes more and more detailed until each specific required characteristic of the software has been challenged in at least one test at some level. Not every requirement can, or should, be tested at every level of the test program. Compliance with some can be tested at the white box level; some cannot be fully challenged until the black box testing is in progress.

The TTM is also very important as the requirements evolve throughout the development of the software system. As the requirements that form the basis for testing are changed, added, or eliminated, each change is going likewise impact the test program. Just as the requirements are the basis everything that follows in the development of the software, so, too, are th the drivers for the whole test program.

Some items of test planning are necessarily left until later in the SDL Such things as the bases for regression testing are determined during t acceptance test period as the final requirements baseline is determine Likewise, as new requirements are determined so are the plans for testi those requirements.

Even though some parts of the test planning will be done later, the ove all test plan is completed during the requirements phase. It is also, therefo one of the subjects of the SRR at the end of the requirements phase. As t approved requirements are released for the design phase activities, t approved test plans are released to the test design personnel for the begi ning of the design of test cases and procedures. Figure 4.3 depicts the flow testing, starting with the test plan and culminating in the test reports.

4.2.2 Test cases

The first step in function testing, and often in input/output (I/O) testing, to construct situations that mimic actual use of the software. These situ tions, or test cases, should represent actual tasks that the software us might perform. These may be the same as, or similar to, the use cases som times used in requirements expression.

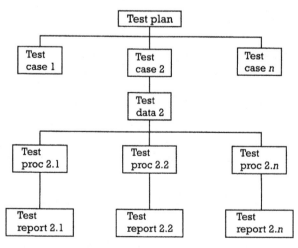

Figure 4.3 Typical testing flow.

Once the test cases are developed, the software requirements that are involved in each test case are identified. A check is made against the requirements traceability matrix to be sure that each requirement is included in at least one test case. If a test case is too large or contains many requirements, it should be divided into subtest cases or scenarios. Test cases—and when used, scenarios—should be small enough to be manageable. Limited size makes sure that errors uncovered can be isolated with minimum delay to and effect on the balance of the testing.

Consider the case of testing the software in a point-of-sale terminal for a convenience store. The store stocks both grocery and fuel products. The test cases, or use cases, might be as follows:

1. *Open the store the very first time.* This would test the requirements dealing with the variety of stock items to be sold, their prices, and the taxes to be applied to each item. It also includes requirements covering the setting of the initial inventory levels.

2. *Sell products.* Sales of various products might be further divided into test scenarios, such as the following:

    a. *Sell only fuel.* This scenario includes those requirements that deal with pump control, fuel levels in the tanks, and the prices and volume of fuel sold. It also tests those requirements that cause the sale to be recorded and the register tape to be printed.

    b. *Sell only grocery items.* Here, the sales events are keyed, or scanned, in on the terminal rather than read from a pump register, so there are requirements being tested that are different from the preceding scenario. The sales recording requirements are probably the same.

    c. *Sell both fuel and groceries.* This scenario, building on the first two, causes the previous requirements to be met in one single sale. There may be additional requirements that prevent the keying of a grocery sale to adversely affect the operation of the pump, and vice versa. It might also be necessary to consider the sequence of sales, such as fuel first and then grocery, or grocery first and then fuel. Other requirements might deal with the interaction of pump register readings with key-entered sales data. Further, a test of the ability to add pump sale charges to keyed sales charges is encountered.

    d. *Provide discounts, coupons, or sales.* An additional scenario might be required to test the proper processing of fleet discounts, bulk sales, cents-off coupons, and the like. Any and all complicatio of the simple sales activity must be tested.

3. *Restock the store.* Having sold sufficient items, it becomes necessary restock shelves and refill fuel tanks. This test case might also de with the changing of prices and taxes and the modification of inve tory levels. It can be seen as an extension of the requirements test in test case 1.

4. *Close the store for the last time.* Even the best businesses eventual close. This test case exercises the requirements involved in determi ing and reporting the value of the remaining inventory. Some these same requirements might be used in tallying weekly or oth periodic inventory levels for business history and planning tasks.

Should comparison of the test cases and scenarios with the RTM reve leftover requirements, additional situations must be developed until eac requirement is included in at least one test case or scenario.

Although this has been a simple situation, the example shows how te cases and scenarios can be developed using the actual anticipated use of th software as a basis.

4.2.3 Test procedures

As design proceeds, the test plans are expanded into specific test cases, te scenarios, and test procedures. Test procedures are the step-by-step instru tions that spell out the specific steps that will be taken in the execution the test being run. They tell which buttons to push, what data to inpu what responses to look for, and what to do if the expected response is n received. The procedures also tell the tester how to process the test outpu to determine if the test passed or failed. The test procedures are tied to th test cases and scenarios that actually exercise each approved requirement

The software quality practitioner reviews the test cases and scenario the test data, and the test procedures to assure that they all go together an follow the overall test plan and that they fully exercise all of the require ments for the software system. Figure 4.4 presents a sample of a test proce dure form.

4.2.4 Input sources

Input of test data is the key to testing and comes from a variety of source Traditionally, test data inputs have been provided by test driver software c

TEST C/S/T _____ TEST DIRECTOR _____ DATE & TIME _____

HARDWARE CONFIG ID _____ SOFTWARE CONFIG ID _____

SET UP_____ INITIALIZE _____ TERMINATE _____ RESTORE _____

PROCEDURES		RESULTS		PASS / FAIL	
NO.	ACTION	EXPECTED	ACTUAL	P	STR

Figure 4.4   Sample test procedure form.

tables of test data that is input at the proper time by an executive test control module specially written for the purpose. These methods are acceptable when the intent is to provide a large number of data values to check repetitive calculations or transaction processors. The use of these methods does diminish the interactive capability of the test environment. The sequential data values are going to be presented regardless of the result of the preceding processing.

As the software system being tested becomes more complex, particularly in the case of interactive computing, a more flexible type of test environment is needed. Test software packages called simulators, which perform in the same manner as some missing piece of hardware or other software, are frequently used. These can be written to represent everything from a simple interfacing software unit to a complete spacecraft or radar installation. As data are received from the simulator and the results returned to it, the simulator is programmed to respond with new input based on the results of the previous calculations of the system under test.

Another type of test software is a stimulator, which represents an outside software or hardware unit that presents input data independently from the activities of the system under test. An example might be the input of a warning message that interrupts the processing of the system under test and forces it to initiate emergency measures to deal with the warning.

The final step in the provision of interactive inputs is the use of a keyboard or terminal that is being operated by a test user. Here, the responses

to the processing by the system under test are (subject to the constraints
the test procedures) the same as they will be in full operation.

Each type of data input fulfills a specific need as called out in the t
documentation. The software quality practitioner will review the varic
forms of test data inputs to be sure that they meet the needs of the test ca:
and that the proper provisions have been made for the acquisition of t
simulators, stimulators, live inputs, and so on.

4.2.5   Expected results

Documentation of expected results is necessary so that actual results may
evaluated to demonstrate test success or failure. The bottom line in any t
program is the finding of defects and the demonstration that the softwa
under test satisfies its requirements. Unless the expected results of each t
are documented, there is no way to tell if the test has done what the t
designer intended. Each test case is expected to provide the test data to
input for it. In the same way, each test case must provide the correct answ
that should result from the input of the data.

Expected results may be of various sorts. The most common, of course,
simply the answer expected when a computation operates on a given set
numbers. Another type of expected result is the lighting or extinguishing
a light on a console. Many combinations of these two results may also occu
such as the appearance of a particular screen display, the starting of a moto
the initiation of an allied software system, or even the abnormal end of t
system under test when a particular illegal function has been input, f
example, an invalid password into a software security system.

It is the responsibility of the software quality practitioner to review t
test documentation to ensure that each test has an associated set of expect
results. Also present must be a description of any processing of the actu
results so that they may be compared with the expected results and
pass/fail determination made for the test.

4.2.6   Test analysis

Test analysis involves more than pass/fail determination. Analyses of t
expected versus actual results of each test provide the pass or fail determin
tion for that test. There may be some intermediate processing necessa
before the comparison can be made, however. In a case in which previo
real sales data is used to check out the new inventory system, some adjus
ments to the actual results may be necessary to allow for the dating of t
input data or the absence of some allied software system that it was not co

effective to simulate. In any case, the pass/fail criteria are applied to the expected and received results and the success of the test determined.

Other beneficial analysis of the test data is possible and appropriate. As defects are found during the testing, or certain tests continue to fail, clues may arise as to larger defects within the system, or the test program, than are apparent in just a single test case or procedure. By analyzing test data over time, trends may appear that show that certain modules to be defect prone and need special attention before the test program continues. Other defects that might surfaces include inadequate housekeeping of common data areas, inappropriate limits on input or intermediate data values, unstated but implied requirements that need to be added and specifically addressed, design errors, sections of software that are never used or cannot be reached, erroneous expected results, and so on.

Software quality practitioners can play an important role in the review and analysis of the test results. It is not as important that software quality practitioners actually perform the analysis as it is that they ensure adequate analysis by those persons with the proper technical knowledge. This responsibility of software quality practitioners is discharged through careful review of the test results and conclusions as those results are published.

4.2.7 Test tools

Many automated and manual test tools are available to assist in the various test activities.

A major area for the application of tools is in the test data provision area. There are commercially available software packages to help in the creation and insertion of test data. Test data generators can, on the basis of parameters provided to them, create tables, strings, or files of fixed data. These fixed data can, in turn, be input either by the test data generator itself or by any of several test input tools. General-purpose simulators can be programmed to behave like certain types of hardware or software systems or units. Stimulators that provide synchronous or asynchronous interrupts or messages are also available. It is more likely, though, that most of these tools will be created in-house rather than obtained outside so they can be tailored to the test application at hand.

Another area in which tools are available is that of data recording. Large-scale event recorders are often used to record long or complicated interactive test data for future repeats of the tests or for detailed test data analysis. In association with the data recorders are general- and specific-purpose data reduction packages. Large volumes of data are often sorted and categorized so that individual analyses may be made of particular areas of

interest. Some very powerful analysis packages are commercially availab
providing computational and graphical capabilities that can be of great ass
tance in the analysis of test results and trend determination.

Tools of much value in the test area include path analyzers. These to
monitor the progress of the test program and track the exercising of t
various paths through the software. While it is impossible to execute eve
path through a software system of more than a few steps, it is possible
exercise every decision point and each segment of code. (A segment in tl
context means the code between two successive decision points.) A pa
analyzer will show all software that has been executed at least once, poi
out any software that has not been exercised, and clearly indicate thc
code segments that cannot be reached at all (as in the case of a subrouti
that never gets called or a decision point that cannot take one branch f
some reason).

Many of these tools are commercially available. Most applications
them, however, are in the form of tools specifically designed and built fo
given project or application. Some development organizations will custor
build test completeness packages that software quality practitioners will u
prior to acceptance testing or, perhaps, system release. Whatever th
source or application, the use of test tools is becoming more and more ne
essary as software systems grow in size, complexity, and criticality. Softwa
quality practitioners should monitor the application of test tools to be su
that all appropriate use is being made of them and that they are being us
correctly.

4.2.8 Reviewing the test program

An important part of the software quality practitioner's activity is to revie
the test program. As discussed in Section 3.3.3, review of the test docume
tation is important. In fact, the full test program should be reviewed reg
larly for status, sufficiency, and success. Such reviews are expected to be a
integral part of the major phase-end reviews, as explained in Section 3.1.
It is reasonable to hold less formal, in-process reviews of the test program
testing progresses and more of the software system is being involved.

The development test documentation permits this review of the who
test approach as it is formulated. Without a documented approach to tl
problems of testing the software, the testing tends to become haphazard ar
undisciplined. There is a strong tendency on the part of many project ma
agers to commit to a firm delivery date. If the project gets behind schedu
the slippage is usually made up by shortening the test phase to fit the tin
remaining, adding more testers, or both. Shortening the test phase al

happens in the case of budget problems. The great, mythical woodsman Paul Bunyan told of a tree that was so high that it took a man a full week to see its top. But, if he had six of his friends' help, they could see it in one day. This probably would not work in the real world, and having more testers is usually not a solution to a test phase that is too short either.

If a well-planned and well-documented test program is developed, the temptation to shorten the testing effort to make up for other problems is reduced. By having a software quality practitioner review and approve the documentation of the test program, there is even more impetus to maintain the program's integrity.

The documentation of the test program should extend all the way to the unit and module tests. While these tend to be more informal than the later tests, they, too, should have test cases and specific test data recorded in, at least, the UDF. The results of the unit and module tests also should be recorded. Software quality practitioners will review the results of the unit and module tests to decide, in part, whether the modules are ready for integration. There may even be cases in which the module tests are sufficient to form part of the acceptance test.

4.3 Who does the testing?

Until recently, the common preference concerning who actually performed the testing favored the independent tester. While this is still valid in some very critical software situations, the definition of independent has been changing for most applications.

On the basis of the concept that everyone is responsible for their own work and that this responsibility also applies to groups, the task of testing is being returned to the developers. This is not to say that programmers should test all their own work, but that the development group is responsible for the quality of the software that they deliver.

A programmer should test only that software for which he or she has sole responsibility. Once the work of more than one person is to be tested, an independent tester, that is someone other than the persons involved, should carry out the testing. Even at this level, though, the testers should come from within the development group responsible for the full set of software. Outside testers are only necessary at the full software system test level when all the developers have an investment in the software.

Unit, module, and most integration testing are the proper tasks of the development organization. This is consistent with total quality concepts and the idea that every person (or in this case organization) is responsible for the

quality of his or her own work. The very early testing is in the form
debugging, and as the unit tests cover more of the software, they flow in
module tests. Module tests, too, are primarily debugging in nature. Even th
initial integration tests can be thought of as advanced debugging, althous
this is more of an organizational decision than an industrywide convention

The characteristic of debugging that separates it from rigorous testing
that defects are generally fixed on the spot without much formal chang
control. At whatever time the organization institutes some level of chang
control, the testing is usually considered out of the debugging process ar
into rigorous testing. This is not to say that there is no configuration contr
up to this point. Configuration control is already in effect on the documer
tation. Any change that affects the requirements or design must be pro
essed formally to maintain the integrity of the documentation and th
system as a whole. Changes that merely fix mistakes in the code can l
made with minimum control at this stage, since the only elements involve
are individual units or modules, or small groups of two or three close
interfacing modules prior to actual integration.

There should, however, be at least an audit trail of the changes mai
tained in the UDF. This will be used for error and defect history analysis a
the development proceeds. Software quality practitioners should monite
the testing at the unit and module level to be sure that such an audit trail
provided. Software quality practitioners are also an appropriate resour
for the error and defect history analysis. Conclusions reached as a result
the analysis should be fed back, as improvements, into the developmer
process.

As the time for full-scale integration and system testing arrives, a te
team that is organizationally independent from the producers should tak
over the testing. Because the goal of the test program is to find defects, th
objectivity of an independent test team greatly enhances the quality of th
testing. The independent testers will perform the testing tasks all the way t
user or acceptance testing. This team is probably the group that produce
the formal test program documents. User or acceptance testing should b
performed by the users themselves, preferably in the user's environment, t
help ensure that the software meets the user's expectations, as well as th
officially approved requirements. Table 4.1 suggests appropriate testers fc
each type of testing described above. As each organization's test progran
matures, the identification of the testers for each type of test will be base
on the organization's experience and testing approach.

Regression tests are conducted by many different persons involved in th
SLC. The developers will regressively test changes to modules and subsys
tems as they make changes in response to trouble reports generated durin

Table 4.1   Who Tests What

Type of Testing	Tester
Debugging	Programmer
Unit testing	Programmer
Module (or object) testing	Programmer
Module (or object) integration testing	Third party
Subsystem and system integration testing	Third party
System testing	Developer test team
User/acceptance testing	User test team

formal testing or maintenance. The test team will also have occasion to use regression testing as they verify that new modules or subsystems do not adversely affect the system as a whole. Software quality practitioners can even use regressive testing techniques as they perform some of their audit and review tasks.

The software quality practitioner's primary role in the testing process, aside from reviewing and approving the test documents, is to monitor the testing as it progresses. The software quality practitioner will audit the tests against their plans and procedures and report the status of the test program to management. There are added benefits if software quality practitioners have been doing more than just cursory reviews of the documentation as it has been produced. The cross-fertilization of the technical knowledge of the system and the test planning for the system can produce better results in both areas.

.4   **Summary**

Testing has as its goals the finding of defects and verifying that the software meets its requirements. The cost of finding and correcting a defect goes up dramatically with the length of time the defect is present. The basic types of testing are unit, module, integration, user or acceptance, and regression.

Unit testing is primarily a debugging activity that concentrates on the removal of coding mistakes. Module integration and testing examine the functional entities of the system. As modules pass their individual tests, they are brought into increasingly larger functional groups. Testing of the integrated modules is designed to find latent defects, as well as interface and database defects. User testing is primarily intended to demonstrate that the software complies with its approved requirements as they are perceived by the user. Regression tests are usually a subset of the user or acceptance tests.

They are maintained to verify that changes made to the software do r result in failures in other parts of the system.

As the requirements for the system are prepared, the original pla ning for the test program also is started. During software design, the t plans are expanded into specific test cases, scenarios, and step-by-step t procedures.

Expected results are an important part of the test procedures. Unl the expected results of each test are documented, there is no way to jud whether the test has performed as intended. Analyses of the expect versus actual results of each test provide the pass or fail determination that test.

A necessary part of the software quality practitioner's activities is t review of the test program. The software quality practitioner's additior role is to monitor the testing as it progresses. The practitioner will audit t tests against their plans and procedures and report the status of the test pr gram to management.

Tests follow the natural progression of the SLC. The testing progra begins in the requirements phase and, effectively, never ends, since regre sion tests continue for as long as there are changes and enhancements bei made to the software system.

4.5   The next step

Testing takes on many forms and must adapt to every type of software, fro traditional data processing applications through embedded real-time sy tems to client-server and distributed systems. Starting points for your testi efforts could be the following texts:

William E. Perry. *Effective Methods for Software Testing,* New York: John Wiley & Sor 2000.

Matthew A. Telles. *The Science of Debugging,* Scotsdale, AZ: Coriolis Group, 2001.

Additional reading

Beizer, Boris B., *Black Box Testing: Techniques for Functional Testing of Software Systems* New York: John Wiley & Sons, 1995.

Bourne, Kelly C., *Testing Client/Server Systems,* New York: McGraw-Hill, 1997.

Haug, Michael (ed.), *Software Quality Approaches: Testing, Verification, and Validation,* Berlin: Springer-Verlag, 2001.

Kaner, Cem, et al., *Testing Computer Software, Second Edition*, New York: John Wiley & Sons, 1999.

Myers, G., *The Art of Software Testing*, New York: John Wiley & Sons, 1979.

Perry, William, *Effective Methods for Software Testing*, New York: John Wiley & Sons, 2000.

Schulmeyer, G. Gordon, and Garth MacKenzic, *Verification and Validation of Software Intensive Systems*, Upper Saddle River, NJ: Prentice Hall, 2000.

CHAPTER

5

Contents

Defect Analysis

Most organizations use the term quality to mean no, or few, defects. Some consider quality to mean meeting users' or customers' expectations. In the context of this book, both are correct. Any time that the software does not perform as the user expects, a defect has been encountered. It matters little to the user whether the problem is a coding error, a missed requirement, or just a function that would be nice to have but is absent.

It is no secret that defects occur in the SLC from the beginning of the concept phase through the final removal of the software system from use. Each defect that is found is expected to be corrected. The recording and tracking of defects ensures that all defects found are, in fact, addressed. Defect analysis applies to all defects and is intended to lead to the correction of current deficiencies and the elimination of defects in the future. Analysis of defects is the primary road to defect reduction. It can show where we started, where we are, and where we are going,

Defect analysis is the bridge between product-oriented software quality control activities and process-oriented software quality assurance activities of the SQS. Defect analysis is a combination of detecting product flaws so that they can be removed, and the analysis of defect and error data so future defects can be prevented. Defect reporting, tracking, and removal are adjuncts to configuration control (see Chapter 6).

While it useful to analyze defects in the system currently being developed, analyzing long-term trends also should be conducted to give clues to weak areas in the software development process. As a history of defect data is accumulated, it can

97

provide indications of where modifications to the software developme
process can be effective. It is these problem analyses that provide the brid
from quality control—(detecting product errors) to quality assurance
(detecting process weaknesses).

This chapter concentrates on the quality assurance application of defe
analysis and the metrics that can be developed.

5.1 Analysis concepts

Defect analysis is the discipline of measuring software development and us
The measures can come from surveys, defect data, schedule and budg
plans and records, system characteristics, help line usage, and so on. Eac
organization will discover and determine the sources of measurements be
suited to their own needs and situations.

Metrics are an essential part of any software quality system. They a
relationships between measures that turn the measurement data into appl
cable, quality management information. However, they are too ofte
merely an exercise in collecting numbers without developing any usef
information. The role of the quality assurance practitioner is to bring
decision-making, action-capable managers the information they need
beneficially affect the software development process, and metrics are on
useful when they contribute to that information base.

5.1.1 Measures

A number, such as 6 or 1,000, is not a metric. It is merely a number, usuall
with no information value. When a dimension is added to the number, suc
as lines of code (LOC) or critical errors (CE), a measure is created that
more descriptive than a number by itself but still without significant utilit
Six CEs and 1,000 LOCs are both measures, but they hold no informatio
until they are related to something.

5.1.2 Metrics

In this book, a metric is defined as the ratio of, or relationship between, tw
measures. Thus, a defect density of 6 CEs per 1,000 LOCs (KLOC) begins t
take on the characteristic of information. Ratios of metrics finally reac
real information status. For example, one could compare a defect density c
6 CE/KLOC before institution of software inspections to a defect density c
2 CE/KLOC after inspections begin.

Defect metrics are, not surprisingly, those metrics composed of measures dealing with defects. The measures might include number of software system failures, number of calls made to the help line, time spent recoding after a failure, and cost of lost sales after a bad press review based on too many errors found by the reviewer. The list could go on and on. A typical defect metric is number of problem reports closed versus the number of new problem reports recorded.

Nondefect metrics are just that; metrics that are not based on defects. Budget overruns, schedule shortfall, size of the software system in lines of code or function points, module complexity, cost of computer time, and the like are representative of nondefect measures. Nondefect measures are combined to develop nondefect metrics. An example of a nondefect metric might be LOC developed per person-month.

5.1.3 Product analysis

Product analysis is the first area for most organizations to begin to measure. Error frequency, software product size, development cost, number of tests run successfully, and the like are often the kinds of things measured in the beginning. Most of these product metrics can be developed directly from the software trouble reports (STR) and project planning documentation. Product metrics deal with the attributes of the product, defect characteristics, and other data about the product.

Using product metrics, the software quality control practitioner can locate error-prone areas of the code, design weaknesses, testing flaws, and so on. These metrics also help the quality assurance practitioner identify efforts that can beneficially affect the specific product being analyzed. In the longer run, product analysis will build up a body of information that can be applied to process-oriented analyses.

5.1.4 Process analysis

It is the goal of the software quality assurance practitioner to improve the process by which the various software products are produced. Process improvement models and process assessment models are becoming important throughout the software industry. International standard ISO 9000 is a family of quality standards that require stable and improving processes. The SEI's CMMI is a model for assessing the ongoing improvement in the software development process of an organization. Another international effort, ISO 15504, is under way and it, too, is a process assessment and improvement approach. These and other efforts are based on the concept process identification, definition, and continuous improvement.

Process understanding and improvement depend heavily on the resu of product analysis. As each product is reviewed, tested, operated, a maintained, a history of its defects and changes can be kept. By itself, t record of analysis of defect and nondefect data for a single product will n be especially useful on a process basis. It is the continuing analysis of mul ple products' data that leads to the body of information that describes t process. At this point, the software quality assurance practitioner can beg to describe the process and its behavior.

Analysis of defect detection methods and their results can give insig into their value. Comparing when and how defects are detected as oppos to when they were introduced into the software products is one view of th process. Comparing budget and schedule actual values with estima reflects on the estimation and management processes. Analysis of def types gives insight into the development process strengths and weakness Tracking the levels of the costs of the quality program versus its effects pr vides information about the quality process. Once an understanding of t behavior of the process is achieved, intentional modification to the proce will result in identifiable changes in the products it produces. In this wa the software quality assurance practitioner is able to suggest benefic process changes based on data and information rather than on guesses.

For example, if defect records show that walk-throughs are finding mo defects than testing, the quality practitioner may do further research determine if the walk-throughs are finding most of the defects and th fewer exist for testing to uncover, or if the testing process is not sufficient robust.

5.2   Locating data

The collection of data, in the form of measures, is a necessary task if we a to develop metrics. Most data will come from easily available sources, su as budget and schedule reports, defect reports, personnel counts, help li call records, and the like. The data usually reflects defect experience, proje planning and status, and user response to the system.

5.2.1   Defect reporting

When software systems and programming staffs were small, the usu method of trouble reporting was to note the location of the defect on listing or note pad and give it to the person responsible for repair. Documentation defects were merely marked in the margins and passed back to the author for action. As organizations have grown, and software and its defects have become more complex, these old methods have become inadequate. In many cases, though, they have not been replaced with more organized, reliable techniques. It is clear that the more information that can be recorded about a particular defect, the easier it will be to solve. The older methods did not, in general, prompt the reporter for as much information as was available to be written down.

Figure 5.1 depicts a typical defect reporting form. It is a general software defect report. The actual format of the form is less important than the content. Also of less importance is the medium of the form; many organizations are reporting troubles directly on-line for interactive processing and broad, instant distribution.

SOFTWARE TROUBLE REPORT

```
┌─────────────────────────────────────────────────────────────────────────┐
│CONTROL NO. _____   PRIORITY - E H M L  PAGE ___ OF ___  │
│DATE _____ TIME _____       TYPE - ___ A I L  D _____  │
│SOURCE - R D C T O _____       SEVERITY - C S M T _____   │
│PHASE -  R D C T O _____       EST: HRS _____ $_____   │
│METHOD - Q W I D TA U _____       ACT: HRS _____ $_____   │
├─────────────────────────────────────────────────────────────────────────┤
│PROBLEM APPEARS IN:                                                        │
│SYSTEM    _____      SUBSYSTEM _____   │
│MODULE    _____      UNIT _____   │
│DOCUMENT  _____      DOCUMENT NO._____   │
│PAGE NO. _____ PARA _____     LINE NO._____   │
├─────────────────────────────────────────────────────────────────────────┤
│PROBLEM DESCRIPTION:                                                       │
│                                                                           │
│                                                                           │
│                                                                           │
├─────────────────────────────────────────────────────────────────────────┤
│PROPOSED SOLUTION:                                                         │
│                                                                           │
│                                                                           │
│SUBMITTED BY _____ ORG. _____ TEL. NO. _____         │
├─────────────────────────────────────────────────────────────────────────┤
│PROBLEM ACCEPTED ☐ PROBLEM REJECTED ☐ PROBLEM COMBINED WITH ___           │
├─────────────────────────────────────────────────────────────────────────┤
│DISPOSITION:                                                               │
│                                                                           │
│RESPONSE BY _____ ORG. _____ TEL. NO. _____          │
├─────────────────────────────────────────────────────────────────────────┤
│ACCEPTED - SCN NUMBER _____ DISPOSITION REJECTED ☐                    │
└─────────────────────────────────────────────────────────────────────────┘
```

Figure 5.1 Software trouble report.

It can be seen that the STR in Figure 5.1 is a combined document/so ware defect report. While many organizations maintain both a docume and a software defect processing system, there is much to suggest that such separation is unnecessary. Using the same form, and then, logically, t same processing system, eliminates duplication of effort. Further, all defe reports are now in the same system and database for easier recording, trac ing, and trend analysis. Table 5.1 defines the codes used in the samp shown in Figure 5.1.

The STR form shown in Figure 5.1, when used to report documentatio defects, asks for data about the specific location and the wording of t defective area. It then calls for a suggested rewording to correct the doc mentation defect, in addition to the simple what's wrong statement. In th way, the corrector can read the trouble report and, with the suggested sol tion at hand, can get a more positive picture of what the reviewer had mind. This is a great deterrent to the comment "wrong" and also can help avoid the response "nothing wrong." By including the requirement for concise statement of the defect and a suggested solution, both the auth and the reviewer have ownership of the results.

As a tool to report software defects, the STR includes data to be provid by both the initiator (who can be anyone involved with the softwa

Table 5.1 Software Trouble Report Codes

Code or Field	Meaning
Control number	Usually a sequential number for keeping track of the individual STRs.
Priority	An indication of the speed with which this STR should be addressed:
	E = emergency; work must stop until this STR is closed.
	H = high; work is impeded while this STR is open.
	M = medium; some negative impact on work exists until this STR is closed.
	L = low; This STR must be closed, but it does not interfere with current work.
Source	The phase in which the error was made that introduced the defect being described (these will depend on the organization's actual life cycle model and its phase names):
	R = requirements
	D = design
	C = code
	T = test
	O = operation

Table 5.1 (continued)

Code or Field	Meaning
Severity	An estimate of the impact of this defect had it not been found until the software was in operation: C = critical-persons could die or a firm could go out of business S = Serious = grave injury to persons or organizations M = Moderate = injury or loss, but not permanent T = Trivial = little or no impact
Phase	The phase in which this defect was detected (typically the same names as for source): R = requirements D = design C = code T = test O = operation
Estimate: hours and money	An estimate of the costs of correcting this defect and retesting the product
Method	The defect detection technique with which this defect was detected (each organization will have its own set of techniques): Q = quality audit W = walk-through I = inspection D = debugging or unit testing T = testing A = user acceptance testing O = operation
Actual: hours and money	The actual costs of correcting this defect and retesting the product

throughout its life cycle) and the corrector. Not only does it call for location, circumstances, and visible data values from the initiator, it asks for classification information such as the priority of the repair, criticality of the defect, and the original source of the defect (coding error, requirements deficiency, and so on). This classification information can be correlated later and can often serve to highlight weak portions of the software development process that should receive management attention. Such correlations can also indicate potential problem areas when new projects are started. These potential problem areas can be given to more senior personnel, be targeted for tighter controls, or receive more frequent reviews and testing during development.

5.2.2   Other data

Other, nondefect measures are available from many sources. During devopment of the software system, project planning and status data is availab.
These data include budget, schedule, size estimates (such as lines of cod
function points, pages counts, and so on).

After installation of the system, data can be collected regarding custom
satisfaction, functions most used and most ignored, return on investmer
requirements met or not met, and so on.

5.3   Defect repair and closure

An important aspect of the trouble report, in whatever manner it is impl
mented, is that is provides a means to assure that each defect is address
and the solution recorded. The closure of trouble reports should follow
prescribed procedure. Defects that are reported, but never resolved, ca
resurface at a later, and perhaps much more damaging or expensive, poi
in the SLC. The software quality practitioner is responsible for monitorir
all open trouble reports and keeping management informed as to the
status. In this way, there is less chance for a defect to escape notice ar
become lost. There is also a check and balance with the developers to l
sure that they are not letting defects go unheeded in favor of further deve
opment activities.

The forms in Figures 5.1 and 5.2 both provide for recording the dispos
tion of the defect. The trouble report is not considered closed until this are
is filled in. Defects can get lost in the system if they are not tracked to the
closure and reported as finished. Each organization should have standar
that govern the reporting and tracking of defects. One of these standar
should specify the length of time a defect may remain unaddressed befo
further activity is halted and the defect is specifically addressed. The use (
on-line defect recording and status reporting can make this task quite eas
and give it increased visibility.

Each trouble report, for either documentation or software in genera
should provide a forward reference to the formal record of disposition of th
defect and its resolution. As stated, defect reports can directly record th
defect dispositions. In some organizations, there is a separate report for th
disposition of a defect correction or change. One format for a separat
record is the software change notice (SCN), shown in Figure 5.2. This coul
be used if a separate form is required to formally implement the change. I
this way, the report-fix-implement-report loop is closed, and a complet
trail is formed of the treatment of each reported defect.

Software Change Notice

SCN #:	DATE:	AUTHORIZED BY:	
		INSTALLED BY:	
		CM APPROVAL:	

STR / DTR #	MODULE / DOCUMENT TO BE CHANGED	REGRESSION TEST BY:
		PAGE _____ OF ___

Figure 5.2 Software change notice example.

The closure of a trouble report usually describes the action taken to correct the defect. Of course, not all trouble reports are correct themselves. There can be instances in which what was perceived as a defect was not a defect at all. Perhaps an incorrect keystroke caused a result that looked like a software defect. The trouble report still exists, however, and even though there is no change spelled out, the report must be formally closed. As a side observation, should later correlation of defect data show a high number of

no-defect trouble reports, some attention may be needed on the topic
defect reporting itself.

In projects under formal CM, trouble report closures that require C
processing, especially approval of the change before implementation (s
Section 6.3.2) will reflect any CM action involved. The defect tracking act.
ity will show when the defect and its planned solution were presented
CM processing, what was done, and the results. Once CM approval I
been obtained, the defect returns to the regular processing path
implementation.

Figure 5.3 depicts a typical defect reporting, tracking, and closure proc
dure. Each organization will have some version of this procedure that
suited to its own situation. All aspects of this procedure should be prese:
though. In some of the topics covered in this book, the breadth of applie
tion of the topic within a given organization of project is left up to the d
cretion of the organization or project. Defect reporting and tracking is
sufficiently important topic that only the actual technique used for each
the activities is seen as discretionary. The presence of a complete defe
reporting and tracking system is not optional in an effective SQS.

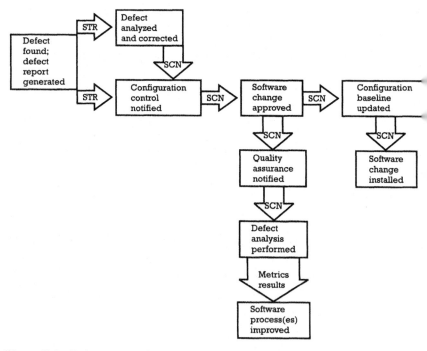

Figure 5.3 Defect processing example.

.4 Selecting metrics

The goals of the SQS lead to questions about defects and their effects. Those questions, in turn, lead to metrics that may provide defect information. The metrics then lead to the measures that must be collected.

In some organizations, a record of unrepeatable defects is kept. While a suspected defect could not be repeated on one project, it might occur again on another project, and its root cause eventually determined.

5.4.1 Available metrics

It is possible to create any number of metrics. In the most trivial sense, every measure can be combined with every other measure to create a metric. Metrics, in and of themselves, are not the goal of a beneficial SQS. Just because one organization uses a metric does not mean that metric will have meaning for another organization. An organization that does not use CICS will not be interested in a metric expressing CICS availability. One that uses LOC as their size measure will not want to compute function points per person-month.

Other metrics may be too advanced for some organizations. Organizations just starting to develop metrics will likely be ready to monitor open and closed problem reports. They are not likely to use metrics that attempt to express the validity of the software system development estimation algorithm until they have been using metrics for some time. In the case of estimation, a new metrics-using organization may not even have a repeatable method of estimating the size and cost of software systems development.

The selection of specific metrics to develop is a function of the goals of the SQS. This book does not intend to imply that there are certain metrics that all organizations should use. This section merely introduces a few sample metrics that some organizations have found useful. A more detailed discussion of specific metrics is given in Section 5.4.3. The metrics identified here are not all-inclusive by any means. They are intended to give the new defect analysis or SQS implementer ideas of what metrics to use and what questions to ask.

5.4.2 Applicable metrics

Most metrics are either product oriented or process oriented.

5.4.2.1 Product-oriented metrics

Of significant interest to software quality assurance practitioners is the product defect experience of the current software development project and its predecessors. For a given software product, defect experience can serve an indication of its progress toward readiness for implementation. Sor metrics can lead to identification of error-prone modules or subsysten Others indicate the reduction in defect detection as defects are found a removed.

Rework generally is considered to be any work that is redone because was not done correctly the first time. Most frequent causes of rework a corrections needed to resolve defects or noncompliance with standar Monitoring rework metrics can help the software quality assurance prac tioner demonstrate the advisability of better project planning and clos attention to requirements.

5.4.2.2   Process-oriented metrics

Of historical interest are much the same set of metrics, but for the body software products already completed rather than for just the current proje or products. Long-term defect experience helps us understand the develo ment process and its stability, predictability, and level of improvability. Tl software quality assurance practitioner will track trends in defect detectic and correction as indicators of process maturity.

Productivity metrics give indications of process effectiveness, quality estimation techniques, quality of defect detection techniques, and the lik Some are based on defects, some on nondefect data.

Trend analysis is the long-term comparison of measures and metrics determine how a process is behaving. Statistical process control, error dete tion rates, output over time, cost of quality, and help line usage are examples of measures and metrics that can be studied over a period of tim Such study looks for trends that will describe the development process or reaction to intentional change. The use of process control charts for softwa can help describe the behavior of the development process. The char can also help identify process behavior changes in response to intention changes made to the process.

5.4.2.3   Cost of quality

The cost of quality (COQ) is often used to measure the value of the SQS. B combining the costs of resources expended to prevent errors from happen ing and to appraise the quality of a product, we can find the cost of achiev ing quality (COA). This value is added to the costs of resources expende because quality was not achieved—the cost of failure (COF). The sum (COA plus COF represents the COQ.

Prevention costs include such items as training, the purchase of methodology, the purchase of automated tools, planning, standarc development, and other similar items. These are costs incurred to reduce the likelihood that an error will be made in the first place.

Appraisal costs result, for the most part, from reviews and testing. These are costs incurred to look for errors once the product has been produced.

Failure costs are incurred when a product manifests an error. It is important to recognize that only the first review of a product, or the first test of a piece of code, counts as an appraisal cost. Any rereviewing or retesting required because a defect has been found and corrected is a COF. This is a cost that would not have incurred had the task been done correctly the first time.

Failure costs include the cost of rework, penalties, overtime, reruns of applications that fail in production, lawsuits, lost customers, lost revenues, and a myriad of other costs. The COF in most companies may be found to contribute half to three-quarters of each dollar spent on the overall COQ.

Table 5.2 presents some typical components of the COQ.

5.4.3 SQS goal-oriented metrics

There is a seemingly unending list of metrics that can be developed. It is important that the organizational goals and those of the SQS be understood before metrics are haphazardly chosen and applied. The metrics types mentioned so far are reasonable for consideration by organizations just

Table 5.2 Quality Cost Contributors

COQ Category	Representative Contributing Costs
Prevention	Training and education
	CM
	Planning
	Standards
Appraisal	Reviews (until defect found)
	Testing (until defect found)
Failure	Rework
	Rewriting specifications and plans
	Rereviewing (after defect correction)
	Retesting (after defect correction)
	Scrap
	Customer complaint handling
	Lost customers
	Missed opportunities

beginning to use metrics in their SQSs. As each organization grows in exp rience with its SQS, additional goals, questions, and metrics will becom useful. More advanced metrics will come to light as the SQS is applied ov time.

Table 5.3 suggests possible goals of the SQS and some representativ metrics that could apply or be beneficial in reaching those goals.

Table 5.3 Goals and Metrics

SQS Goal	Applicable Metric
Improved defect management	COQ changes/SQS implementation schedule
	Cost of rejected software (scrap)/ total project cost
	Cost of defect corrections/cost of defect detection
	Defect density/software product
	Defect density/life-cycle phase
	Defects found by reviews/defects found by testing
	User-detected defects/developer-detected defects
	STRs closed/total STRs opened
	STRs remaining open/STRs closed
	STRs open and closed/time period
	Mean time between failures
	Software product reliability
	Help line calls/software product
Improved requirements	Changed requirements/total requirements
	Implemented requirements/total requirements
	Requirements errors/total errors
Improved defect detection	Tests run successfully/total tests planned
	Defects found by reviews/defects found by testing
	Defect density/software product
	Defects inserted by life-cycle phase/ defects detected by life-cycle phase
	User-detected defects/developer-detected defects
Improved developer productivity	KLOC or function points/person-month
	Schedule or budget actuals/estimates
	Budget expenditures/schedule status
	Mean time to repair a defect
	Defects incorrectly corrected/total defects

Table 5.3 (continued)

SQS Goal	Applicable Metric
	Software product defects/software product complexity
Improved estimation techniques	Schedule or budget actuals/estimates
	Mean time to repair a defect
	Budget expenditures/schedule status
Increased data center throughput	Incorrect corrections/total corrections
	Mean time to repair a defect
	User-detected defects/developer-detected defects

None of the metrics suggested in Table 5.3 should be construed to be required or even desirable for all organizations. No text on metrics could cover the vast array of potential metrics available to the developer of an SQS. Even less likely is that a book could guess the exact set of metrics that applies to every possible organization. The intention of this chapter is to identify typical metrics so that the implementing organization will see the types of concerns that its SQS could address.

.5 Collecting measurements

Once an organization has decided which metrics to use, it can turn its attention to collecting the necessary measures. From the SQS's point of view, most measures will be related to defects.

5.5.1 Classification of defects

As defects are detected, analyzed, and corrected, much data are available that is of use to the software quality assurance practitioner. Classification of defects aids in the use of defect data to guide defect resolution now and to identify software development process weaknesses or predict problem areas in the future. This is the connection or bridge between software quality control—finding and fixing defects—and software quality assurance—analyzing and improving the development process. Defects can and do occur in any phase of the SLC. The data gathered with respect to defect classification can direct additional testing of software, point out inherent anomalies in requirements or design, call attention to needs for enhancements to operational software, and give guidance in the correction of current defects.

Defects can be classified according to their various basic characterist (see Figure 5.1), which should include at least the following:

- Severity of the defect if encountered in operation;
- Priority of immediate repair;
- Source (life-cycle phase) of the defect;
- Type of defect;
- Phase (life-cycle phase) in which the defect was found;
- Method by which the defect was found;
- Estimated and actual costs to repair the defect.

The severity of a defect is an indication of the impact of not fixing immediately. A defect that presents a life-threatening situation or cou result in the loss of property if not fixed is a very severe defect indeed. (the other hand, some defects may result in a wrong answer from a calcul tion but do not, for instance, hold up further testing until they are correcte Such defects would be fairly nonsevere until they began to impact the te program itself. (This shows that some factors are a function of situation well as immediate impact.)

Related to, and sometimes dependent on, the severity of a defect is t repair priority that is assigned to it. Usually a life-threatening defect will addressed immediately, and a noninterfering defect will be addressed wh there is time. This, of course, is not a hard and fast rule. There will be occ sions in which a severe defect can be isolated so that work can continue other areas. Some defects may be of such complexity or wide-reachi effect that they cannot be repaired without extended study or serio impact on resources. These defects may be addressed immediately b require a solution that is a long time in coming. Recognition that work ca continue while the defect in question is being solved can give it a lower pi ority. Other factors may affect the priority as well, not the least of which visibility. A relatively minor screen format defect may become a top priori defect if it is in a highly visible demonstration that will affect the futu funding of a software project.

A piece of classification data that is often overlooked is the source, genesis, of the defect. This is an indication of where the original error w made and where the defect entered the product. It also points to areas in tl SDLC that may profit from increased attention by software quality practiti ners. When later correlation of defects shows a high concentration of defec that can be traced back to the requirements, it is probably wise to sper more effort in the generation and review of requirements in future projec

Likewise, a preponderance of coding errors may indicate the need for better programmer training. By looking at the data collected on multiple projects, the quality assurance practitioner can suggest changes to management that affect the software development process. New data from projects begun after the process changes have been made can provide information of the effectiveness of these modifications.

The type of defect encountered is one indication of weakness in design, implementation, or even support software. I/O defects involve the transfer of data into or out from the object, module, or other part of the software system. These transfers may be internal to the system or external to the software, as with a key entry or printer action. When seen frequently, I/O-type defects may suggest an operating system that is difficult to use. Arithmetic defects are problems in computations that may indicate weak support routines or less-than-desirable coding practices. Arithmetic defects are also caused by incorrect requirements, such as specifying an equation incorrectly. Control defects occur primarily in decisions within the software. Indexed loops, wrong exits from decision points within the software, and improper transfers of control between objects or modules are examples of the control type of defect. Control defects are often indicative of design or requirements deficiencies.

Two additional characteristics are less defects-based and more indicative of the benefit of the detection techniques being used. The phase in which defects are found, that is, in what part of the SLC, can be compared with the source to evaluate the various review methods being used. Capturing the method by which defects are found permits direct comparisons of the efficiency of the different methods and can also indicate which defect detection methods are more successful against various types and sources of defects.

Finally, the estimated and actual costs to repair lead to evaluations of the estimation techniques employed and can be useful in calculating the COQ (see Section 5.4.2.3).

5.5.2 Other defect measures

Certainly not all the measures will be restricted to defect classifications. Countless other defect-related measures can be made. The following list is not intended to be complete, but rather to suggest some potentially useful measures:

- Number of defects;
- Defect frequencies;
- STRs open and resolved;

- Time between defect detections;
- Defects resulting from correction of previous defects;
- Size of change;
- Incorrect defect reports (incorrect information on STRs).

The number and frequencies of defects can be used to detect defe prone products or processes. These measures are usually taken with refe ence to specific parts of the system or its documentation. Once the system in production, these counts may be used to monitor the system's maturi or its need for maintenance. Modules or documents with higher-tha average defect counts may need redesigning or rewriting. In addition, hi defect counts or frequencies in a particular product may require a compa to redeploy its defect detection efforts.

Defects tend to clump. A quality control adage is that if a defect is foun look in the same area for more. Since defect detection resources are alwa limited, this adage can give an organization clues as to where to concentra quality control activities. High counts or frequencies spread more or le evenly across products may indicate a development process problem. T quality assurance practitioner should always be alert to process flaws th may be indicated by inordinate defect experience.

Open and resolved STR counts can be used to determine defect detectic and correction productivity, identify poor defect analysis and isolatic methods, detect flawed defect correction techniques, and so on. T number of resolved STRs can be compared to the number of newly opene or still open, STRs to monitor correction activities.

The time between defect detections, either directly indicated by date ar time or via mean time to failure can be used in several ways. Longer tim may indicate a reduced defect level or reduced defect detection success effort. Stable, or shorter, times might indicate the addition of defects durir the making of modifications or of increased defect detection efforts improved detection processes.

Defects resulting from the resolution of other defects are known to frequent. This measure will aid in the identification of poor defect resolutic processes or insufficient quality control of software modifications.

The size of the change is often one of the comparative measures used develop various metrics. In combination with other measures, size can be normalizing factor. Do not compare data from small, short projects wi data from large or long schedule projects. Such comparisons are ofte invalid and can lead to erroneous conclusions. For example, if two projec both have 10 STRs opened per day, one might presume that the defect leve were about equal. However, when it is discovered that the first project is only a 3-month project involving two people and the second is a 3-year project with 25 participants, a rather different conclusion about their respective defect levels will likely be made.

Not all reported defects are defects. In some cases, the detected operation of the system is not wrong, just unexpected; for example, incorrect expected results in the test case or an inexperienced system user. In other cases, the data entered on the STR may be incorrect—(i.e., wrong module name, incorrect document reference, wrong version, and so on). The quality assurance practitioner will want to determine what causes the incorrect STRs. Training users or defect reporters may be necessary, or better user documentation might be the answer. In any case, it is not productive to try to correct defects based on incorrect reports.

5.5.3 Nondefect measures

Defect analysis depends on defect data, but defect data alone is not sufficient for most metrics. Nondefect data is usually the basis for product and process metrics. In some cases, it forms the whole metric, as noted in Section 5.4.2.

Some nondefect measures are readily available and are in hard numbers. These include project size, budget and schedule figures, clock and processor time, number of people involved in an activity, and the like. These measures can be taken directly, and no interpretation of them is usually needed.

For the software quality practitioner, some measures are not available in hard numbers but rely on quantification of subjective data. These soft measures include customer impressions, perceived quality on some subjective scale, estimates of quality, and so on. Soft measures should be used with care, for there is often no precise way to quantify or validate them.

Derived measures include those that cannot be determined through either hard or soft means. One such derived measure might be quality, which ranks as good (a soft measure) since 90 users out of 100 (a hard measure) do not return survey forms and, thus, must not be dissatisfied. Great care must be exercised with measures such as these. Only organizations with significant experience in metrics should consider using derived measures.

5.6 Quality tools

The representation of measures and metrics may take many forms. Even their collection must be considered. The following tools are most often used for measure collection and measure and metric use:

- Tally sheet;
- Scatter diagram;
- Graph;
- Histogram;
- Pareto diagram;
- Flowchart;
- Cause and effect diagram;
- Statistical control chart.

None of these tools is new. The hardware quality practitioner has h. such tools available for many years. Some, such as the tally sheet and th scatter diagram, have been regularly used in software quality activities. Ot ers, like the cause and effect diagram and statistical control charts, are rel tively new to software quality applications.

5.6.1 Tally sheet

The tally sheet is the simplest form of data collection. Each occurrence some event or situation is tallied as it happens or is detected. The example Figure 5.4 depicts a collection of data for defects detected in several modul of software being reviewed. Note that this is merely a collection detected-defects data. Taken by itself, the collection gives little or no info mation about the modules beyond pure defect counts. It is usually benefici to chart or graph the numbers for comparison.

Module	Defect count	(× five)	Total
1	‖‖		20
2	‖‖‖ ‖		30
3	‖‖‖ ‖‖‖	Plus 4	54
4	‖‖‖	Plus 2	27
5	‖‖‖ ‖‖‖		40
6	‖‖‖ ‖‖‖	Plus 2	52
7	‖‖‖ ‖‖‖ ‖‖‖ ‖‖‖		90
8	‖‖‖ ‖‖		35
9	‖‖‖ ‖‖‖	Plus 3	43
10	‖‖	Plus 2	12
11	‖‖‖ ‖	Plus 1	31
12	‖‖‖ ‖‖‖	Plus 3	53

Figure 5.4 Tally sheet.

5.6.2 Scatter diagram

Figure 5.5 presents the data from the tally sheet in a more mathematical form. The numbers are the same, but some people find this representation more understandable. The scatter diagram gives a visual comparison of the numbers from the tally sheet. Sometimes, it is useful to plot the trend line or least-squares curve that summarizes the scattered points. The dashed line represents an estimate of the data trend.

5.6.3 Graph

In its simplest form, a graph is just a scatter diagram with the points connected. Continuing the defect count example, Figure 5.6 is a graphical representation of the numbers on the tally sheet. Graphs are often preferred for observing the progress of a process or activity with respect to time. Continuing the example, the modules 1–12 may have been completed in the time sequence shown. More information, such as calendar dates or complexity, can be shown in a graph. We might discover that module 7 was highly complex, while module 12 was completed near year's end.

5.6.4 Histogram

A histogram is similar to the graph, but instead of connecting the points with a line, they are shown as vertical [or horizontal] bars whose lengths represent the numbers. Figure 5.7 is a histogram of the tally sheet data. Histograms are often precursors to Pareto charts and are sometimes expanded to have the width represent an additional condition, such as size or effort.

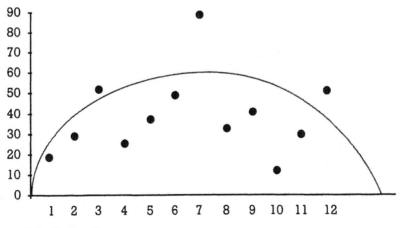

Figure 5.5 Scatter diagram

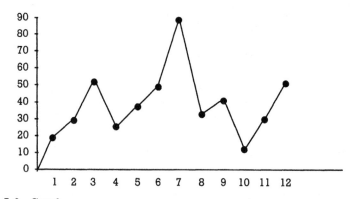

Figure 5.6   Graph.

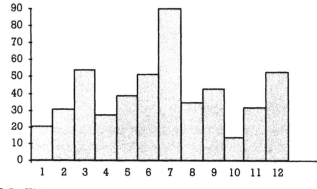

Figure 5.7   Histogram.

5.6.5   Pareto diagram

In the nineteenth century, economist Vilfredo Pareto determined th approximately 80% of his country's wealth was controlled by about 20% the population. Thus was born the 80/20 rule. Although originally directe toward economics, the 80/20 rule has come to be used in many applic tions, including software quality management. The 80/20 rule in softwa quality management suggests that we pay attention to the products th account for 80% or so of the defects. Admittedly not mathematically pre cise, it serves as a good guide to the application of quality effort.

The Pareto diagram is the histogram arranged in (usually) descendin order of bar height. Figure 5.8 is the Pareto representation of the tally she numbers. Also indicated is the approximate 80% point. Software quali

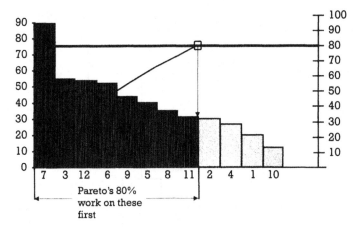

Figure 5.8 Pareto diagram.

practitioners could use a Pareto diagram to prioritize their examination of the causes for the defect numbers associated with each module.

5.6.6 Flowchart

Flowcharts are diagrams that permit users to describe processes. They are not used to represent data, but rather the way in which things are done. Manufacturing, sales, banking, military, software, in fact nearly all processes have been described with flowcharts. The software quality assurance practitioner will use the flowchart to depict the various processes used in software development, maintenance, operation, and improvement. As the metrics begin to suggest flaws in one or another process, the flowchart can help isolate the part of the process that is flawed. Figure 5.9 depicts the format for a typical flowchart.

Continuing our example, the development process for each module might be flowcharted to look for differences that might account for the variations in the defect rates. Alternatively, the defect detection processes might be flowcharted in a search for their variations and the reasons for their differing results.

5.6.7 Cause-and-effect diagram

Another diagram used to locate process flaws is the cause and effect diagram. Defect detection and correction is responsible for eliminating the defect. Cause and effect diagrams are used to determine the actual cause of a

An aid to understanding the process

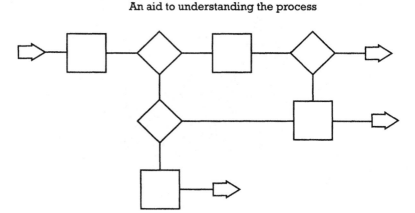

Figure 5.9 Flowchart.

defect. In this way, not only is the defect itself eliminated, but the situatio that permitted it to be introduced is also eliminated, so it will not occ again.

The cause and effect diagram, an example of which is shown Figure 5.10, is also called the Ishikawa diagram after Professor Kaoru Isl kawa, who introduced it in Japan, and the root cause diagram Note that ne ther the flowchart nor the cause and effect diagram is used to depict dat Rather, they help describe processes and analyze defect causes.

In our example, based on the high defect rate for module 7, the softwa quality practitioner might use the cause and effect diagram to seek out th specific causes for the high defect rate, rather than just guessing.

Coupled with the knowledge of the module's complexity, the time year of its creation, the type(s) of defect detection methods applie

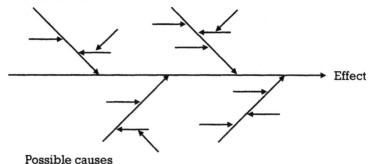

Figure 5.10 Cause-and-effect diagram.

flowcharts of the development and defect detection processes, and, perhaps, its cost and schedule variations from expectations, the cause and effect diagram can assist the quality practitioner in the analysis. One arm might represent all the potential effects of calendar dates, another the effects of schedule or budget changes, still another the effects of requirements changes, and so on. The user of the cause and effect diagram tries to examine each potential cause until the actual root cause of the situation is discovered. The diagram serves to document each potential cause examined and its relationship to other potential causes.

5.6.8 Process control charts

In 1931, Walter Shewhart applied the laws of statistics to production processes and discovered that the process behavior can be plotted. He then showed how the process can be controlled and how that control can be monitored.

5.6.8.1 Run charts

Run charts depict the statistical behavior of a process. Shewhart intended that these be used to show when a process was stable or in control. It is not based on the intended or target behavior of the process but its actual behavior. Figure 5.11 shows a basic process control chart. The center line is the mean level of the described characteristic (perhaps the error rate for a given software system). The upper line is the upper control limit (UCL) and indicates the presence of special causes of defects. The lower line is the lower control limit (LCL) and also reflects special causes, this time because the product is better than it has to be. Shewhart set the UCL and LCL as functions of the mean and standard deviation for the population being plotted.

The idea of evaluating process behavior using a run chart is depicted in Figure 5.12. A process that has an error rate falling consistently between the

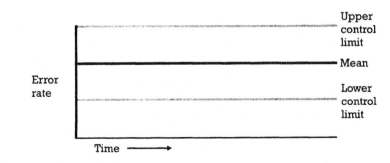

Figure 5.11 Basic run chart.

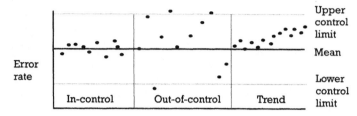

Figure 5.12 Process behavior.

control limits (as in the first section of Figure 5.12) is said to be in contro
An occasional point outside the limits identifies a special case, a target fo
cause and effect analysis. In general, however, the process is considere
sound and repeatable. The second section of Figure 5.12 shows the case
which the points fall randomly around the mean. This process is said to b
out of control. Changes to the process are not likely to be identified wi
changes in the results. The third section of Figure 5.12 shows a process
control but drifting. In the manufacturing world, we might conclude that
tool was getting worn. In software we might suspect that a defect detectio
technique was improving (the drift implies that we are finding more defect
or that the development process was degenerating (and letting more defec
into the products).

Continuous process improvement might be depicted as in Figure 5.1
Based on the Japanese concept of *kaisen* (continuous improvement throug
small changes), the process is continually improved. As a result, the contro
limits, still functions of the mean and standard deviation, tend to mov
closer to the mean.

5.6.8.2 Acceptance control charts

Acceptance control charts are not based on statistical determination of th
mean and control limits. These charts use the desired value, called the ta
get, as the centerline. The upper and lower control limits are chosen base
on permissible variation, not statistical variation.

In software terms, when depicting defects, we would like all three line
to lie on the zero-defects line. That is also the ultimate long-term goal of th
SQS. In the meantime, and in the real world, there are other pressures tha
slow our attainment of the zero-defect goal. Just like in the hardware worl
of Shewhart, costs and risks will define the realistic levels for the target an
control levels. In economic terms, we might say that the UCL is the level a
which the customer will no longer accept the product, and the LCL the leve
at which the costs of finding further defects exceed the costs incurred if th
defect occurs in the use of the software. Stated still another way, the UC

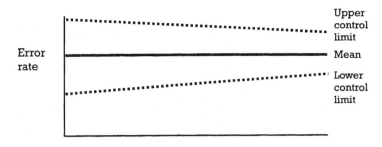

Continuous improvement

Figure 5.13 Kaizen concept.

defines "how bad I dare to make it" and the LCL defines "how good I can afford to make it."

Acceptance control charts are not as statistically valid as run charts, but they do not require the large sample and population sizes on which run charts are usually based. Acceptance control charts are more easily adapted to the uses of the software quality assurance practitioner, however. Figure 5.14 combines the acceptance control chart, the *kaizen* concept, the desire for zero defects, and economic reality into a typical software process control chart. In this chart, the LCL is set as close to zero as is economically feasible. The centerline, the target defect rate, starts at the current experienced value and slopes downward at the goal rate of the SQS. At the same time, the UCL is more sharply sloped to motivate process improvement.

.7 Implementing defect analysis

The creation of a metrics program starts with determining the requirements or reason for measuring something. Just as in the development of software,

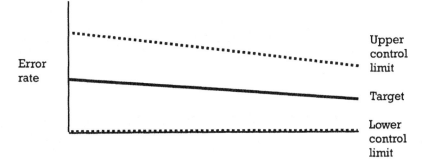

Figure 5.14 Toward zero defects.

defining the problem we wish to solve is the first step. Once we know wh information we might want, we can begin to determine what measures c lead us to our objective.

It is unfortunate that there are few, if any, metrics in common use in t industry. Even those measures that many organizations use, such as LO function points, error counts, time, and so on, are not defined industrywi In effect, each organization that counts something counts it in its own w. For that reason, when one company claims to have one error per thousa delivered LOC, another company may have no idea as to how it compar The reason is that there is no commonly accepted definition of either err or LOC. Even function point users know that there are variations in he function points are defined and counted.

The solution may be for a given company to design its metrics progra for its own situation. When the company has a metrics set that preser information about its software processes, it might offer those measures the industry as guidelines. At some point, other companies may adopt ar adapt those metrics, and a de facto standard may be born. The IEEE has pu lished a standard covering the establishment of a metrics program (IE Standard 1061-1992) that could certainly be a starting point for a compar just starting to develop its own program.

5.7.1 Rules

When preparing to design and implement a defect analysis and metrics pr gram, a few simple but important rules should be observed. Many progran are started, and most fail in the first year or so. In order to have a god chance for success, the following should be considered:

- The program must be instigated and supported from the top of th organization down.
- The metrics must support quality as seen from the custome perspective.
- The measurements must not interfere with the performance assigned work.
- The people being measured must have a role in defining the measur ments and methods.

The primary reason for failed programs is failure to observe these vit considerations.

Support from top management is necessary because, as measurements are begun, they must be seen to be of interest—and value—to top management. If management does not use the metrics, ignores the results of the program, does not provide for the costs of data collections and metrics development, and is not visibly committed to the success of the metrics program, the rest of the organization will soon conclude that metrics do not matter.

Metrics that are developed for the sake of metrics will usually not be used. Metrics that are not used become targets for elimination. The metrics developed must be based on defects and other data that will lead to better customer satisfaction. If the program does not result in increased customer satisfaction, the costs will eventually be determined to have been wasted. That is almost always the end of the program.

Even when top management supports the defect analysis and metrics program, if it gets in the way of job performance, the workers will not cooperate. The persons conducting the data gathering must remember that the rest of the people are busy with the jobs to which they are assigned. They are being paid to do their work, not the measurer's. When pressures mount, the assigned task gets attention, not additional side tasks that do not appear in the worker's job description.

It should not be a surprise that if you are going to measure my productivity, the defect history of my work, and things of that nature, I want some influence over, or at least a full understanding of, what is measured, how the data is collected, and what the metrics and their use will be.

Perhaps even worse than non-customer-focused metrics are those used for personnel evaluations and comparisons. Especially damaging to the metrics program is defect data that is construed to reflect workers' performance. When that is the case, the program will not survive as a useful activity. It must always be remembered that you get what you measure. If my defect data is going to be used against me, there will be very little accurate defect data available to the software quality practitioner or management.

5.7.2 Designing the program

A defect analysis or metrics program should be treated exactly the same as the development of software. It is a project with requirements and must be designed, coded, tested, implemented, and maintained. The following simple five-step approach can be used to define and start the program:

1. Define the goals of the program.
2. Ask questions about the use of the program and metrics.

3. Identify the metrics to be developed and used.

4. Identify the measures that must be made to gather the data for t metrics.

5. Plan the data collection, metrics development, and metr application.

It has been stated that the defect analysis or metrics program must ha established goals before anything else is done. This is analogous to the se ting of vision and mission statements for the organization. The goals of t program lead to questions about customer attitude, product quality, defe experience, process improvement opportunities, and the like. The answe to the questions give insight into what kinds of metrics will be of value. we are just interested in defect analysis, one set of metrics may emerge. we are interested in improved quality and processes, a larger set of metri will be recognized. In every case, the organization must perform these ste in the context of its own maturity, business, and capabilities.

Once the metrics that will be needed are defined, the data and requir measurements can be defined as well. It was noted earlier that some da consists of hard numbers that are collectable directly. Other data is soft subjective, in the form of opinions, guesses, feelings, and so on. The sc data must be quantified for used with the hard data. The organization mu determine the quantification methods and how precise they believe tł quantifications to be.

Throughout the process of defining goals, asking questions, and identif ing metrics and measures, the people whose work and products will be tł subjects of the measures must be involved. Acceptance of the program is n the only thing requiring the participation of the people being measured. Tł persons doing the work are the closest to all the things being mea ured—their effort, products, processes, defects, and so on. They often ca suggest metrics and measures that have even more utility than those cox ceived by the software quality practitioners. If the program is to succeed, it imperative that the voice of the workers be solicited and heard.

5.7.3 Metric characteristics

If the SQS and the metrics program have requirements, so have the metri themselves. Measures and their resulting metrics must be easy to gather an develop. Measures that require extensive investigation or complicated co lection methods will tend to be poorly collected (at least at the beginning ‹ the program). Section 5.4 suggested that many useful metrics compris easily collected measures. These measures and metrics should form the basis of the beginning metrics program. As experience and maturity is gained, more sophisticated metrics and measures can be adopted. In the beginning, *keep it simple* is a good motto.

Metrics must also be easy to understand and apply. It may be possible to determine the number of defects per thousand LOC written from 10 P.M. to 11 P.M. on a cloudy Friday the 13th by developers in Bangalore, India, compared to the same data for developers in Fort Wayne, Indiana. Whether there is useful information in that metric is another question. If there is information, of what use is it? As metrics become more sophisticated, their understandability often becomes more difficult. Many of the metrics being converted from hardware to software quality applications must be redefined for use on software. These metrics are generally applicable after their adaptation but frequently require very large sample sizes to be meaningful. Again, the new metrics program must be useful. Utility of the metrics being developed is more important than whether they comprise the most complete set of metrics.

Validity of the metrics is another key point. Do the metrics correctly reflect their target situation? An example was given in Section 5.5.2 of the need to consider the size of the project in a given situation. Metrics that are sensitive to parameters other than those in the direct equation may not reflect the real situation. The software is tested to determine if all its requirements have been corrected addressed. Metrics, too, need to be tested to ensure that they present the information we want and do so correctly and repeatably. Careful definition of each of the data terms being used, specification of exact data collection methods to be used, and precise equation for the metrics can only reduce the likelihood that the metric is developed incorrectly. The real question being asked is whether the metric is the correct one for the desired application. It must be shown that the metric actually applies to the situation in which we are interested. Is the metric in support of the original goals of the program? Does it address the organization's concerns? Does it give us information that we need and do not have elsewhere? The comparison of defects between Bangalore and Fort Wayne may be available and precise, but if we really do not have a need for that comparison or know what to do with it, it is not beneficial to develop it.

5.8 Summary

Defects can and do occur in any phase of the SLC. Recording and tracking defects in the software makes sure that all found defects are, in fact,

addressed. An important aspect of the trouble report, in whatever manne
is implemented, is that it provides a means to ensure that each defect
addressed and the solution recorded.

Changes require careful control. Every time a change is made, there
the chance that a new defect will be introduced with the change. In proje
under formal CM, trouble report closures that require CM processing, a
especially including formal change approval, will reflect any CM acti
involved.

Classification of defects aids in the use of defect data to guide defect res
lution now and identify software development process weaknesses. Futu
problem areas can also be predicted using error or defect trend analysis.

As defects are found and eliminated, a body of data about the defects c
be accumulated. These data become input for quality assurance analys
Such analysis as trends and metrics can be conducted to help depict t
development process in use and its potential weaknesses. While finding a
fixing defects is the quality control role, and defect analysis aids in the rep
of defects, the quality assurance practitioner needs defect data to help ide
tify potential process flaws. The defect data is also useful as empirical info
mation that can aid decision-making, action-capable management in
process modifications.

5.9   The next step

No text can cover the entire scope of software metrics, but these two a
good starting points:

Robert B. Grady. *Successful Software Process Improvement,* Upper Saddle River, NJ:
Prentice Hall, 1997.

John McGarry et al. *Practical Software Measurement for Objective Decision Makers,*
Boston, MA: Addison-Wesley, 2001.

Additional reading

Burr, Adrian, and Mal Owen, *Statistical Methods for Software Quality: Using Metrics to
Control Process and Product Quality,* Lexington KY: International Thomson Publishing
1996.

Campanella, Jack, *Principles of Quality Cost,* Milwaukee, WI: ASQ Quality Press,
1999.

Feigenbaum, Armand V., *Total Quality Control,* New York: McGraw-Hill, 1991.

Goodman, Paul, *Practical Implementation of Software Metrics*, New York: McGraw-Hill, 1993.

Humphrey, Watts S., *Managing the Software Process*, Reading, MA: Addison-Wesley, 1989.

Kan, Stephen H., *Metrics and Models in Software Quality Engineering*, Reading, MA: Addison-Wesley, 1995.

McConnell, John, *The Seven Tools of Quality, Fourth Edition*, Manly Vale, Australia: Delaware Books, 1992.

Musa, John D., *Software Reliability Engineering*, New York: McGraw-Hill, 1998.

CHAPTER

6

Contents

Configuration Management

CM is the discipline that ensures that the state of the software at any given time is known and reconstructable. CM is a discipline that covers hardware as well as software, but in this book CM will be limited to software unless specifically stated otherwise.

CM comprises three basic elements: configuration identification (CID), configuration control (CC), and configuration accounting (CA). While each element may be invoked without the others, CM is incomplete in the absence of any of them.

CID provides a method for specifically and uniquely identifying each instance (e.g., release, version) of a given software product or set of products. By using a standard naming convention that allows for the identification of every instance of the product, each new draft of a document, each new compilation of a unit, or each new build can be specifically identified.

CC is the element that ensures that each change to an instance of the product is known, authorized, and documented. CC includes the activities of the change control board (CCB), which reviews and authorizes changes to the documents and code as increasingly formal control is placed on the developing software system. The software library may also be included as a function of CC.

CA serves to keep track of the status of each instance of the product. This becomes increasingly important as units and modules are integrated into subsystems and systems. It is obvious that the specific parts of a given system must be known so the system itself can be known. CA also assigns and tracks the status of each baseline of the requirements, test, design, code,

131

and so on, as the software effort proceeds. Another growing requirement
CA is the case of a basic product that is adapted for use in multiple instal
tions, each with slight variations in the total requirements set.

The increased use of reusable code makes all CM elements more imp
tant than ever.

Figure 6.1 presents an overview of CM processing.

6.1 CM components

Traditionally, CM has included identification of the items to be configu
tion managed, control of the changes to the identified items, and main
nance of the status of each item.

6.1.1 Configuration identification

CID permits unique and uniform naming of each component and product
the total software system down to the lowest separable level. Any syste
including software systems, is separable into smaller and smaller parts do

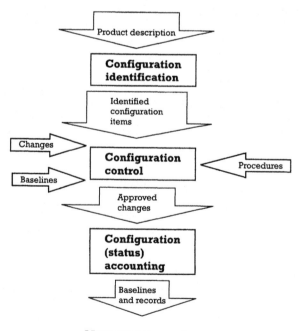

Management overview

Figure 6.1 CM overview.

to some desirable, manageable level. In this book, the lowest level of a software system—that is, the smallest component that can be assembled or compiled—is called the unit. Increasingly larger components are the module, the subsystem (there may be more than one level of subsystem depending on the size of the system), and finally the system itself. The documentation goes through a similar separation from the original requirements statement to the individual module and unit design specifications, the code, and the test procedures.

Each of these subdivisions, code components, and documents will go through multiple issues as they are developed. The primary issue usually is called a release. This is a formal issue and usually represents a baseline. After a release is issued, updates are made. These are often called versions and represent significant changes to the release, but not wholesale modification or replacement.

Finally, in some large systems, there may be reissues of versions that may be little more than recompiles, or document updates to make editorial or minor corrections. These low-level issues may be called editions, patches, dot releases, or any other name with meaning to the organization. Note that the actual terms used are up to the organization. As in most areas of software engineering, there are no industrywide standard names for these levels of products. Figure 6.2 shows an example of a hierarchical structure of these product levels.

It is clear that the management of all of these subdivisions and issues is critical to the development and delivery of a quality software system. The first step in the CM of all the various subdivisions and issues is to give each of them a unique identifier. This is the role of CID.

As each product—a component of code or a document—comes into being, it must be assigned an identifier that will depict its instance, its parent (the next larger component of which it is a part), and its age (when it was created). In this way, users of the product can be sure they have the exact

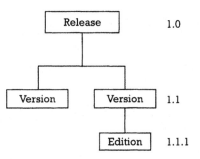

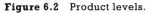

Figure 6.2 Product levels.

issue that is appropriate for their use. As shown in Figure 6.2, each level ca
ries the name of its parent for continuity in identification. Not all identific
tion schemes carry this information, as will be seen in Section 6.2.1.

6.1.2 Configuration control

CC ensures that all—and only—approved changes are made to the baselin
Having established a given baseline, all changes must be acted on wi
increasing formality and control. Early in the development, there are no
mally few products to consider as changes are perpetrated. There is, f
example, usually only one requirements document. Changes to that or
document, early in the requirements phase, may be easy to track ar
record, and so may require less formal control than the entire system durir
acceptance testing. As the system becomes more and more subdivided in
its lower-level products or component parts, defects become more exper
sive to correct. Therefore, control of changes becomes more stringent.

When the software system is under formal CM, changes are proposed i
a formal manner (e.g., a change request form or a software trouble report
These requested changes are reviewed by a software CCB that evaluate
such things as impact on other software components, cost, and schedul
Approved changes are then prepared and tested, and, if successful, a:
implemented into the affected component by means of an SCN (as describe
in Section 6.3.3). The SCN gives formal notice that the software or docu
ment has been changed. The SCN is also notification to the CA element th.
a change has been made to the current baseline.

It is the intent of all of CM, but especially CC, to be sure that the softwa
products (the code and the documentation) stay in step with one anothe
and that no changes are made without proper consideration and approval.
is the software quality practitioner's role to verify that the CM program
sufficient to accomplish this task and that it is being followed.

6.1.3 Configuration accounting

CA maintains and records the status of each baseline and its history. It ma
also be called on to account for multiple instances of the products, such
those in Figure 6.2.

6.1.3.1 Baselines

The establishment of a baseline generally occurs as the result of a maj
phase-end review (see Section 3.3). The importance of a baseline is that
represents the starting point for all subsequent changes as the produ

evolves. As shown in Figure 6.3, five commonly recognized baselines should be established. These baselines and their phase-end reviews are as follows:

1.   Functional (SRR);

2.   Allocated (PDR);

3.   Design (CDR);

4.   Product (FA/PA);

5.   Operational (implementation of system).

Other, informal, in-process baselines may be established if they are necessary for a particular development consideration.

6.1.3.2   Instances

Instances of a product may occur when changes occur, variations evolve, or the software product exists in multiple forms. The simplest of the instances are those that happen each time a product undergoes any change. Quite often, especially during the development of drafts of a document, these instances are not recorded and disappear. Only when CM is required do the instances take on names and recorded existence. New instances arising from the modification of an existing product—usually as a result of correction or enhancement—are called successors. Figure 6.4 depicts the creation of a successor.

When different installations of the software system require minor variations in the functional or other requirements, but the basic system is intact, variants are created, as depicted in Figure 6.5. CM of variants is extremely important in situations such as the same software running on various

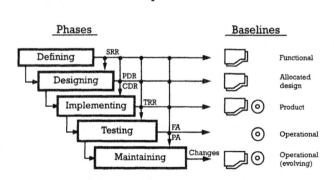

Figure 6.3   Common baselines.

Successors are revised instances of an item

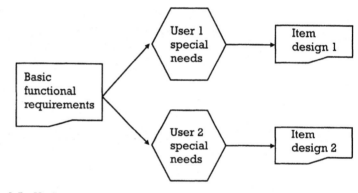

Figure 6.4   Successors.

Variants are alternate versions of an item

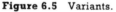

Figure 6.5   Variants.

platforms and having to perform identical functions with slightly differer
platform-dependent differences. Another instance of variants might be th
weapon system software running on identical computational platforms b
on different weapons platforms such as aircraft versus shipboard install
tions. GUIs and client-server installations often need slight modifications
permit implementation on multiple hardware configurations without affec
ing the users' perception of software performance.

   Equivalents are multiple instances of a product in which the content
identical. Equivalents are normally associated with multiple copies of
product, such as purchased applications that are reproduced on discs
other media. Equivalents are also created when a document or softwa
application is copied from a floppy to a hard disc, for example. The specif
medium of the equivalent is not a factor, other than to those customers wh

want a specific medium. The key to equivalence is identical content, not medium. Figure 6.6 shows equivalents on various media.

CA keeps track of the instances of the individual products and their relation to the established baselines. It also records which smaller or lower-level components comprise each higher-level component; that is, which specific units go together to make up which specific module. Further, CA records all approved changes made to the current baseline. Accounting for all approved, but outstanding, changes is also provided. In this way, the CM requirement for providing for reconstructability is met.

.2 Configuration identification

CID involves selecting the items to be configuration managed and giving each of them a unique identifier or name.

6.2.1 Configuration item

Each component of the software is a manageable configuration item. Each project will decide the level of component that will become the lowest managed item.

A configuration item (CI) is any product—any component of the software, documentation, code, and in some cases storage medium (e.g., memory chip)—that has a unique CID. Thus, CID can be applied to everything produced during the software life cycle. In fact, for most large-scale software systems, this is true. Compilers and assemblers usually are constructed so as to append an updated CID to each new assembly or compilation.

Equivalents

Must have identical content
May exist in different media

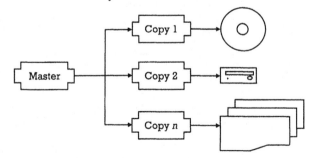

Figure 6.6 Equivalents.

Each CI must have a unique identifier to differentiate it from all of predecessors and successors. The identifier should show the CI's parent; th is, the next higher level of configuration and the specific issue at this lev There must also be a clear indication of the status of the CI. The CID must least show the release and version and, if used, the edition of the CI. documentation, this is generally a simple document name followed an issue indicator. For code CIs, it is much more important to show t sequence of compilation or assembly, so that work may be performed on t most recent or up-to-date instance of the CI. As integration proceeds a delivery is made, the situation becomes more critical. The software syste being tested must be exactly known, down to the unit level, so that wh changes are made, only the correct instance of each component is affected

In the simplest form of identification, each CI is sequentially numbere starting with 1 and continuing until the last CI has been created. This syste does fulfill the requirement of unique identifiers for each instance of ea CI, but there is little intelligence contained in the name. Clearly, a table numbers versus the CIs would be needed to be able to tell which produ was which. This base-level naming scheme would be suitable for only th smallest of software projects. In a slightly more informational scheme, date and time-of-creation tag could be used. This scheme presumes that tv CIs cannot be created at the same instant. As in the case of the sequenti numbering approach, though, a table showing the correspondence betwee a specific name and the exact CI to which it applies will be required.

Figure 6.7 depicts two examples of simple schemes, as well as a mu more elaborate identification scheme. This is more likely to be of the ty most software projects would use. Each level of the system has its identifi included in the name. With some care, a certain amount of intelligence ca be built into a naming approach such as this. The characters chosen for eac of the level names can be related to the level so that the user can recogni products without an elaborate cross-reference table. Of course, if th number of CIs is large, a reference list may be necessary just to keep track what the codes in each field stand for.

In any case, the CID must be suited to the software system being deve oped. Clearly, very large software systems will require more elaborate nam ing schemes than very small systems. Further, the CID should, to the exter possible, be based on a standard CID method throughout the organizatio Using a single scheme throughout the organization makes it easier for th CM practitioner to operate on more than one project at a time. Having separate naming approach for each project, or even groups of several pro ects, may increase complexity unnecessarily.

A simple scheme is one in which
the name is not intended to convey
any information about the item other
than a unique identifier.

Examples

-0001   (sequence)

-200201271042   (date-time-elements
                         cannot occur in parallel)

An intelligent scheme is one in which
characters are assigned to describe
selected characteristics of the product.

Character meaning is position-dependent.

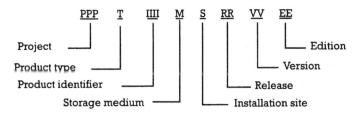

Figure 6.7 Naming schemes.

6.2.2 Release

A release is a major instance or issue of the product. Releases usually occur at a milestone point and often are the baseline of the product as defined at the milestone. Once the software is placed into operation, a release represents an entire new issue of the software product. The term release is usually applied to the reissue of a product at its highest level.

6.2.3 Version

Each time a component is formally reissued, recompiled, or assembled for inclusion in its parent, a new version of all higher-level components is created.

The concept of version is usually rather subjective and is reflective of the needs of the organization and the project. In general, a new version is created anytime there is a major update to a component. A revision to a document is usually considered to be a new version. (This is a smaller case than the release, which is the issuance of the document with all revisions to all components fully integrated.) A new compilation of a code component for

inclusion in the next higher-level component is also generally considered
be a new version.

Each component of the system, down to the unit level, may be consi-
ered to be a replaceable part of the whole. A code CI at the unit level is
part of a code CI at the module level. A module is a part of a subsystem, ar
so on. There is a less clear inclusive relationship between documents, b
the same principle applies. A design specification describes the detaile
response to some portion of the requirements. When the design change
there may be an impact on the related requirements. Within a document,
chapter or major section is clearly a part of the whole document.

When a large number of changes (and this is a subjective term, som-
times determined by an arbitrary standard suitable to the software of th
organization) are made as a group, a new version is created. This is ofte
associated with a set of changes to a functional aspect of the software. Fe
example, if a new module is introduced into a subsystem, a new version e
the subsystem is created. If a new chapter or major section of a document
inserted, there is a new version of that document. Changes that corre-
defects but do not change the basic design or functional intent of the component might not cause the designation of a new version.

6.2.4 Edition

Some organizations may find it useful to define a third level of produ-
instance, called the edition. Each time any component of the system is re-
reated, a new edition is formed.

The creation of a new edition is any action that changes any componer
of the system. While this is a true statement, not all projects or organization
use this concept for CID. On small projects, it is sometimes not worth th-
extra effort to manage the configuration at this level. In most cases, thougl
the information is available if it is wanted. Most compilers and assembler
now include some type of new edition indication as a part of their norma
processing, even if it is only a date and time record.

The use of the edition is important when working with larger system,
since several editions of the whole system may exist at any one time
Remember that any variation in any component is also a variation in ever
superior level of which that component is a part. Thus, if a change is mad-
to a unit, that change must be reflected in the CID of every level above tha
unit all the way to the system level if integration is in progress.

At some point, there are sufficient editions present within a version t-
make the creation of a new version appropriate. Thus, a new issue of the
component will be made with the version identifier increased and the

edition identifier reset to its starting point. The new version will also cause ripples up through the system, since its change must be reflected by all components of which it is a part. Whether the superior components become new releases, versions, or editions is a decision based on the overall CM philosophy for the project or the organization.

.3   Configuration control

CC is that part of CM concerned with the processing, approving, and installation of changes to the software products.

6.3.1   Change processing

Without an effective change processing mechanism, the software can easily become unidentifiable and unmanageable. Change processing mechanisms must be effective (effective does not necessarily mean complicated or bureaucratic). Figure 6.8 presents a very straightforward process for incorporating changes.

Changes come from two primary sources: defect corrections and enhancements. To the change processing system, it matters little which source is involved. Each change must be requested, prepared, tested, approved, and implemented. It is the change processing activity that ensures that all required steps have been taken.

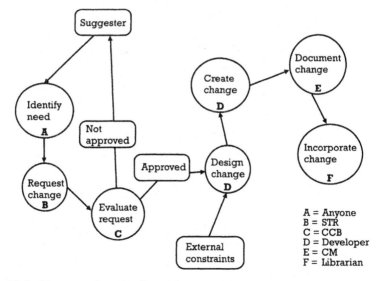

Figure 6.8   Incorporating changes.

Once the software is baselined, all changes are referenced to the baseli in effect. It is important that all changes be controlled so that their effe can be tracked. The control of the changes is dependent on the stage in t SLC, various organizational factors, standards, and project priorities. T customer, who may have to pay for the changes, also is interested in chan processing. The trail of the change, from its inception as the result of a def or an enhancement request, must be clear. All steps in the change proce are important, and ignoring or skipping one or more of them can introdu mistakes and cause further changes to be necessary.

Defects make changes necessary. Obviously, changes are the methods which defects are corrected. The full defect tracking process was discussed Chapter 5, so suffice it to recognize here that the change process is not li ited to defect correction alone.

Enhancements are a major source of changes as the deployed softwa matures and new capabilities are needed. There are many cases in which t software system is implemented in a phased manner, starting with a smal capability and gradually adding functions until the full required system available. These changes are processed in the same manner as defects. Th is, they are proposed, designed and tested, approved, and implemented.

The software CCB can be seen here as playing an important role. T CCB makes the final determination as to whether the change is made at a and, if so, when it will be made. The CCB is responsible for making sure th changes are carefully analyzed and that all associated software effects a considered. The software quality practitioner is usually is a member of t CCB and can report on the quality aspects of the change and whether t quality requirements have been met.

Figures 5.1 and 5.2 introduced forms designed for the purpose of initia ing and tracking a change through its processing. Change processing al often uses automated tools, such as spread sheets, database manageme systems, or full CM systems, to assist in the management of changes.

6.3.2 Change control boards

The software CCB is the final approval authority for the implementation o software change. This board is responsible for coordinating changes ar their intercomponent effects.

The CCB's size and membership depend on the standards of the organ zation and the needs of the project. All affected functions should be repr sented on the CCB in order for it to adequately review requested changes. most cases, members come from each functional area (usually subsyste level), CA, CC, and the hardware areas involved, if appropriate. In additio the software quality practitioner is expected to be a member of the CCB. In some organizations, a representative of the internal audit group is also an appropriate member.

Size is a factor in the efficacy of the CCB. If the group is too large, there may trouble getting things done in a timely manner. If, on the other hand, the proper areas are not represented, changes may be approved that adversely affect other parts of the system.

It is the responsibility of the CCB to review all proposed changes for their correctness and their effect on the baseline. Interactions with other parts of the software system are considered, as well as impacts on the schedule and cost. Especially in the case of cost and schedule, the customer is a necessary member of the CCB. There may also be cases in which a change will impact the system requirements. In these cases, the customer or user must be present in order to agree that the change and its impact are permissible.

The impact of the change on the documentation is also considered by the CCB. Any change that impacts higher-level components than itself probably also affects documentation of that level. Some changes may affect documentation all the way back to the requirements of the system. If the documentation is not updated as changes are made, the task of the software maintainer is made much more difficult. If the documentation is not up-to-date, the maintainer must regenerate it before beginning useful work on the next change.

There are instances where multiple CCBs are convened. This may be especially true in the case of very large or multiple-contractor projects. At the software development level, an informal CCB may review changes within subsystems and the overall system as the changes are proposed. These informal boards serve to prepare the changes for the more formal software CCB to which the changes will be submitted for final approval. At the same time, there is likely to be a hardware CCB working with the proposed changes to equipment involved in the system.

In the case of large systems involving hardware as well as software, there will be hardware CCBs paralleling the software CCBs. In addition, there will be an overall system CCB to review changes that affect performance, cost, schedule, hardware/software interface, and other global concerns beyond the scope of the lower CCBs. In the case of multiple CCBs, it is imperative that a written description of the relationships among the CCBs be prepared. This will ensure that there are no conflicts over authority and that no areas of concern are left unheeded.

The software quality representative to the CCB must make certain that all software quality system requirements for the project are being met. Of particular interest to the software quality representative will be the test

plans for the change and the regression tests on the rest of the system
ensure that no unexpected impacts are being felt. Changes are to be test
to the same, or even greater, rigor as original development.

6.3.3   Software libraries

Ultimate access to configuration-controlled products is through the softwa
library.

The library is the repository of the official issues of all documents a
code. The librarian is responsible for the control of the baselined system a
all current issues of the documents and code. There must be formal proc
dures for the entry of a particular issue of a component into the libra
Equally formal procedures are used to gain access to the official issues of t
components.

Provisions will be made for authors and programmers to access worki
copies of the official issues, but not to enter them back into the curre
library. There will also be procedures for maintaining cognizance of whi
working copies are being used, so that multiple changes are not being ma
to the same component at the same time without the knowledge of t
changers.

Once the formal change procedures have been followed, and the CC
has authorized the implementation of a change, an SCN will be generat
that tells the librarian to update the current official issue of the affect
component. In a well-controlled library, the SCN is the only way to effect
change to the baselined system. Finally, it is the library that prepares the f
system for formal delivery to the customer. Along the way, the library w
prepare official issues for testing and operation. Figure 5.3 suggested a fo
mat for a software change notice.

As reuse of existing software products becomes more prevalent, the sof
ware library's responsibilities are usually increased to include the manag
ment and control of reusable items. Not only the item or product itself, b
the applicable documentation describing the item and its appropriate u
must be available and configuration managed. Reuse of items usua
requires some sort of modification to the item in order that it correctly fit i
new use. These modifications create variants of the item that will be mai
aged and controlled just like the original. It is worth repeating that eac
instance of any configuration item or product must be carefully manage
and its status and baseline records maintained.

It is frequently the additional task of the library to be the repository of a
documentation for the software system. In some cases, even contracts an
correspondence between the organization and the customer are kept in th

central library. The use of the library as a documentation center is an effective way to be sure that copies of requirements and design documents are available when needed and are of the most current issue.

.4 Configuration accounting

Baselines mark major CI status levels of the software. However, while the creation of baselines is of major importance in CA, the baselines only form the basis for the actual accounting process.

6.4.1 Baselines

As shown in Figure 6.3, several baselines can be identified, but three (functional, design, operational) are the most common. Further, each baseline usually is associated with a major review marking the end of an SDLC phase. Again, there is no industrywide standard for the names of the baselines. The names used here are common in the defense arena.

The functional baseline is established at the SRR. At this point in the SDLC, the requirements have been documented and reviewed, at the end of the requirements phase, for compliance with the criteria discussed in Chapter 3. The functions that will perform the processing necessary to achieve the requirements, in a hardware/software system, are analyzed and assigned to the hardware and software as appropriate. Documenting the software requirements specifies the tasks assigned to the software and what the software is going to do in performing those tasks.

The requirements are then allocated to functions, and the design process determines how each requirement is going to be fulfilled. This phase is typically called preliminary design and may not be necessary for simple software projects. When it is included in the system development methodology, it culminates with the PDR. The conclusion of the PDR results in the allocated baseline.

At the end of the full design phase, the code-to design has been completed. It is validated in the CDR that determines the design baseline. The design baseline determines the specification for the coding activities.

Prior to acceptance testing on which user approval of the product is based, an analysis of the results of all preceding testing is performed. Upon the satisfactory completion of this TRR, the product baseline is established. The product baseline is that instance of the software that will undergo acceptance testing.

Upon completion of acceptance testing, completion of the FA and P
and installation of the software, the operational baseline is established. Th
baseline identifies the software as it is going to be delivered to the user
customer. It is occasionally called the as-built baseline, since it represer
the actual system being delivered. (This is frequently not the system th
was originally specified in the initial requirements documentation.) Aft
installation of the software system, the operational baseline will continue
evolve as the software is maintained and enhanced throughout its usef
life.

Other baselines have various names and are instituted for specific pu
poses within the organization. There are no hard and fast rules about ho
many baselines there should be (other than those that are called out in so
ware development contracts). Each project or organization will determi
the applicable level of control needed for the project and will then impo
those baselines that fulfill the control needs.

Baselines are defined so that change control may be instituted. The bas
line reflects all previous changes to the given CI and determines the point
departure for all subsequent changes to that CI. It is a fixed reference poir
and all changes are made to that reference point. As CM is imposed wi
increasing rigor, the baselines become more important as well. It is obvio
that if the basis for changes is not known, there is a good chance that th
wrong component or instance of the component will be changed. There
also the danger that two changes may be made to the same part of a comp
nent without the knowledge of each other.

6.4.2 Accounting

Given the baselines and the imposition of CC, the CA element keeps track
the status of the software as it goes through the SDLC and operatio
Records of all changes, reviews, and action items affecting the configuratio
of the software are maintained by CA.

CA must monitor such things as the baselines themselves, where an
how they were established, and by whose authority. CA maintains th
records of changes made to the current baseline and notes the date of th
change request, action of the CCB, status of the change in progress, and da
about the ultimate installation of the change.

6.4.2.1 Instance collaboration

An important record maintained by CA is the exact composition of eac
instance of each software component. The name, release, version, an

edition of each product and each of its subordinate components is closely monitored so that when changes are made, all CIDs of affected components can be updated. Not only is this important in the changing of software components, but it is critical to the coherence of the testing and delivery activities. To test and accept one version of a component and then deliver a different version is not conducive to quality software development or installation.

Figure 6.9 depicts a situation in which different versions of products were delivered. In this case, without more information, the user would not know whether the products were internally consistent or not. Rigorous CA will lessen the likelihood that incompatible instances of related software products will be delivered and used.

6.4.2.2 Instance tracking

As newer technologies, such as client-server, are implemented, the role of CM, and especially CA, becomes even more important. In the mainframe environments still in use throughout the world, most software products exist in only one or two instances. CM is important but not as heavily taxed as in the newer, distributed information processing installations. It is critical to keep track of environmental software such as operating systems, languages, database managers, and so on so that applications will be subject to the environments for which they were prepared.

Multiple application instances are also frequently present in distributed systems. CM, and particularly CA, must ensure that the expected instances of processing applications are called by the user. Maintenance of the environments and applications also depend on CM to ensure that modifications are correct for the product concerned and are applied to the intended products. Coordination of modifications between variants of products becomes a serious concern, especially as distributed and client-server processing and e-commerce applications become the norm.

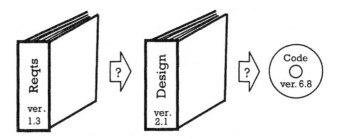

Figure 6.9 Mismatched products.

6.5   Summary

CM is the discipline that ensures that the state of the software at any giv
time is known and reconstructable. It comprises three basic elements: ide
tification, accounting, and control.

CID permits the uniform naming of each software component and pro
uct, down to the lowest separable level.

Baselines, specific points of departure for a new set of developme
activities and changes, are constructed by the CA portion of CM. CA ma
tains and records the status of each baseline and its history. Baselines ma
major CI status levels during the SLC. They are usually associated w
major milestone events (such as a formal review) in the development cycl

CC ensures that all approved changes are made to the software. It I
the equally significant obligation to ensure that no changes are made th
have not been properly approved. It must be noted that as technolo
evolves and software development techniques and methods evolve, it
often necessary to configuration manage the development and testing pl.
forms, as well as the intermediate and end products.

A CI is any product of the software development process that is to
configuration managed. Each CI must have a unique identifier to differen
ate it from all other software development products and other instances
the item itself.

Ultimate access to the SLC products, so that changes can be made,
through the software library, which is the repository of the offici
approved issues of all documents and code. Changes to the products of t
software development process come from two main sources: defect corre
tion and enhancements. Without an effective change processing mech
nism, the software can easily become unidentifiable and unmanageable.

Coordination of changes and their intercomponent effects is the task
the CCB. The CCB is responsible for determining that all effects of the pr
posed change have been anticipated and reconciled. Especially important
the control that the CCB exercises over the creation of new instances or ve
sions of the various software system products. Once CM has been impos
on the project, it is the CCB that has the authority to approve changes ar
permit the updating of the various issues of the products. It is the respons
bility of the software quality practitioner to monitor the functioning of tl
CCBs.

.6 The next step

To begin your CM program or to see if it is up-to-date, consult the following texts:

Susan Dart. *Configuration Management: The Missing Link,* Norwood, MA: Artech House (CD-ROM), 2002.

Fletcher J. Buckley. *Implementing Configuration Management: Hardware, Software and Firmware, Second Edition,* New York: IEEE Press, 1995.

Additional reading

Babich, W. A., *Software Configuration Management Coordination for Team Productivity,* Reading, MA: Addison-Wesley, 1986.

Berlack, Ron H., *Software Configuration Management,* New York: John Wiley & Sons, 1992.

Compton, Stephen B., and Guy R. Conner, *Configuration Management for Software,* New York: Van Nostrand Reinhold, 1994.

Daniels, M. A., *Principles of Configuration Management,* North Babylon, NY: Advanced Applications Consultants, 1985.

CHAPTER

7

Contents

Associated Quality Concerns

Some issues, while of concern to software quality practitioners, are usually outside of their direct responsibility and authority. These issues have no less impact on the quality of the software system, however. This chapter discusses four important software quality issues. The role of the software quality practitioner with respect to these issues is to ensure that decision-making, action-capable management is aware of their importance and impact on the software system during its development and after its implementation. These important issues are security, education of developers and users, management of vendors, and maintenance of the software after implementation.

7.1 Security

Security is an issue that is frequently overlooked until it has been breached, either in the loss of, or damage to, critical data or in a loss to the data center itself.

Security has three main aspects. Two of these deal primarily with data: the security of the database and the security of data being transmitted to other data centers. The third aspect is that of the data center itself and the protection of the resources contained therein.

The software quality practitioner has a responsibility not to protect the data or the data center but to make management aware of the need for or inadequacies in the security provisions.

151

7.1.1 Database security

The software quality data security concern is that the data being used by t·
software is protected. Database security is two-fold. The data being pro·
essed must be correct, and, in many cases, restricted in its disseminatio·
Many things impact the quality of the output from the software, not t·
least of which is the quality of the data that the software is processing. T·
quality of the data is affected in several ways. The correctness of the data
be input, the correctness of the inputting process, the correctness of t·
processing, and, of interest to security, the safety of the data from modific·
tion before or after processing is a database security issue.

This modification can be in the form of inadvertent change by an inco·
rectly operating hardware or software system outside the system und·
consideration. It can be caused by something as simple to detect as t·
mounting of the wrong tape or disk pack, or as difficult to trace as faul·
client-server communication. From a security point of view, it can also ·
the result of intentional tampering, known as hacking or attacking. An·
thing from the disgruntled employee who passes a magnet over the edges·
a tape to scramble the stored images to the attacker who finds his or her w·
into the system and knowingly or unknowingly changes the database can ·
a threat to the quality of the software system output. Large distributed con·
puting installations are often victims of the complexity of the data stora·
and access activities. While quality practitioners are not usually responsib·
for the design or implementation of the database system, they should ·
aware of increasing security concerns as systems become more widely di·
bursed or complex.

The physical destruction of data falls into the area of data center securi·
that will be discussed later. Modification of data while they are part of t·
system is the concern of data security provisions.

Database security is generally imposed through the use of various pas·
word and access restriction techniques. Most commonly, a specific passwor·
is assigned to each individual who has access to the software system. Whe·
the person attempts to use the system, the system asks for identification ·
the form of the password. If the user can provide the correct password, the·
he or she is allowed to use the system. A record of the access is usually ke·
by a transaction recording routine so that if untoward results are encour·
tered, they can be backed out by reversing the actions taken. Further,
there is damage to the data, it can be traced to the perpetrator by means·
the password that was used.

This scheme works only up to a point. If care is not taken, passwords ca·
be used by unauthorized persons to gain access to the system. For th·

reason, many systems now use multiple levels of password protection. One password may let the user access the system as a whole, while another is needed to access the database. Further restrictions on who can read the data in the database and who can add to it or change it are often invoked. Selective protection of the data is also used. Understanding databases and the logical and physical data models used will help the quality practitioner recommend effective security methods.

One typical system of data protection is shown in Figure 7.1. The first control is the unlisted telephone number that accesses the computer. A user who has the telephone number and reaches the computer must then identify himself or herself to the computer to get access to any system at all. Having passed this hurdle and selected a system to use, the user must pass another identification test to get the specific system to permit any activity. In Figure 7.1, the primary system uses a remote subsystem that is also password protected. Finally, the database at this point is in a read-only mode. To change or manipulate the data, special password characteristics would have to have been present during the three sign-on procedures. In this way, better than average control has been exercised over who can use the software and manipulate the data.

Another concern of database security is the dissemination of the data in the database or the output. Whether or not someone intends to harm the data, there is, in most companies, data that are sensitive to the operation or competitive tactics of the company. If those data can to be accessed by a competitor, valuable business interests could be damaged. For this reason, as well as the validity of the data, all database accesses should be candidates for protection.

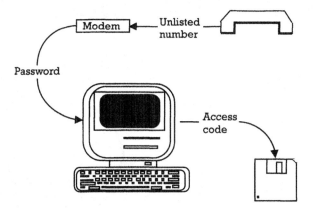

Figure 7.1   Dialup protection.

7.1.2 Teleprocessing security

The data within the corporate or intercompany telecommunications n
work are also a security concern.

Data contained within the database are vulnerable to unauthoriz
access but not to the extent of data transmitted through a data netwo
These networks include such things as simple, remotely actuated processi
tasks all the way to interbank transfers of vast sums of money.
e-commerce becomes common, personal data are increasingly at risk
well. Much effort is being expended to create secure sites for on-line trar
actions. Simple password schemes are rarely satisfactory in these cases.
be sure, they are necessary as a starting point, but much more protection
needed as the value of the data being transmitted increases.

Two concerns are of importance in regard to telecommunications. T
first concern, usually outside the control of the company, is the quality
the transmission medium. Data can be lost or jumbled simply because t
carrier is noisy or breaks down, as is depicted in Figure 7.2. Defenses agair
this type of threat include parity checking or check sum calculations wi
retransmission if the data and the parity or checksums do not coincic
Other more elaborate data validity algorithms are available for more criti
or sensitive data transmissions.

Unauthorized access to the data is the other main concern of transm
sion security. As data are being transmitted, they can be monitored, moc
fied, or even redirected from their original destination to some oth
location. Care must be taken to ensure that the data transmitted get to the
destination correctly and without outside eavesdropping. The metho

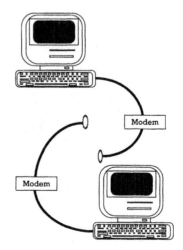

Figure 7.2 Interruption.

used to prevent unauthorized data access usually involve encryption (see Figure 7.3) to protect the data and end-to-end protocols that make sure the data get to their intended destination.

Encryption can be performed by the transmission system software or by hardware specially designed for this purpose. Industries in the defense arena use highly sophisticated cryptographic equipment, while other companies need only a basic encryption algorithm for their transmissions.

As in the case of prevention of loss due to faulty network media, the use of check sums, parity checking, and other data validity methods are employed to try to assure that the data have not been damaged or tampered with during transmission.

Prevention of the diversion of data from the intended destination to an alternative is controlled through end-to-end protocols that keep both ends of the transmission aware of the activity. Should the destination end not receive the data it is expecting, the sending end is notified and transmission is terminated until the interference is identified and counteracted.

The proliferation of the use of the Internet and Web sites has immensely complicated and exacerbated these problems. It is the responsibility of software quality to monitor the data security provisions and keep management informed as to their adequacy.

7.1.3 Viruses

A frequent entry into the threat scenario is the computer virus. A virus is software that is attached to a legitimate application or data set. It then can commit relatively benign, nuisance acts like blanking a screen or printing a

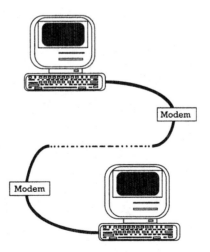

Figure 7.3 Encryption.

message announcing its presence. It also can be intended, like some mo
recent viruses, to be malignant, in that it intentionally destroys software
data. Some can even erase a full hard disk.

Viruses are usually introduced by being attached to software that, oft
in violation of copyright laws, is shared among users. Downloading softwa
from a bulletin board is one of the more frequent virus infection metho
Data disks used on an infected system may carry the virus back to an oth
wise healthy system, as shown in Figure 7.4.

Some viruses do not act immediately. They can be programmed to w
for a specific date, like the famous Michelangelo virus, or, perhaps, son
specific processing action. At the preprogrammed time, the virus activa
the mischief or damage it is intended to inflict.

Many antiviral packages are available. Unfortunately, the antiviral va
cines can only fight those viruses that have been identified. New viruses
not yet have vaccines and can cause damage before the antiviral software
available.

The best defense against viruses, although not altogether foolproof,
to use only software fresh from the publisher or vendor. Pirated so
ware—software that has not been properly acquired—is a common sour
of infection.

7.1.4 Disaster recovery

A specific plan of recovery should be developed and tested to ensure conti
ued operation in the case of damage to the data center.

Figure 7.4 Virus introduction.

Even the best risk analysis, prevention, detection, and correction are not always enough to avoid that damage that can prevent the data center from operating for some period of time.

Many companies are now so dependent on their data processing facility that even a shutdown of a few days could be life-threatening to the organization. Yet, the majority of companies have done little or no effective planning for the eventuality of major damage to their data center. Sometimes a company will enter into a mutual assistance agreement with a neighboring data center. Each agrees to perform emergency processing for the other in the event of a disaster to one of them. What they often fail to recognize is that each of them is already processing at or near the capacity of their own data center and has no time or resources to spare for the other's needs. Another fault with this approach is that the two companies are often in close physical proximity. This makes assistance more convenient from a travel and logistics viewpoint if, in fact, they do have sufficient reserve capacity to assist in the data processing. However, if the disaster suffered by one of them was the result of a storm, serious accident, an act of war, or a terrorist attack, the odds are high that the backup center has also suffered significant damage. Now both of them are without alternate facilities.

One answer to these threats is the remote, alternative processing site. A major company may provide its own site, which it keeps in reserve for an emergency. The reserve site is normally used for interruptible processing that can be set aside in the case of a disaster. However, because a reserve site is an expensive proposition, many companies enroll in disaster recovery backup cooperatives. These cooperatives provide facilities of varying resources at which a member company can perform emergency processing until its own center is repaired or rebuilt.

To augment this backup processing center approach, two conditions are necessary. The first condition, usually in place for other reasons, is the remote storage of critical data in some location away from the data center proper. That way, if something happens to a current processing run or the current database, a backup set of files is available from which the current situation can be reconstructed. The backup files should be generated no less frequently than daily, and the place in which they are stored should be well protected from damage and unauthorized access as part of the overall data security scheme.

The second necessity in a disaster recovery program is a comprehensive set of tests of the procedures that will enable the emergency processing to commence at the remote backup site. All aspects of the plan, from the original notification of the proper company authorities that a disaster has occurred through the actual implementation of the emergency processing

software systems at the backup site should be rehearsed on a regular bas
Most backup cooperatives provide each member installation with a certa
number of test hours each year. These need to be augmented by a series
tests of the preparations leading up to the move to the backup site. Notific
tion procedures, access to the backup files, transportation to the backup sit
security for the damaged data center to prevent further damage, provisic
for the acquisition of new or repaired data processing equipment both f
the backup site and the damaged data center, provisions for telecommunic
tions if required, and other types of preparations should be thorough
documented and tested along with the actual operation at the backup site.

Software quality practitioners are natural conductors for these tes
since they must ensure that the disaster recovery plan is in place and th
the emergency processing results are correct. Software quality is the repor
ing agency to management on the status of disaster recovery provisions.

7.1.5 Security wrap-up

Security has three main aspects: the database, data transmission, and th
physical data center itself. Most companies could not last long without th
data being processed. Should the data become corrupted, lost, or know
outside the company, much commercial harm could result.

The failure of the data center, no matter what the cause, can also have
great negative impact on the organization's viability. A disaster recover
plan should be developed and tested by the organization, with the softwa
quality practitioner monitoring the plans for completeness and feasibility

As systems increase in size and complexity and as companies rely mo
and more on their software systems, the security aspects of quality becom
more important. The software quality practitioner is responsible for makin
management aware of the need for security procedures.

7.2 Education

Education of personnel in the proper performance of their tasks is essenti
to the production and use of quality software systems.

Education, while rarely provided by the software quality organization,
a necessary step in the provision of a quality product. The software qualit
practitioner is responsible for monitoring the educational activities that su
round the development and use of software systems. Education is one of th
elements of the SQS that is most often delegated to another organizatio
within the company. While software quality practitioners will monitor an

report on the educational status with regard to each development project, they are rarely the educating facility. Most companies use an in-house education group, video courses, outside instructors, outside seminars, and hands-on or on-the-job education and training methods.

Programmers must be taught the proper use of programming languages and software development facilities for their assignments. Users must be taught the proper ways to use the software system and its results. Operations personnel need to learn the correct procedures for running the system. And, finally, the various support organizations, including software quality, must be educated in the proper performance of their tasks.

7.2.1 Developer education

The production of a quality software system depends heavily on the performance of the producers.

Developers—the designers, analysts, coders, and testers—must know their jobs in order to contribute to the production of a quality software system. All participants must have the proper training and background to permit them to do their jobs correctly. Inadequate education, missing experience, and lack of training all can contribute to lower than acceptable performance and, thus, lower than acceptable quality in the end product.

It is obvious that a system designer who knows little about the system being designed can bring little insight into the solution of the problem. To expect a designer well schooled in accounting systems to be a top performer on a radar guidance system, without specific education in radar theory and practice, would be an invitation to a product with questionable reliability. There are new techniques for design and programming being developed at a rapid pace. While not every new technique can, or should, be applied to every project, the more experience and education in the various techniques that a staff has, the more likely it is that the best approach will be taken. Some techniques, like structured design and object-oriented programming, have been widely accepted as standard approaches to be taken in all cases. Newer techniques are now beginning to show that, while they are fine methodologies in many situations, structured design and object-oriented programming are not always the best methods. Techniques such as rapid prototyping, automated design, and extreme programming are being shown to be superior in a growing number of applications. Better techniques usually mean better results and higher productivity. Education of the development staff can lead to the implementation of software development methodology that is best suited for the specific application.

Equally important to the development of quality software systems is t
fluency of the programming and coding personnel in the language in whi
the system is being written. One of the more important education concer
of the software quality practitioner is that the developers be knowledgea
in the language to be used for the system. While emphasis is genera
focused on the coders, it is also important that designers and testers be w
trained in the language. This will help designers express design conside
tions in terms more understandable to the coders, as well as help the test
understand the intricacies of the code itself.

Another area of educational concern is the background environment
be used during the development. Such things as operating systems and da
base management systems greatly affect the design and implementation
the software and should be well understood by the developers. Failure
recognize the various characteristics of the software environment can cau
many headaches later in operation and testing. Even the operation of t
desktop terminal cannot be overlooked in the educational process.

Software development is a labor-intensive activity, and many too
techniques, and methodologies are coming forth. Computer-aided softwa
engineering; object-oriented techniques; client-server and distributed pro
essing; local-, wide-, and municipal-area and value-added networks; t
tools; database management applications; visual development languag
internets and intranets; GUIs; and the like are all areas of challenge to t
information technology developer. The quality of the development and t
productivity of the developers depend to a large extent on the level of ed
cation, training, and experience of the developers.

7.2.2 Support training

Support includes both the development environment that must be mai
tained and the ancillary activities such as software quality, CM, test, a
security.

As already mentioned, there is a need for developers to be schooled
the programming environment such as the operating system and the dat
base management system. They need to know how the environment
going to affect the software being developed and vice versa. Care must
taken, though, that the personnel charged with the creation and maint
nance of that environment are well educated in their tasks. In addition, t
developers must be well educated in the specific development methodolo
to be used on a given project. Development methodologies such as stru
tured and object-oriented analysis and design techniques and fourt

generation languages all require detailed understanding if they are to be applied beneficially.

As Figure 7.5 shows, the development staff is at the center of, and supported by, a much larger environment. Failures in any of the surrounding fields can seriously impact the ability of the developers to accomplish their assigned tasks.

The area commonly known as systems programming includes the operating systems and various language systems. Without these, there is no software development at all and effectively no maintenance. The software quality practitioner is responsible for ensuring that an adequate and ongoing education program is provided for the systems programming staff.

Database administration, security measures, and telecommunications are also present in most organizations. Poorly trained or inexperienced personnel in these groups must also receive the necessary training and education to keep them able to cope with the advances being made in those disciplines and the growing dependence of the total organization on them.

The testing group is a frequently overlooked area for education. The test group should be knowledgeable in the system as a whole, the programming language being used, and the programming environment. Armed with such

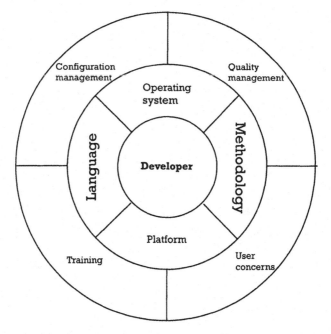

Figure 7.5 Developer's world.

information and knowledge, the testers are able to see areas of potent weakness in the code and can test for those weaknesses.

Finally, software quality practitioners cannot ignore themselves ensuring that all software personnel have adequate education and traini for their jobs. The software quality people must know how to revie documents, the standards being imposed on the various projects, how communicate their findings upward to management, how to accompli the various audits for which they are responsible, and all the rest of t SQS tasks.

7.2.3 User education

The best system will not perform well if incorrectly used. It is worth rest ing that if the users of a system do not have full knowledge of how to u the system, the system will not perform up to its capabilities. The syste may be underused, which effectively wastes some of the effort put into creation. It may not work at all, making the whole system a waste. Worst all, incorrect use of the system may negatively affect other systems bei run; sometimes even to the extent of bringing a halt to the whole processi activity. It should be clear that user education is at least as important developer education.

The two main areas of user education are the inputting of data and tl use of the outputs from the system. Data input includes starting the syste and telling it what it is required to do for any particular processing exercis Some systems need only be started, and they then perform a series of pres functions. Such things as process control or standard data reduction systen may fall into this category. Knowing how to start the system is the impo tant point. Other systems require parameters or additional data to be pr vided. Payroll systems, for example, need to have time records input an may have to have parameters, such as special bonus equation value entered. The proper provision of existing databases is important in bo cases. Finally, some systems are interactive, and the user must respond the system while it is running, perhaps by providing additional input or gi ing directions to the systems based on the system's computations or que tions. A simple example is the word processing package on which this te was generated. The user entered text into the package, and the packag occasionally asked for directions on what to do in certain situations, such reaching the limit of the working memory allotment.

The use of the produced information is of equal importance. If a securit system detects an attempted breach of the secure area, the user must hav full instructions as to what action to take. This is true whether the breac attempted is of a data security system or of a building. If the system has not been designed to respond with some action on its own, the user must take the appropriate action.

More often, though, the output is in the form of business or scientific data in one format or another. Business users and users of scientific data must understand what they are receiving and what to do with it. At other times, education in the use of the output will be as simple as informing the user to whom a particular printer report is to go. Whatever the specific system requires, though, with respect to inputs and outputs, the user must be properly trained in its use.

Other user educational considerations include such things as the limits of the system. These may involve valid input data limits, number of entries that the system can accept at one time, the speed of input, limits on the size or type of outputs, access control passwords, frequency of use in a particular time period, and so on. Each user must be aware of the capabilities built into the system so those capabilities are not violated or underused. Asking more of the system than it can provide may lead to errors or crashes, while underutilization may lead to underestimation on future projects.

Dr. W. Edwards Deming was a strong proponent of employee training and development. Implementation of new software products and systems normally brings change to the way users perform their jobs, or the environment in which they work. New jobs and tasks may be created, while existing jobs and tasks may be vastly altered or even eliminated. Management of this type of change offers many educational and development opportunities.

The software quality practitioner's role in user education is much the same as his or her role in developer education. That is, the monitoring of the user education plans and progress so that the proper education is provided. Software quality control practitioners may even take the education themselves as a part of the acceptance test procedures. By exercising the system in the same manner as the intended users, the test team can often find flaws not only in the software but also in the educational programs.

7.2.4 Operations training

If a system is not run properly, results are suspect and users cannot rely on the information provided. Operation includes everything from computer power-up to report delivery. Virtually anything outside of the user, at the terminal at his or her desk, can be thought of as the domain of the operations organization. Operations loads the data media, starts the various applications, monitors throughput, puts paper in the printer, delivers reports to their intended recipients, and keeps the operational environment sufficient

for the processing load being demanded by the developers and users. Trai
ing in this area encompasses an extremely wide range of activities. And,
course, there is a correspondingly wide range of potential problems if t
personnel are not properly and completely trained in their functions.

In the early days of computer centers, the operations group had to co
tend with only the running of the jobs. The jobs were generally run in t
order in which they were submitted, and the reports were placed in
mailbox-like slot for someone to retrieve. As the computing industry h
matured, the complexity of the computer center activities has increas
many fold. Multiple processors are running multiple jobs, many of whic
were submitted at the same time with multiple priorities. These, in tur
may be generating multiple outputs on multiple media. Operations perso
nel must be knowledgeable in job sequencing, computing hardware oper
tion, data entry and validation, report distribution, remote job entry ar
computing, security, job control languages, defect reporting and correctio
long-range and short-range facilities planning, space allocation, safety, ar
a multitude of other considerations. Training must be provided in most
these fields, since on-the-job training often takes too long for a new persc
to become proficient and productive.

In some cases, generally in very large or very small data centers, on-the
job training is feasible. In a large shop, new employees are assigned to sma
specialized tasks such as tape or disk loading and unloading. They are the
rotated through the various tasks until they have learned them all. A sma
shop usually has a simple, small-scale computer whose operation can b
learned quickly. A small shop also has a correspondingly small set of appl
cations with which to deal. The bulk of computer centers, however, usual
include multiple central processing units or servers, distributed printer st
tions, dial-up and Internet equipment, and several types of data medi
When experienced personnel cannot be hired, they must be trained by th
organization.

Software quality practitioners should monitor the operations activit
and the levels of training present within it. Close coordination with th
manager of the operations area will ensure that proper training is provide
to the operations personnel.

7.2.5 Education delivery

Various educational needs are met in different ways, but there are six majc
methods of delivering the needed education. Each of the following method
is applicable to one or more of the education and training needs discusse
so far:

1. On-the-job or hands-on experience;

2. Formal classes;

3. Seminars and workshops;

4. Videotapes and demonstrations;

5. Conferences and user group meetings;

6. Web-based courses.

Developer education should include all the methods that are suited to the individuals' needs. On-the-job experience is the slowest method for most development tasks, but it can be of value to the new employee who has had some formal education in computer programming, computer science, or the specific application area being developed. Formal classes, either in an actual atmosphere classroom, via the World Wide Web, or through less formal events such as seminars, workshop, or conferences, are valuable to both the learning of new applications areas and the gaining of familiarity with features of new development environments. Languages are best learned through a formal classroom experience coupled with hands-on exercises. New design techniques are often the subject of seminars or workshops. Demonstrations can be used to show how new equipment, such as a workstations or desktop terminals, is to be utilized.

Support personnel have much the same educational requirements as do the developers, though in different areas, of course. The methods that seem to best serve support education are also similar to the developers. Classrooms are appropriate for operating system and language familiarization, as well as database operation. For highly experienced personnel, seminars and workshops are sometimes sufficient. If the subject to be learned is an extension of a system already in place in the organization, hands-on experience and demonstrations can be used.

User education can sometimes be provided with demonstrations or in-house seminars, or even on-the-job learning if the system is simple or similar to or an extension of existing systems. New, large-scale systems frequently need formal classroom education when the range of user opportunities is wide or there is much user system interaction. In the latter case, hands-on experiences are justified as well. Videotapes are less usefulunless they are an adjunct to demonstrations or formal classroom presentations.

Operations training is almost always a series of demonstrations of the proper way to perform a particular task. This method is usually enhanced by hands-on or on-the-job experiences. For new equipment, formal classroom and videotapes presentations are often appropriate. When new environment systems (operating systems, languages, database manageme systems, and the like) are being installed, more formal training is need and the classroom may again be the preferred method. Finally, hands-experience and demonstrations will be an almost regular part of the routi in a large data center as additional data storage media are installed a enhancements to the environment are made.

Once more, it should be made clear that the role of the software qua practitioner in the training of personnel is monitoring and reporting t status of the various training situations. The actual delivery of the educati and training is normally the responsibility of the education department the individual group, such as development or operations. The softwa quality practitioner keeps management aware of the need for education a training and their status. Table 7.1 suggests typical types and sources training and the recipients for whom they may be suited. There are no ha and fast rules; each organization must use the means at its disposal.

7.2.6   Education wrap-up

While rarely provided by the software quality practitioner, education is necessary step in the provision of a quality product. It is one of the elemer

Table 7.1   Training Needs and Sources

Training Need	Recipient	Training Source
Application area	Developer	Classroom/Web
Design methods	Developer	Classroom/Web/vendor
	Quality group	Demonstration
Operating systems	Developer	Classroom/Web/vendor
Database management systems	Data administrator	Vendor
Language	Developer	Classroom/Web
Testing	Tester	Seminar/on-the-job training
SQS	Quality group	Seminar
	Developer	Demonstration
Operation	Operator	Demonstration
Application use	User	Demonstration/classroom/Web
	Customer service	Classroom/Web
Networks	Developer	Seminar/demonstration
	User	Demonstration

of the SQS that is most often delegated to another organization within the company.

Fluency of the programming and coding personnel in the language in which the system is being written is very important. So, too, is familiarity with the background environment to be used during the development.

Training for the support environment must not be overlooked either. Systems programming (the operating systems and compiler-assembler software), database administration, and the testing group should be thoroughly trained in their tasks. Software quality practitioners must not forget themselves in ensuring that all software personnel have adequate knowledge in their responsibilities.

If the users of a system do not have the proper education in its use, the system may perform inadequately and be seen as less than acceptable. The operations staff must also be schooled in the operation of the system in order for it to supply the expected outputs.

The software quality practitioner must keep management aware of the needs for training and education.

.3   Vendor management

Purchasing software is often risky business at best. While there are many reasons for an organization to buy software rather than write it in-house, the role of the software quality practitioner often is reduced. Thus, the risks increase that the software will not meet its requirements.

When software is purchased, much, if not all, control over development is lost. The risks run from slightly more than those for in-house development all the way to what-you-see-is-what-you-get (WYSIWYG). The role of the software quality practitioner changes when software is purchased. Since visibility into the development process is diminished, if not lost altogether, other avenues must be found to investigate and ascertain software quality. The software quality practitioner must be innovative in selecting quality methods to apply and firm in insisting that those methods are applied. There are many packages and methodologies that can help with software product acquisition, but the basic quality concerns remain the same.

Three basic types of software purchase are available: off-the-shelf, tailored, and new development. Each type presents a different challenge to the software quality practitioner. Visibility and influence over the development process change as each type of purchase is exercised. Table 7.2 presents examples of purchased software and the quality approaches that could be applied to them.

Table 7.2 Purchased Software Quality Approaches

Type	Source	Quality Approach
Graphics application	Off the shelf	Vendor reputation
		Trial-use period
Database manager	Off the shelf	Vendor reputation
		Trial-use period
Operating system	Vendor	Trial-use period
		Vendor maintenance
Tailored application	Application customizer	Partial purchaser SQS
		Test records
		Vendor maintenance
Contracted application	Third-party developer	Full purchaser SQS
		Vendor maintenance
	Off-shore developer	Full purchaser SQS
		On-site inspection
		Vendor maintenance

Each type of purchase presents different maintenance situations. W▌ will maintain the purchased software is an important consideration for t▌ software quality practitioner in evaluating purchased software.

7.3.1 Off-the-shelf software

Purchasing off-the-shelf software allows little or no insight into t▌ processes involved in its development.

Software purchased off-the-shelf, such as an operating system, a co▌ piler, or database management system, whether for a mainframe or a po▌ able computer, usually comes as-is. Usually, there are no guarantees a▌ sometimes there are blunt denials of any liability on the part of the vend▌ This type of software offers the greatest challenge to software quali▌ practitioners.

Few traditional quality assurance steps can be taken with off-the-sh▌ software. Often, the only evidence of a vendor's software developme▌ process is its reputation and, in some cases, life span, in the marketplac▌ The quality and availability of documentation can also provide clues. Ho▌ ever, even in the best of cases, visibility into the development process is d▌ and unreliable. Software quality practitioners must resort to emphasis ▌ other aspects of software development in order to do their job.

The primary step is to clearly identify the requirements for a software package that is needed. Software quality practitioners must make every effort to determine what the organizational needs are for a software purchase. For example, many database packages exist for personal computers. If a company or organization decided to provide its employees with PC workstations, including a database package, software quality practitioners must urge as much specificity in the requirements of the database as can be determined. Once the actual, intended use and application of the database package are determined, evaluation of candidate vendors and their products can commence. It is no different from traditional software development at this point. Until the software requirements are known, software development, or in this case purchase, should not begin.

Having settled on the requirements, vendor and product evaluation can begin. Vendors with the reputation of developing sound packages and packages that best appear to meet the requirements will be identified. When one or more possible packages have been identified, two more SQS activities that should take place: the specific testing of the packages and consideration of future maintenance. Either or both of these actions may be impossible for a given vendor or product. In that case, that product should be dismissed.

The vendor should provide for a period of real-world use of a potential package. Most acceptable vendors will allow a trial-use period in which the buyer has a chance to see if the product really meets the requirements for it. Unless there are serious, overriding conditions, software quality practitioners should counsel against purchase of off-the-shelf software from a vendor that will not allow such a test. Test or demonstration portions of many packages are also available for trial use. Some vendors sell the demonstration package and give credit for the demonstration package price against the purchase of the full software package. It should be noted that demonstrations may gloss over or skip potentially troublesome characteristics or weaknesses.

When permitted by licensing terms or provisions, reverse-engineering techniques can be applied to establish design methods or data models. These can then be assessed for compliance to the approved requirements. Such techniques must only be undertaken when the vendor grants permission. The quality practitioner should alert management that such activities may result in legal action on the part of the vendor for copyright infringement.

The second action is the review of vendor software maintenance provisions. A package that provides for vendor support, free updates when latent defects are found and corrected, reduced cost for new versions offering enhanced capability, and the like, should receive special attention. Vendors that agree to nothing, once the package has been bought, should be viewed

with a suspicious eye by software quality practitioners. The most likely ca
is a negotiated agreement as to the costs involved in various kinds
maintenance situations. Again, the vendor's marketplace reputation shou
influence this activity.

All in all, purchase of off-the-shelf packages is risk intensive. Of cours
there are situations when it is the proper method of providing softwa
capability to users. Software quality practitioners must recognize the ris
involved, however, and act to reduce those risks with whatever means a
available. One rule of thumb might be if you can't try it, don't buy it, and
they won't fix it, deep six it.

7.3.2 Customized shells

Software can often be purchased as a shell, which is generic and off-th
shelf. Its advantage is that the purchaser's unique needs are then custo
built into the shell and the total package tailored to the specific application

As in pure off-the-shelf software, software quality practitioners will hav
little influence over the generic shell portion. These shells are usually pr
built and act as a foundation for the customized software to be added. Sof
ware quality practitioners should encourage negotiation of developme
control over the customized portions.

The reputation of the vendor often is a good clue in this type of softwa
purchase, just as it is for off-the-shelf software. During early evaluation
potential vendors and shells, software quality practitioners can review ma
ketplace reports to help identify leading vendors for particular applications.

After-purchase maintenance also must be considered. Unlike most of
the-shelf software, a purchaser may be able to take over some or all of th
maintenance of a tailored package. Cost of source documentation for th
shell, postpurchase vendor maintenance announcements, and the buyer
ability to maintain the software should be investigated by software qualit
practitioners and corresponding recommendations made to management.

It is entirely acceptable to request that the vendor's proprietary sourc
code be placed in escrow against the possibility that the vendor become
unwilling or unable to continue maintenance of the software. In such a
event, the customer would receive the code from the escrow and take ove
maintenance at that point. In some cases, the source code would becom
the property of the customer after some contractually agreed period of tim
has passed. In that way, the vendor's proprietary property is protected, an
the customer is at less risk of loss of maintainability of important software.
is also important to have the right to ensure that the source code in escrow
does, in fact, match the object code being run.

Testing of the custom portion of the software is commonplace, so the software quality practitioner's main concerns in this area are the quality of the software requirements and the adequacy of the test program. Software quality practitioners must urge the preparation of an adequate statement of requirements for the software and then ascertain that the test program will, while finding defects, give confidence that the software meets the requirements.

Finally, software quality practitioners should encourage management to secure warrantees or guarantees with respect to at least the custom portions of the software.

7.3.3 Contracted new development

Purchase of total software packages, developed as new software for a specific buyer, provides the greatest opportunity for involvement of the purchaser's software quality practitioners.

The purchase of, or contract for the development of, a new software package is similar to an in-house development effort. All the same activities in the software development process must be accomplished under the auspices of the software quality practitioners. It is expected that the buyer's software quality requirements will cause the invocation of at least as stringent software quality requirements on the vendor as are followed by the buyer. Even when more strict software quality requirements are placed on the vendor, the buyer's software quality practitioner's visibility is probably hampered.

Remembering that the purchase of new software permits (in fact, requires) the buyer to specify all of the software requirements, the software quality practitioner should be certain to have all of its quality program requirements included in the contract. Not only should the vendor be contractually required to provide a strong software quality program, the buyer's software quality requirements must demand visibility into that program and its conduct. The buyer must have the right to conduct regularly scheduled and unscheduled reviews and audits of the vendor's development process and controls at the vendor's facility. Too often, these reviews and audits are held at the buyer's facility and amount to little more than dog and pony shows at which the buyer is assured that everything is fine. Only later does the buyer discover that costs are overrun, schedules have slipped, and the software does not work. The buyer's software quality practitioners must be provided the contractual right to visibility into the vendor's activities.

Maintenance of the software continues to be a concern of software quality practitioners. If the vendor will be contracted to maintain the software,

software quality practitioners should continue their regular level of visibil
into the vendor's processes. When maintenance becomes the responsibi
of the buyer, software quality practitioners must be sure that training, do
mentation, and the in-house facility to maintain the software are in pl
prior to delivery of the new software.

Finally, software quality practitioners should be sure that all new s
ware being purchased is subject to rigorous, requirements-based acceptar
testing prior to approval and acceptance by the buyer.

7.3.4   Remote development

More and more development is becoming a remote activity. Beginning
off-shore coding vendors, many companies in so-called developing cou
tries were formed to receive detailed design specifications from softw
developers and deliver the source code for them. It became apparent t
some of these off-shore companies were also ready, willing, and able
provide detailed design specifications from architectural design. Now, so
of the companies are doing all the design and coding based on receiv
requirements specifications.

Naturally, the remoteness of the work being performed was, is, and co
tinues to be a problem for coordination and oversight. Various techniqu
and approaches to this situation are being used. Certainly, very close revi
of the products as they are received is a necessity. Vigorous and rigoro
testing is also demanded.

Even closer coordination techniques include regular on-site visits to t
suppliers to establishing offices in the suppliers' locations.

The economies of lower labor costs and higher productivity can be neg
tively affected by poor quality products from remote suppliers. Softwa
quality practitioners need to take an aggressive role in reviewing and testi
remotely developed products.

7.3.5   Vendor management wrap-up

All purchased software carries risks not present in software developed i
house. Software quality practitioners must be innovative in both identifyi
the various risks associated with the different types of software purcha
and finding ways to meet and blunt those risks.

Software quality practitioners must be aware not only of the develo
mental risks but also of the maintenance requirements for the softwa
after delivery. Maintenance training, suitable maintenance-oriented doc
mentation, and the hardware and software facilities to support softwa

maintenance must be available. Placing the vendor's proprietary source code in escrow should also be considered. Software quality practitioners are responsible for ascertaining the availability and sufficiency of software maintenance needs. If anything is lacking in this area, software quality practitioners need to make management aware of those issues.

.4 Maintenance

A frequently quoted fact of the software industry is that something like 70% of the SLC is devoted to maintenance. There may be empirical data somewhere to back this up, or it may just be someone's off-the-cuff observation. The important thing is that it indicates that many companies expend a large share of their software resources in maintenance activities.

Clearly, the heavy majority of effort in the SLC is expended in the maintenance phase. One bank interviewed by the author asserted that no new code had been developed in 15 years. All development activity involved maintenance and enhancement of existing software. While maintenance is considered to be composed of both defect correction and enhancements to the original system, most maintenance is the result of requirements or design deficiency or planned obsolescence. (Planned obsolescence is usually termed phased implementation.) Certainly there will be occurrences of latent coding defects that remained hidden through the testing process, but the majority of defects usually are found to be faulty requirements and design.

Two points about maintenance should be made. First, except for the very simple correction of a very simple coding defect, maintenance is usually a repeat of the SDLC activities. Second, the cost of maintenance is almost never clearly known or recorded.

The role of software quality practitioners is also two-fold: (1) monitor the SDLC-type activities the same as was done in original development, and (2) try to help management realize the true cost of the maintenance effort. Once management can see and understand the cost of maintenance, the task of justifying the SQS activities will become much more achievable.

7.4.1 Types of maintenance

Four broad categories of maintenance are repairs, adaptations, enhancements, and polishing. Repairs are necessary to resolve latent defects that survived the best efforts of the testing program and add improvements to make the system do those things that were wanted but were left out of the

original requirements or design. As shown in Figure 7.6, repair of act
defects that were found after the system was placed in full operati
account for about 20% of the maintenance activity. Another percentage
the result of additions made to bring the system up to the level of capabi
originally desired, which might be called polishing. Little definitive d
exist to express the degree of effort expended in making these changes, t
at least a portion of the enhancement number will include requireme
corrections as well as new requirements.

Enhancements, shown as the largest category in Figure 7.6, are the
changes to give the system capabilities that were not originally foresee
Often, enhancements come at the request of the user who finds that ad
tional capabilities would be desirable. While new requirements and nee
frequently do arise over the life of a software system, it is likely that ma
corrections are being identified as enhancements. Requirements that we
overlooked or ignored during the original development often come back
enhancements. That may happen even though they probably were caus
by errors in the requirements analysis or design portions of developme
Maintenance that is deemed an enhancement should not include a
changes that help the system perform as it should have originally.

Adaptations, another large category, are generally in response to char
ing environmental conditions or the outside world. Environmental con
tions might include a change to a different computer or a new operati
system. Outside conditions could include a change in government regu
tions relating to an insurance or banking system.

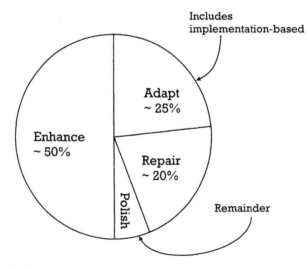

Figure 7.6 Maintenance types.

Software quality practitioners must be closely involved in the maintenance activity to ensure that proper control of the software and documentation configurations is enforced. In a protracted maintenance period, the loss of control of the configuration can mean the introduction of new defects as the existing ones are being found and corrected. Software quality practitioners will monitor and audit the defect reporting and tracking system reports and ensure that the CM function is in operation throughout the maintenance period.

7.4.1.1 Repairs
Repairs reflect defects identified by and reported from all sources. Repairs are the changes made for every defect from the simplest latent coding mistake, such as a misspelled data name, to a requirements deficiency. While repairs consume a minority percentage of the overall SLC costs, they do represent the most expensive tasks. Defects that must be repaired in the maintenance phase almost always affect more than just the code. As stated in Section 7.4.1, those requirements that were known but not addressed should be categorized as defects and processed as repairs.

Each repair will result in the reentry of the development cycle, as shown in Figure 7.7. Each repair must go through the full life cycle as the requirements of the repair are determined: that is, design, code, test, and implementation. The type and impact of the defect will determine how far back into the development products the repair will reach. In the large majority of cases, the ramifications go back through code to design and sometimes requirements. This, in turn, means corrections to

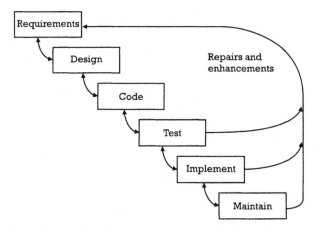

Figure 7.7 Repeating the life cycle.

documentation, sometimes corrections to other parts of the system in ord
to accommodate the repair, testing of the changed areas, and regressic
testing of the entire system. The cost of repairing a requirements defect
the maintenance phase may be as much as 100 times the cost to repair th
defect if it had been found in the requirements phase.

Estimates are that about a third of all corrections themselves introdu
new defects. Introduction of new defects is the case especially when shc
cuts are taken in the repair process. If CM procedures are skipped or testir
is slipshod or incomplete, the chances of introducing a new defect a
greatly magnified.

7.4.1.2 Adaptations

Adaptations are the modification of capabilities to meet changes from ou
side the original system. Activities such as these include changes to me
new government regulations, modifications to company procedures, incl
sions of new products, and similar conditions that did not exist at the time
the development of the original system.

Adaptations also include those changes made to accommodate imple
mentation approaches. A typical type of implementation approach is th
phased implementation. This is usually done when the schedule, the con
plexity of the system, or outside situations such as hardware availability w
not permit implementation of the entire capability of the system all at onc
The adaptations are the changes to the edges of the implemented softwa
to interface with the next phase of software being implemented. Since son
of the total software system has been missing up to this point, somethir
has been done to allow the existing software to operate until the new sof
ware is added. These allowances must be removed when the next softwa
is ready for implementation.

Most often, the problem is in the development planning for the systen
Resources, generally schedule resources, are miscalculated and run ou
before the system is ready for implementation. In this case, the system
partitioned into functional groups that can be implemented one or a few at
time. Some subset of the system is installed, and then, at a later time, add
tional system partitions are installed piecemeal until the full system is i
place. This has the advantage of permitting more attention to the variou
phases of the SDLC, but it usually is a repair in the context of this chapter.

Only in those cases where there was good reason at the outset to plan fc
a phased implementation can this not be considered a repair. One cas
would be an experimental system in which each step is a major evalua
tion—and possible termination—point of the development. Other case
would be those in which the system has a large number of outside interface

that become available at inconvenient times or where the complexity of the system dictates that smaller sections be installed one by one. It is probably appropriate to exclude these cases from the realm of maintenance altogether, since they were planned to occur from the beginning of the project.

Adaptations carry significant risk in some cases. There is small risk when the adaptation takes the form of a simple change to a job-entry routine or a spreadsheet formula. They become more threatening when they entail modifications as great as database reconfiguration. Software quality practitioners must monitor adaptations as closely as the other types of maintenance.

7.4.1.3 Enhancements

Enhancements usually follow the full SDLC.

Enhancements occur because the original requirements did not address some need of the user or customer. They are limited to those needs that became visible or recognized after the system has been installed and running. Enhancements cover the addition of new capabilities and the removal of obsolete capabilities. Work performed to modify the software to meet original requirements that were overlooked or misleading is more correctly classed with repairs.

Again, Figure 7.7 shows the return path to the SDLC. Enhancements always reenter the SDLC at the requirements phase, since new requirements are almost always involved, and the entire SDLC traversed. New development planning must take place, which must include planning for the transition to the improved system once it is ready. There may also be some consideration given to provision of the needed capabilities until the software is ready to support them. The entire SDLC is then followed, just as in the original development. Testing and CM play a large role in the enhancement process, just as they do in the repairs process. As discussed in Section 4.1.5.1, regression testing is especially important as well.

The software quality practitioner has the same set of functions in the repair and enhancement processes as in the original development. Since the SDLC is being followed, so must the SQS procedures.

7.4.1.4 Polishing

Polishing may be some of the most difficult of maintenance to perform. Most polishing is performed to increase the operating speed of an application or to reduce its memory requirements. Quite often, these changes can be extremely far-reaching, as loops are removed from the code to increase speed or added to reduce size. When both goals are present, large-scale reengineering of the system may be required. The software quality practitioner should be sure that all participants in the polishing main nance activities are aware of the breadth of the effects their changes m have. If the polishing is being performed to more closely meet origin requirements, it should probably be called a repair. If it is modifying t software in response to external changes, it is more likely an adaptatic Often, polishing may be change for change's sake and not justified at all

7.4.2 Documentation

Regardless of why or where the SDLC is reentered, it is essential that t system documentation be maintained. It cannot be stressed too much th the documentation of the system is the key to the ease of repair or enhanc ment. The better the documentation, the more easily the maintenance p sonnel can find and correct a defect or properly install an enhancement. the needed documentation is lacking, the maintainer must either recreate or try to find the affected portion of the system through detective wor When the issues of the documents for the various phases are out of step, discussed in Section 6.4.2, the maintainer has more work to do in the doc mentation of his or her work as well.

If more that one change is in progress at one time, such as both enhancement and a repair, poor documentation practices may allow t two activities to operate on different issues of the system or to conflict wi each other. If the documentation is up-to-date and correct, both maintai ers can recognize any areas of overlap in their work and can work togeth during the change process rather than creating another defect that must repaired.

Software quality practitioners perform an important monitoring a reporting function in the maintenance phase by keeping manageme informed as to the quality and status of the documentation.

7.4.3 Regression testing

The software quality practitioner has an additional concern in the maint nance phase, that of ensuring that regression testing is accomplished. Whi the software quality practitioner must monitor the regular SDLC testi function, the maintenance phase introduces the regression testing activit Although the SDLC is used to create repairs and enhancements, these no mally affect only a portion of the entire system. Once the change has be tested for its own correctness, the full system must undergo overall testi to ensure that the changes have not had some unexpected negative effe on the operation of the system as a full entity.

As stated in Section 4.1.5.1, regression testing should be a part of the overall test plan developed for the system during its original SDLC. As the system acceptance test is designed, and data for the test is prepared, a subset of the acceptance test data should be preserved for future regression tests. The expected and actual results should also be preserved. In that way, the correct performance of the original system is known. When regression testing is needed, the same test data that were used for the acceptance test are used. The original results should be received from unchanged parts of the system, showing that unintentional changes have not been made or new defects introduced.

For those changed portions of the system, new regression test data must be prepared for use in future change activity. The software quality practitioner has the responsibility of ensuring that the regression tests are prepared in the beginning and that they are kept up to date during the full SLC. Further, the practitioner must ensure that all differences from the expected results of the regression tests are accounted for.

7.4.4 Maintenance wrap-up

The great majority of effort in the SLC is expended in the maintenance phase.

Repairs make up a significant portion, if not the majority, of the maintenance effort. Repairs include latent defects that survived the testing program and implementing enhancements or improvements required to make the system perform those tasks that were wanted but were left out of the original requirements or design. True enhancements are those additions or modifications that enable the software to perform functions not originally wanted or needed.

Software quality practitioners must be closely involved in the maintenance activity to ensure that proper control of the software and documentation configurations is enforced and that regression testing is fully performed. The software quality practitioner has the responsibility of ensuring that the regression tests are prepared in the beginning and that they are kept up-to-date during the full SLC.

Software quality practitioners perform an important monitoring and reporting function in the maintenance phase by keeping management informed as to the quality and status of the documentation and code.

7.5 Summary

Security has three main aspects; the database, data transmission, and the physical data center itself. All purchased software carries risks that are present in in-house developed software. Education, while rarely provid by the software quality practitioner, is a necessary step in the provision quality product. The heavy majority of effort in the SLC is expended in maintenance phase.

As in all other areas, the ongoing responsibility of the software qual practitioner is to monitor each situation or activity and report on its stat and needs to decision-making, action-capable management.

7.6 The next step

To find out more about several of the topics in this chapter, consult the following texts:

Martin Wieczorek and Dirk Meyerhoff (eds). *Software Quality: State of the Art in Management, Testing, and Tools*, Berlin: Springer-Verlag, 2001.

T. M. Pigoski. *Practical Software Maintenance*, New York: John Wiley & Sons, 1997.

Additional reading

Bryan, W. L., and S. G. Siegel, *Software Product Assurance*, New York: Elsevier, 198

Guide International, *Quality Assurance of Purchased Packages—GPP 145*, Chicago: Guide International, 1986.

Lobel, Jerome, *Foiling the System Breakers*, New York: McGraw-Hill, 1986.

McConn, Charlotte Eudy, *Business Computer Systems: Design, Programming, and Maintenance with Case Studies*, Englewood Cliffs, NY: Prentice Hall, 1989.

Westwater, Keith, *The Earthquake Business Plan*, Wellington, NZ: Ministry of Civil Defense, 1990.

CHAPTER

8

Contents

Software Safety

Not that long ago, software safety was not a hot topic. Certainly, the safety of space flight software was important and the defense industry was interested, at times, in software safety, but the general public gave no more thought to software safety than to the safety of their tap water. Users presumed that software was safe as long as it had been debugged and performed pretty much as expected. Besides, even if someone's bank messed up his or her checking account because of erroneous software, it was deemed a nuisance, not a catastrophe.

However, actual software-related catastrophes began occurring, such as a train crash due to faulty signal control software, the death of a cancer patient because of failed radiation limiting software, and so on. Spectacular failures like the space probe that flew to the sun and the Mars lander that crashed, both due to simple coding errors, were also reported.

Software safety is an issue that is growing in importance as more and more of our lives are directly or indirectly affected by computers and software. With software an integral part of everything from wristwatches and automobile dashboards to nuclear power plants and medical devices, we are increasingly at personal risk from unsafe software.

IEEE Standard 610.12 defines critical software as "software whose failure could have an impact on safety or could cause large financial or social loss."

The standard defines safety-critical software as software that falls into one or more of the following categories:

> ▸ Software whose inadvertent response to stimuli, failure to respo
>   when required, response out-of-sequence, or response in combin
>   tion with other responses can result in an accident.
>
> ▸ Software that is intended to mitigate the result of an accident.
>
> ▸ Software that is intended to recover from the result of an accident

The demand for safety-critical software has increased significantly in t last few years. Aircraft, such as the Boeing 777, now employ fly-by-wi controls where computers, and not humans, are in direct control of t flight surfaces. Automobiles have become rolling systems of distribut computing that controls the engine and power train, break system, ar other critical components. To avoid failure in safety-critical areas, softwa developers now need to pay close attention to the various aspects of so ware criticality and safety.

8.1   Aspects of software safety

The following are four of the most important aspects of software safety:

1. Software whose failure could damage hardware or equipment;

2. Software whose failure could hurt the business or enterprise;

3. Software whose failure could cause harm to the environment;

4. Software whose failure could cause harm to people.

Of course, some software might impact more that one aspect of safet such as software involved in weapons systems, the medical field, or nucle power generation.

8.1.1   Damaging hardware

An example of hardware damage might be damage caused when the sof ware embedded in a generator fails to respond to a high temperature signa This could permit the generator to overheat and fail in several ways (i.e seizing the armature, catching fire, fracturing the housing, and so on). more disastrous failure could be the meltdown of a nuclear power plar caused by an incorrect software action or response.

8.1.2   Business or enterprise damage

Software is often used to make important business decisions and actuall run the business. Something as simple as a spreadsheet failure could resu in management making a bad decision based on incorrect information. A retail store chain could lose track of its inventory and discover its automatic ordering system is ordering the wrong products. A warehouse management system could store products incorrectly and not be able to account for them when needed.

8.1.3 Environmental damage

The software monitoring an oil pipeline could fail to detect, or react incorrectly to the detection of, a leaking or burst section of the line. The resulting oil spill into the ground or sea could cause grave damage to the environment and, perhaps, the animals that inhabit it. Navigational software failure could cause an oil tanker to run aground and spill millions of gallons of crude oil into the sea.

8.1.4 Damage to humans

The safety-criticality of medical and air traffic control software is often recognized. For example, an air traffic control system failure could result in the collision of aircraft or the software controlling a morphine intravenous injection system could result in a patient's overdose.

However, with software being used in so many seemingly benign areas, we may overlook other hazards. For example, a faulty readout on an automobile speedometer could permit a driver to enter a curve too fast and crash. A computerized refrigeration temperature sensor could fail and permit the growth of dangerous bacteria in food.

.2 Safety issues

The software quality practitioner must be aware of the following issues surrounding software safety:

- Improper or inadequate analyses of potential safety problems;
- Failure to recognize safety needs during the system or software requirements definition and design efforts;
- Inadequate planning for the mitigation of safety concerns;
- Inadequate training in safety-critical software development techniques;
- Inadequate monitoring of safety assurance efforts;
- Inadequate testing of safety critical software and systems.

8.2.1 Inadequate analysis

One company violated a coding standard by taking a shortcut, which caus
a weapon system to fail. Because the company did not perform an analy
of the possible consequences of this shortcut, the system encountered a $
million failure in testing.

8.2.2 Failure to recognize safety needs

In one example, the danger of overheating in a microwave oven was r
recognized. The overheating caused several serious house fires before t
ovens were recalled for repair. The manufacturer suffered millions of doll
in repair costs and in restoring lost customer trust and confidence.

8.2.3 Inadequate planning

Identified hazard threats are sometimes built into the software in an attem
to avoid or minimize the hazard's effects should it be encountered. F
example, avionics software that evaluates airspeed and rates of climb
descent is expected to warn the pilot if these values are out of corr
ranges. Failure to program the software to properly combine the speed a
descent rate could result in a crash during landing.

8.2.4 Inadequate training

Little formal education or training is available in the specialized area
safety-critical software development. While research is being conducte
most training is on the job or based on experience. Major enterprises such
NASA and the military conduct in-house training in certain cases. Peop
who manage and develop safety-critical software can also attend occasion
conferences. Beyond that, however, training and educational opportuniti
are scarce.

8.2.5 Inadequate monitoring

Most safety-critical software failures encountered by the author have be
the result of inadequate quality management efforts. The application
non-safety-critical software quality efforts are not sufficient for critical so
ware that exhibits any or all of the aspects identified in Section 8.1. Mu
more extensive reviewing and testing is necessary to reduce the likeliho
of failure in critical situations.

8.2.6   Inadequate testing

Testing of safety-critical software must go beyond the does-it-meet-the-requirements level to the how-could-it-fail, or what-if, level. All of the software's safety requirements are rarely known, even by the time testing is thought to be complete.

For example, a home security system had been shown to be impervious to electrical storms. Only after the system had been installed was it found to be susceptible to the magnetic field surrounding a vacuum cleaner.

8.2.7   Combination of issues

The following situations are examples of a combination of safety issues discussed so far.

The developers of the rod lifter, a mechanism that raises and lowers control rods in a nuclear reactor, decided to attach a computer to the rod lifter to download various data elements collected by the mechanism. Management was assured that there would be no interaction between the computer and the rod lifter. The computer was attached, and several tests of the combination were run. An alert quality practitioner asked the following what-if question: What if the operator happens to press a key on the computer while the rod lifter is raising or lowering a rod? The reply was that there is no connection between the computer and the rod lifter. The practitioner asked that the rod lifter be put into action, with the computer attached. As the rod was being lifted, he hit a key on the keyboard. In response, the rod lifter raised the rod three increments but did not record the motion, leaving the rod in a different position from that displayed to the operator. The same result was experienced when the rod was being lowered.

In that case, there was a failure to analyze the possibility and recognize the potential for interaction between the computer and the rod lifter. In fact, such an interaction was summarily dismissed as a possibility. Because it was decided that the situation could not exist, no plans were included for software checks or operator training to preclude any interaction during the movement of the rods. Further, since no safety situation was deemed to exist, no testing was done to determine what would happen if there actually was an interaction.

Another, more software-specific example deals with the modification of an alarm-sensing program. In that case, the software had been in operation for a number of years when it was noticed that, during 15 seconds of each hour, the software was in self-test mode and could not detect alarms during that time. A seemingly simple modification was made to the software and the change tested. The software could now sense alarms during self-test,

and the new software was installed. Some time later, an operator noti
that two lamps were illuminated on the console. One lamp indicated t
an alarm had been sent to the software, while the other indicated that
software had detected no alarm. The operator immediately shut down
reactor. The problem in that case was the lack of recognition that the mo
fication to the software carried important safety implications. Because
change had been tested, and the software clearly could recognize alar
during self-test, no regression testing of the unchanged software was cc
ducted. It was not seen that the modified software could no longer det
alarms during the non-self-test periods (59 minutes and 45 seconds
each hour).

8.3 Safety requirements

Safety requirements are both obvious and subtle. Some, like the need fo
dose limiting section on a radiation system, are obvious. Others, like the r
lifter dangers, are less intuitive. As part of any requirements gathering a
analysis effort, the quality practitioner should be involved in trying
anticipate and record any safety issues.

Some safety requirements will be imposed from outside the proje
Medical, nuclear, space, traffic (air, rail, sea, and highway), defense, a
other agencies have various rules, regulations, standards, guidelines, a
required practices that become safety requirements. However, other are
may involve safety issues that are not imposed by another domain.

No standards would have precluded the interaction between the cor
puter and the rod lifter, nor would standards have prevented the alar
error. In those cases, experienced quality practitioners responsible for fin
ing defects were able to look at the situation from a how-might-it-not-b
safe bias rather than the more common this-will-work-just-fine view.
that way, quality practitioners can be of great value in seeking potenti
safety failures during requirements gathering and analysis and desig
review. IEEE Standard 730 lays out the required contents of a softwa
quality assurance plan (see Appendix B). Section 15, entitled "Risk Manag
ment," describes the quality system procedures that deal with safety issues.

IEEE Standard 830 (see Appendix D) calls for the inclusion of safe
requirements in Section 2.5 (constraints, part k, and safety and security co
siderations).

Finally, IEEE Standard 1228 (see Appendix K) describes the require
content for a software safety plan. For safety-critical software, this pla

defines the specific roles, resources, responsibilities, and activities to be used in software development.

Requirements for safety typically arise in all parts of the SLC:

- Requirements gathering, analysis, and expression (recognize hazards);
- Design (discover hazards);
- Coding (avoid hazards);
- Testing (probe for hazards);
- Operation (react to hazards).

8.3.1 Requirements period

During the requirements effort, clear hazards to be encountered or caused by the software are recognized and stated in the requirements documentation. During this period, situations that must not be allowed or must be addressed are stated. This could be called "the software must not cause or allow harm" period. Any known or anticipated hazards will be spelled out in the requirements and the safety plan.

An example from the space shuttle software might be "All computers must be in synchronism prior to engine ignition." In that case, it is recognized that the software must take action to determine whether or not the various computers are in sync.

During the requirements period, quality practitioners find themselves asking the what-if questions. Practitioners will often be testers who are knowledgeable in the concepts of the system or experienced in other safety-critical systems or software.

8.3.2 Design period

As design proceeds, hidden hazards may be exposed and discovered. This might be called the "the software could have caused or allowed harm" period.

Continuing the space shuttle example, it might be discovered that not all computers are linked and capable of being synchronized. While this may be intentional, it might also be discovered that one or more computers must be linked. New or additional software may be needed to accomplish the required linking.

In another example, a design review could determine that, under certain-processing loads, low-priority tasks could be interrupted for higher

priority tasks to the extent that the low-priority tasks are never complet
and the system will fail.

During the design period, the quality practitioner is a reviewer and ch
lenger of the design against the requirements and continues to ask, what if

8.3.3 Coding period

Some of the most costly failures of critical and safety-critical software ha
occurred during the coding period. The Mars lander crash, the space pro
that went to the sun, and the weapon test failure were all caused by simp
yet undetected, coding errors. These errors could all have been detected
properly phrased what-if questions. What if the data description is wro
and uses miles versus kilometers? What if the looping is miscoded and cr
ates a variable rather than a loop? What if the priority interrupt rules a
violated and stores priority-four data in the priority-one field? Unfort
nately, none of those questions were asked.

8.3.4 Testing period

Testing of safety-critical software must not only evaluate the softwa
against its requirements, but must also look for previously unidentified ha
ards. This is the "the software would have caused or allowed harm" period

Presuming that computers that should be linked have been identifie
and that those not required to be linked are also known, the quality pract
tioner should test the linkages and synchronizations and check for missir
synchronizations and improper and missing linkages to verify that prop
alarms are provided for failure cases.

During the testing period, anomalous situations should be presented
the software to probe for unanticipated situations that could lead to th
exposure of additional hazards in the software or system.

8.3.5 Operational period

The operational period is when as-yet unexposed hazards and defens
against them can be found. This is the "the software nearly did or did cau
or allow harm" period. It is hoped, but not really expected, that all hazar
to be detected, avoided, corrected, reduced, or otherwise treated by the sof
ware will be discovered, considered, and managed.

As has happened more than once on the space shuttle program, lack
synchronism among computers can cause launch delays.

The quality assurance practitioner must constantly review problem and anomaly reports, looking for situations that could become hazards, as well as those that are encountered. During the previous periods, the quality practitioner concentrated on quality control, or defect detection and correction, in the software and system. While quality control continues in the operational period, as well as the quality assurance practitioner's defect prevention activities, the emphasis has clearly shifted. The operational period is the source of the majority lessons learned that can be applied to subsequent system and software projects.

.4 Safety management

The following three major elements are involved in the area of safety management:

1. Previous hazard experience;
2. Hazard analysis;
3. Safety planning.

8.4.1 Experience

Two kinds of experience are applied here: lessons learned and intuition. Lessons learned come from experience with prior or similar systems or software. Each space shuttle mission becomes less hazardous due to the lessons learned on earlier flights. Some of the same hazards still exist, but those hazards and how to manage them are known. The example of the undetected alarm (see Section 8.2) led to a lesson learned regarding better analysis of a situation requiring a software change and better review and regression testing of the change and the affected system prior to operation.

In the case of new systems or software, there is a greater reliance on intuition and asking what could go wrong rather than knowing what did go wrong. The story about the rod lifter (see Section 8.2) is an example of intuition on the part of the quality practitioner. He had no prior experience with such a system but knew that the casual addition of the computer had not received close scrutiny and acted on a hunch that a hazard might exist. Had the hazard not been detected by his action, a serious nuclear incident could have occurred.

8.4.2 Analysis

IEEE Standard 1228 defines the content and format of the software saf
plan and includes an entire section on software safety analyses. These ana
ses reflect the information in Section 8.3 and discuss activities to be cc
ducted during the coding phase.

At each step in the development of safety-critical software, attenti
must be given to the identification, evaluation, documentation, and amel
ration of the following types of hazards:

> ◦ Those to be avoided by software;
> ◦ Those caused by software;
> ◦ Those incorrectly controlled by software;
> ◦ Those incompletely responded to by software;
> ◦ Those overlooked by software.

Each type of analysis will be determined by the period of the life cy
involved, the type of hazard being considered or expected, the severity a
probability of the hazard, and other factors specific to the project. The so
ware safety plan will spell out these issues and their treatment.

8.4.3 Planning

In most, if not all, safety-critical system and software development effor
planning for special attention to the safety aspect and issues is necessary.
there are only one or two relatively obvious and simple hazards to consid
the project plan itself may provide adequate attention to the issues.

Beyond the simple and obvious, though, specific and detailed attenti
should be paid to safety. This is best done with a planned approach
addressing safety issues. The preparation of a software safety plan, accordi
to the IEEE standard, is one way to increase the quality and safety of critic
and safety-critical software.

8.5 Summary

The following are the four aspects of safety-critical software:

1. Damage to hardware or equipment;
2. Damage to the business or enterprise;
3. Damage to the environment;
4. Damage (harm) to people;

Safety-critical software includes software that can contribute to, reduce the effect of, or recover from the occurrence of one or more of those aspects.

All software is subjected to applicable quality system activities. Safety-critical software requires the application of more extensive quality measures. Large projects will benefit from a separate software safety plan that specifically defines the appropriate quality measures.

6   The next step

To find out how to deal with safety-critical software, the following are good sources to consult:

S. Gardiner (ed.). *Testing Safety-Critical Systems*, Berlin: Springer-Verlag, 1998.

Debra Herrmann et al. *Software Safety and Reliability*, Piscataway, NJ: IEEE, 2000.

Additional reading

Friedman, Michael A., and Jeffrey M. Voas, *Software Assessment: Reliability, Safety, Testability*, New York, Wiley Interscience, 1995.

IEEE Standard 1228-1994, "IEEE Standard for Software Safety Plans," Piscataway, NJ: IEEE, 1994.

Kramer, Bernard J., *Safety-Critical Real-Time Systems*, Boston: Kluwer Academic Press, 1997.

Leveson, Nancy G., *Safeware: System Safety and Computers*, Reading, MA: Addison-Wesley, 1995.

Neumann, Peter G., *Computer-Related Risks*, New York: ACM Press, 1995.

9

Risk Management

Risk is an ever-present factor in software and its environment, but what is risk?

IEEE Standard 1228-1994 defines risk as "a measure that combines both the likelihood that a system hazard will cause an accident and the severity of that accident."

Merriam Webster's Collegiate Dictionary, Ninth Edition includes a definition of risk as "a dangerous element or factor."

Both definitions suggest that risk is the threat of a negative situation and an evaluation of that threat.

In this book, we recognize the difference between risk and safety. Chapter 8 addresses safety issues. In this chapter, we will consider risks to successful projects and the quality practitioner's roles in helping to reduce or eliminate those risks.

9.1 Types of risk

Technical, managerial, operational, environment, and testing risks all represent threats to the success of a software product. While other risks exist, these are the most prevalent, identifiable, and addressable in a software development or maintenance project.

9.1.1 Technical risk

The first type of risk a software project faces is that of the problem itself. Two major questions need to be asked: (1) Do we really know what the problem is? and (2) Is the problem solvable?

Defining the problem is done during the business analysis and softwa requirement gathering and definition phase. Too often, a software project begun with only a vague suggestion of the business needs to be address and the outcomes expected. Thus, at the very outset, developers are aimi at a hazy and moving target. They do not know where they are going how to get there, but they are on the way. The quality practitioner has t responsibility of assisting management to ensure that a complete definiti of the business needs and subsequent software requirements is provide This is not to say that all requirements must be known prior to the start any work, but all must be known prior to claiming that the project complete.

Just because a problem is known does not mean it can be solved. Sol tions may be too expensive or could turn out to be a negative contributic to the overall business. These risks need to be analyzed and the proble defined during the project initiation period.

Another aspect of technical risk is the potential that the desired solutic to the business need is beyond current technological capabilities. While th teleportation of the Star Trek crew is a viable solution on a television pr gram, that technology is not readily available today. Although not expecte to be an expert in all technologies, the quality practitioner is responsible fe ensuring that technology questions are answered by the appropriate peopl

If a company does not know what the real problem is or whether it beyond the scope of current technology, the project is doomed before starts. Ensuring that technical risks are addressed is an important area responsibility for quality practitioners.

9.1.2 Managerial risk

The following managerial risks are faced throughout the life of the project:

 > Schedule risk;

 > Financial risk;

 > Personnel risk;

 > Quality risk;

 > CM risk.

9.1.2.1 Schedule risk

Perhaps the biggest risk in project management is scheduling and the managing that schedule. Schedule risk starts with the initial (and ofte unchangeable) estimates of the size, criticality, complexity, importance, necessity, and feasibility of a project. Stories abound of runaway projects that are woefully late or incomplete.

Quality practitioners should be closely involved in the estimation process to aid in the schedule determination. They should also counsel management to monitor and adjust the schedule as the software is designed, coded, and tested. Each step along the way should provide better visibility into the development effort, with associated better schedule reality.

9.1.2.2   Financial risk

Clearly tied to schedule risk is financial risk. Poorly estimated and determined schedules will have a negative effect on the veracity of financial estimates. This is not to say that schedules are the only contributor to financial risk. Many of the same factors affecting schedule estimation are also factors in financial estimation. These must be considered when project cost estimation is performed.

Another financial risk is incorrect or neglected consideration of the costs involved in merely deciding to accept or undertake a project. Yet another major financial risk is faced when the project overruns its schedule or budget.

The quality practitioner has the task of bringing to decision-making, action-capable management information regarding the threat and occurrence of financial risks.

9.1.2.3   Personnel risk

While technical risk occurs due to problem understanding and technological capabilities, it may roll over into personnel risk. Project management and quality practitioners should ask the following questions:

- Do we have sufficient staff to address the problem?
- Do we have sufficient skills to solve the problem?

Too few or inexperienced staff can threaten the successful completion of a project.

9.1.2.4   CM risk

Developing and delivering a product requires that all parts of the product are mutually consistent and meet the currently approved product requirements. This is obvious if the product is a stand-alone software product. However, software is virtually never stand-alone. At the very least, it must perform its functions on a computational platform in the company of other

software, such as an operating system. In some projects, the software i
part of a larger system that may involve other software and include ha
ware as parts of the deliverable product.

From the smallest software change to the largest total system, ensur
that the delivered software is correct for its surroundings is a major CM ri
The quality practitioner will work with developers, management, and C
practitioners to help ensure that configuration concerns do not pose thre
to the project's success.

9.1.2.5 Quality risk

It would be nice to think that all projects result in software that exhibits z
defects and delivers exactly as expected. Not only is this almost never t
case, but it is sometimes not desirable from a business perspective. None
the managerial risks can be solved independently of the others. Ov
running the budget to achieve schedule goals or acquire training
staff, lengthening the schedule to provide better CM, hiring costly t
specialized staff to increase quality and so on show the interactions amo
the risks.

An important risk question is, how good must the delivered product b
Trade-offs often exist between quality and timeliness or cost. In some cas
the business decision is to deliver a product that is close to its quality go
in order to meet market pressures or customer demands. In other cas
the criticality of the product dictates that budget or schedule or both
exceeded to deliver a high-quality product.

It is the quality practitioner's role to ensure that all aspects of a situ
tion are considered when making trade-off decisions involving prodt
quality. Parties to the trade-off decisions may include management, m
keting, finance, user, operations, and so on, depending on the speci
situation.

9.1.2.6 Project monitoring

Managerial risks are best addressed by recognizing threats and then mo
toring the project to detect a threat's occurrence. Initial recognition of t
threat potential should lead to intentional planning for addressing the ris
As the project proceeds, continuous monitoring of the risk potential w
expose those risk situations and call for the execution of risk manageme
plans.

The quality practitioner can play a large role in assisting in identifyi
risk potential, planning how to address encountered risk situations, ar
executing risk responses.

9.1.3 Operational risk

The following are three important operational risks:

1. Inadequate user education or training;
2. Misuse, intentional or unintentional, of the product;
3. Inadequate maintenance of the product.

9.1.3.1 User education

User education is the most easily addressed of the three risks. Understanding the role of the user as the project is being initiated is expected. This understanding should indicate potential training or educational requirements for the correct and skillful use of the new product. The quality practitioner may be called on to assess training needs, try the product to find potential user confusion or error, or even conduct a dry run and operate the product using only the provided user manual or instructions.

9.1.3.2 Software Misuse

A more difficult risk to address is misuse of the product by its intended user. Anticipation of, and built-in software protection against, common unintentional mistakes on the part of the user is a risk response that is often possible.

The intentional misuse of the product usually cannot be foreseen and is hard to stop even if it can be foreseen. In these cases, clear statements of the proper scope and use of the product and specific cautions about the potential results of misuse may be a company's only defense.

The daunting role of the quality practitioner is to keep management aware of the potential for and possible consequences of product misuse.

9.1.3.3 Maintenance

Maintenance of software products is often more risk laden than the original development. Both quality control and quality assurance practitioners have direct roles in identifying and addressing maintenance risks.

The quality control practitioner's role is to make certain that every maintenance activity is checked, tested, reviewed, and configuration managed prior to the completion of the maintenance action.

The quality assurance practitioner's role is to monitor maintenance activities to detect signs of defect-prone portions of the product, identify weaknesses in the maintenance process, and anticipate potential, but as-yet unencountered, maintenance problems.

9.1.4 Environment risk

The best software systems in the world are not useful if they cannot ru
This seems like a rather basic concept, but the security of the data cen
itself is often the last area that an organization is concerned about. The da
center is at constant risk from fire and water damage, and if any precautio
are taken, it is usually in this area. Beyond that, most data centers overlo
the potential for interrupted processing due to severe damage. Unfort
nately, few data centers make provisions for temporary processing facilit
in the case of damage to the center.

A formal risk analysis will expose the various types of damage to whi
the specific data center is vulnerable and the degree of protection that
appropriate.

There are many physical risks that may threaten a particular data cent
Fire is the most widely acknowledged threat, and provisions are nearly ur
versal for prevention, detection, and extinguishing of fire. A second cor
monly recognized threat is water, usually from above in the form of ra
leakage or a burst water pipe. Here, too, provisions for detection and prote
tion are common. Unfortunately, protection frequently stops once fire ar
water issues are addressed because other risks are not recognized or give
credence. A risk analysis can point out additional risks that may require pr
tection against.

Such an analysis may show that the potential for severe weather damai
is a real factor in hurricane and tornado areas, as well as in areas whe
heavy snow can damage roofs. The potential for fire damage may be show
to exist not only within the data center, but immediately outside it in su
areas as adjacent warehouses or offices. The proximity of landing aircraft
railroad sidings presents the possibility of damage from accidents outside th
center. Electrical power transmission lines in the immediate vicinity cou
break in a storm and fall onto or into the data center.

Intentional damage is a real threat as well. A recently discharge
employee flooded his former employer's data center by going to the buil
ing's top floor and opening the fire hose connection. This occurred on
weekend when the bulk of the building was deserted. By the time the bas
ment data center noticed the water's arrival, there was sufficient water o
the way to flood the center with five feet of water. A risk analysis performe
prior to the installation of the data center may have warned against placi
the data center in the basement, where water would have nowhere else
go. A second data center had no thought of intentional damage being dor
to it until a terrorist bomb destroyed a nearby data center. Again, risk anal
sis could have shown the danger of building the data center in its curre
location.

Not all risks are preventable. In fact, some are inevitable and no real prevention can be provided. Others will cause such little negative effect that they can be ignored. Each risk must, however, be identified before such judgments can be made. Risk analyses help the diligent data center determine the best places to spend its protection dollars. It is equally as important to determine that a particular factor is of little or negligible risk as it is to find those factors that do present risk. Once the risks and their costs of occurrence known, preventive or protective action can be taken.

9.1.5 Testing risk

The quality control practitioner plays a key role in addressing the testing of risk. A well-constructed test plan and test process combine to reduce incomplete or redundant testing. However, the question of how much testing is enough falls to the responsible risk identifier and responder.

When to stop testing involves consideration of the types of defects still being detected by testing, the penalty to be suffered if such defects are encountered by the user, the cost of additional testing, and so on. The quality assurance practitioner will analyze the defect detection experience of the quality control activities. Consideration will be given to the potential for delivering unknown or undetected defects; the consequences of delivering known but uncorrected defects; and the costs associated with continued testing.

The results of the analysis will be presented to responsible management for the final decision as to whether to accept the risk or end testing.

.2 Risk management process

A simple and effective risk management process consists of the following four steps:

1. Identifying the risk;
2. Assessing the risk's magnitude;
3. Determining the response to the risk;
4. Planning for the addressing of, and reporting on, the risk if encountered.

9.2.1 Risk identification

There is no widely accepted standard method to identify risks. Experience on other, similar projects or products is a valuable tool in risk identification.

Brainstorming, what-if questioning, and the like can sometimes lead to t discovery of risk potential. An important technique is to look for the wo possible situations that might occur and try to determine their likelihoc In addition, asking how could the product or project fail will frequen uncover unexpected threats.

Once a risk or risk potential, however remote it may seem, is identifie it should be recorded and passed on to risk assessment.

9.2.2   Risk assessment

Risk assessment includes making the following determinations:

1. The cost potential of the risk's occurrence;

2. The probability of the risk occurring;

3. The risk exposure;

4. The cost to respond to the risk.

9.2.2.1   Cost-potential determination

Some costs can be computed or estimated directly. The costs of damage equipment, overpayment of invoices, untimely submission of invoices payments, and the penalties for budget or schedule overruns are general predictable to a degree. Other costs such as lost customers or customer co fidence or the cost of the loss of human life cannot be well determined. the greatest extent possible, each identified risk should be assigned a co potential.

9.2.2.2   Occurrence-probability determination

As in the determination of cost potential, some risk probabilities can determined easily. Historical records of tornado frequency are available fe many areas. Testing history or previous operational experience can lead the likelihood that a given risk might occur. Some risks may just be assigne a value based on one's gut feel. In any event, a probability will be stated fe each identified risk.

9.2.2.3   Risk-exposure determination

Risk exposure is the product of the cost potential and the probability of th risk. The exposure for each risk will be calculated and used in risk manage ment planning to assign priorities and response methods to them. In som cases, such as the loss of human life, the cost may be deemed infinite and a infinite exposure value assigned.

9.2.2.4 Response-cost determination

This task is similar to the cost and schedule estimation for the project itself. An estimate of the cost—and its impact on the budget and schedule—to respond to each identified risk will be calculated.

9.2.3 Risk response

Once the risk exposure is calculated, a response to that risk must be determined. Based on the exposure, and the estimated cost to respond, each risk will be assigned one of the following response types:

- Elimination;
- Avoidance;
- Mitigation;
- Acceptance.

9.2.3.1 Elimination

Elimination of the risk is called for when the exposure is unacceptably high or when the cost of elimination is not prohibitive. In the case of risk to human life, every effort is expended to eliminate the risk. In the case of low or negligible cost to respond, the risk is usually eliminated as well. For example, if potholes in the road pose significant risk to automobiles and their drivers, the risk elimination would be to fill the potholes.

9.2.3.2 Avoidance

As the term suggests, avoidance means taking alternative steps so that the risk probability is reduced to zero or almost zero. In the pothole example, closing the street would be an example of avoidance.

9.2.3.3 Mitigation

Mitigation is the reduction of the exposure to the risk. This can be accomplished by reducing the probability of the risk occurring, reducing the cost of experiencing the risk, or both.

Again, using the pothole example, the probability of risk could be lowered by installing a barrier around the pothole. Installing warning signs about the danger of potholes in the street and advising motorists to seek an alternative route could reduce the penalty, as well as the cost of a potential lawsuit filed by a driver who hits the pothole.

9.2.3.4 Acceptance

In the case of an extremely unlikely occurrence, or very low estimated c of occurrence, the decision might be to ignore the risk and live with : threat. This decision might also be reached if the cost of elimination, avo ance, or mitigation is unacceptably large. In the pothole case, the decisi might be to ignore tiny potholes.

9.2.4 Planning and reporting

The final step in the risk management process is the generation of a spec risk management plan for the project. In this plan, all identified risks a the company's planned responses should those risks be encountered . spelled out. The required reporting concerning the risk management proc and provisions for its improvement are also discussed in the plan.

Appendix L presents a sample risk management plan from IEEE St dard 1540-2001.

9.3 Summary

Risks are present in every facet of software development and maintenane Types of risks include technical, managerial, operational, environment and testing. Each type may impact other types, so none is isolated by itself

Risk management is a four-step process that involves identifying, asse ing, and responding to risks, as well as planning a course of action shou the risk occur. Determining the actual response to each risk is important ar includes consideration of the risk exposure and the cost to respond to th exposure.

The risk management process culminates in the preparation of a ri management plan for both the project and organization.

9.4 The next step

Further information on this topic may be found in the following books:

Martyn A. Ould. *Managing Software Quality and Business Risk*, New York: John Wile & Sons, 1999.

Steve McConnell. *Software Project Survival Guide*, Redmond, WA: Microsoft Press, 1997.

Additional reading

Dorofee, Audrey J., et al., *Continuous Risk Management Handbook*, Pittsburgh, PA: Software Engineering Institute, Carnegie Mellon University, 1996.

Down, Alex, et al., *Risk Management for Software Projects*, New York: McGraw-Hill, 1994.

Jones, Capers, *Assessment and Control of Software Risk*, Upper Saddle River, NJ: Prentice Hall, 1994.

Karolak, Dale Walter, *Software Engineering Risk Management*, Los Alamitos, CA: IEEE Computer Society Press, 1996.

CHAPTER

10

Software Documentation

Contents

Documentation is the record of the translation from the user's needs to the software that satisfies those needs and instructions for the operation and use of that software.

A vast portion of the software being developed lacks adequate records of how it got where it is. The original requirements are poorly stated, design has just evolved as it went along, code tends to simulate the design rather than implement it, testing is based on showing that the code works rather than that it meets the requirements, and user documentation is incomplete to a fault. The SQS can play a large role in improving this situation.

Documentation is like the markers along a highway. Looking ahead, it provides a trail to follow toward the destination. Looking back, it provides a record of the trip thus far. Each phase of the SDLC prepares the directions for the next phase in the form of some sort of documentation. Those same documents are the record of what has happened during the phase itself. The requirements phase is directed by the statement of needs from the concept exploration phase. The design phase is directed by the requirements document, which is a record of the activities of the requirements phase. In turn, the design documentation directs the coding phase while recording the design phase, and so on. In parallel with the development phases, the testing documentation is prepared, leading to the testing effort the way requirements documentation leads to coding.

Software documentation is composed of management, developme. test, and user documentation. It is intended to follow the evolution of t software as it progresses through the SLC.

It is important to note that once a document is written and approved, can—and must—still change. As development proceeds, errors, defec incomplete specifications, and necessary additions and deletions w become known. If the documentation is to serve its purpose on a continui basis, it must be kept current. As discussed in Chapter 6, the documentati must be configuration managed just like the development products ther selves. Many software projects have suffered serious problems, not becau the documentation was poorly written in the first place, but because it w allowed to fall behind the actual situation as development continued. In t later phases, when it was needed to support testing or maintenance, it w no longer current and, thus, was not useful. The actual, currently approv requirements were no longer reliably documented, the design specificati had fallen behind the actual code implementation, and there was no way accurately trace the code back to the requirements. In almost every case li this, the user winds up with a software system that does something, but n what was actually needed or wanted.

Finally, the documentation is the basis for CM. If the documentatic starts out poorly or is allowed to degenerate with respect to the ongoi development activities, the software is out of control. CM loses visibility in what was required and how that has changed. Once the software develo ment effort is out of control, the end result of that development usually not predictable, verifiable, or maintainable.

Table 10.1 offers recommendations for minimum documentation f various project sizes. Other project factors, such as visibility, criticality, ar complexity, will influence the selection of documents each case. (Appe dixes A through L include outlines for the primary documents.)

10.1 Management documents

Every software development project is going to be managed in some way. plan will be prepared, in one form or another, that lays out the expecte schedule and resources. Effort will be expended to review and test the sof ware, at least at the end before delivery, and the components of the sof ware will be identified so that the delivered software and its components ar known.

The following management documents are common to all softwar development projects:

Table 10.1 Software Documentation Recommendations

Project Size	Recommended Documents
Small project	Requirements specification
	Design description (as-built design)
	Test report
	Plans: software development, SQS, CM
Medium project	All small project documents
	Preliminary design
	Detailed design (build-to design)
	Test plan
Large project	All medium project documents
	Test cases (and scenarios)
	Interface requirements and design
Other documents—not project-size specific	Database requirements and design
	User manual
	Operations manual
	Maintenance plan
	Training plan
	Risk management plan
	Software safety plan

- Software development plan;
- SQS plan;
- CM plan.

These documents are the overall software development process control documents. Their size and depth of detail will vary with the size and complexity of the system being developed. They may even be merged into a single document for small projects. Even so, the content, describing how the development project will be managed and controlled, must be present for each software development project. It should not be surprising that the more formal the planning and its documentation, the more complete and effective it will be. Thus, the creation of the software development plan (SDP), the software quality system plan (SQSP), and the configuration management plan (CMP) is a necessary part of each software development project.

These plans for a project leading to 500,000 or more lines of code would probably cost more than a whole 500-line project. Therefore, the level of

detail and control included in each plan must reflect the size and comple:
of the project at hand.

10.1.1 Software development plan

The SDP is the document that lays out the management approach to
software project. In its most basic form, the SDP will include the sched
and resource needs for the project. The milestones for tracking the progr
of the project will be specified, probably as a pictorial of the SDLC. The p
sonnel loading will also be shown so that the required expertise and sk
can be available when they are needed. The SDP should also specify ha
ware and environmental needs such as computer time, special test faciliti
compilers and linkers, other systems, and the like.

For simple systems, the material covering the SQS and CM may also
included as separate sections in the SDP. As system complexity grows,
does the SDP. More and more detail is required to cover the larger scale
the software development activity. Schedules must contain intermedi
checkpoints or milestones, and personnel loading will become more vari
and complicated. Test support facilities will become more elaborate. T
SDP will also begin to address software quality and CM to a level of det
that precludes their inclusion as SDP sections.

The more elaborate the software system, the more it probably interfa
with other systems and the outside world. While these interfaces are p
sented in requirements documentation, provision for their involvement
testing must be ensured and scheduled in the SDP.

Larger systems may require enough people or facilities to justify spec
offices or test laboratories. If so, these must be presented in the SDP so th
their availability is ensured.

Budget control becomes more important as the size of the system grow
The SDP is the appropriate place to present budget considerations and
specify control mechanisms in support of the normal, companywide co
accounting system.

While the software quality practitioner obviously does not generate t
SDP, the practitioner has the responsibility for reviewing it against SI
standards and ensuring that all appropriate information is present. Deficie
cies detected both by the software quality practitioner and any other SI
reviews should be corrected before the project is permitted to commence

The software quality practitioner also monitors the software develo
ment activities against the SDP. Deviations are reported so that correcti
action may be taken by management.

Most corrective action will be to correct the software development process where it has strayed from the plan. Some corrections will be made to the SDP to keep it current with changes in the project. The software quality practitioner will review these changes to ensure that contracted requirements are not being violated and that the plan still complies with the standards for it.

See Appendix A for a sample SDP outline.

10.1.2 SQS plan

The SQSP addresses the activities to be performed on the project in support of the quest for quality software. Being careful not to exceed the requirements of the customer, company standards, or the SDP, the SQSP will discuss all of the activities to be performed on all of the various SLC products. A sample format for an SQSP is shown in Appendix B.

Remember that a software quality group is not necessary for the SQS functions be performed. Thus, the various software quality functions will be assigned, through the SQSP, to be the organizational entities that will perform these functions. All activities to be accomplished in the software quality area should receive the same personnel, resource, and schedule discussion as in the overall SDP, and any special tools and methodologies should be discussed. The SQSP may be combined with the CMP (see Section 10.1.3) for medium-sized efforts.

Whatever the format of the SQSP, it is important that the document (or its information if in another document) be complete and approved by management and the producers. The SQSP becomes the charter for the SQS functions for the particular project when approved by management. It lays out the entire SQS and how it will be implemented.

Without the involvement of and approval by the software developers, the SQSP can be a recipe for ineffectiveness and frustration on the part of the software quality practitioners. Without the cooperation of the developers, software quality practitioners can be severely hampered in their attempts to conduct the review and monitoring activities for which they are responsible. Involving the development organizations in the generation and approval of the SQSP can encourage their cooperation as the project progresses.

The software quality practitioners must also monitor their own plan and their activities according to the plan. Any deviation from the plan or any indication that it is inadequate must be corrected. The software quality practitioner will monitor all the software management and development activities. It is certain that management and the developers will be watching the software quality practitioners to be sure they perform according to the S plan, the whole plan, and nothing but the plan.

10.1.3 CM plan

CM, as discussed in Chapter 6, is a threefold discipline. Each of the thr activities should be discussed in its own section of the CMP. The metho requirements levied on the producers, contracted requirements, and tools be used for software CM all should be spelled out. (See Appendix C fo sample format for a CM plan.)

If the project is small, the necessary information may be included in t SDP. On medium-sized projects, it may be appropriate to combine the Cl information with the SQS plan in a single, dual-purpose document.

While some of the information may be in the personnel and resour sections of the SDP, CM-specific information must be presented in the CM Schedules for baselining, major reviews, and auditing should be show either on the overall project schedule or on the CM schedule.

Any special tools or resources needed to support CM must be called c in the CMP. Another topic that may appear in the CMP is the operation the software development library, which is the depository of all softwa product master copies. If not discussed elsewhere (e.g., SDP or SQSP), t library, its responsibilities, functions, and so forth should be presented in t CMP.

As with the SDP, the software quality practitioner has the responsibili to review the CMP before its release and adoption. The software quali practitioner should ensure that the CMP is complete and appropriate for t project and that it meets any specified format and content standards.

Software quality practitioners will also review the CM activities on ongoing basis. The reviews will ascertain whether the activities described the plan are being performed and if they are still appropriate for the projec

10.1.4 Additional plans

As software becomes an increasingly critical part of our lives, addition plans may be required for some software system development efforts. Su plans might include the software safety plan (Appendix K) and the ri management plan (Appendix L). These plans are certainly not required f all development projects. It is the responsibility of the quality practitioner evaluate their necessity for each new project and to recommend the preparation when appropriate.

0.2   **Development documents**

Each SDLC phase produces development-oriented documentation. These documents are the statements of the increasingly complete solution for the user's needs as development proceeds. Development documentation covers the SDLC and tracks the software from the requirements that grow out of the concept exploration phase through the installation phase. This series of documents, each serving as the basis for the succeeding level, permits the producers to determine when they have completed the task and allow the testers to determine whether or not the software complies with the intended requirements.

The primary development documents are as follows:

▸ Requirements specification;

▸ Preliminary design;

▸ Detailed design (build to);

▸ Design description (as built);

▸ Database specification(s);

▸ Interface specification(s).

There are many formats for each of the basic development documents. The format for each of the basic SLC documents is less important than the content of those documents. Further, the necessity for some specific documents depends on the size and complexity of the specific project. In some cases, the required information can be provided in a higher-level document. Thus, the actual format and content specifications will be a function of the individual organization and the documentation standards that have been adopted.

The requirements document is intended to fully define the overall function to be performed or problem to be solved. It is a mandatory document, without which the project should not even be started. Until the customer or user has clearly stated what is to be provided, and all the external considerations have been identified, the producer has insufficient information with which to start work. Without a clear statement of what is wanted of the software, there is no way to determine completion or how completion is to be achieved.

Design documents, both preliminary and detailed, describe in increasing detail the method by which the problem or function is being addressed. Prior to coding, the design must be such that the coder does not need to make any "I think they meant this" decisions. After coding and testing, a

final design document should be published, which is the as-built docume
that will be used by the software maintainers after installation.

10.2.1 Requirements specification

The requirements specification is the keystone of all software documen
tion. It is the statement of what the software system is to provide.
describes the problem to be solved, any restrictions or constraints on p
formance or environment that may be imposed, time and size restrain
hardware constraints, specific requirements levied on inputs and outpu
and any other information necessary for the complete specification of t
problem or function. Other people besides the end users may levy requir
ments on the software. Without this complete specification of what the so
ware is to accomplish, the producer is put in the position of having to ma
requirements decisions as the design progresses. This removes some of t
control of the system from the customer and may result in the customer n
receiving what was expected. Viewed another way, the producer is also
the position of being unable to provide anything acceptable to the custom
who says, "That's not what I asked for." Appendix D shows a general form
for a requirements document.

There are many ways that errors or faulty requirements creep into t
requirements document. It is the role of the software quality practitioner
carefully review the requirements document, both for adherence to the fo
mat standards for the document and for the correctness of its content. Th
latter may pose a problem to some practitioners who do not have the appr
priate expertise to adequately review the document for technical content.
those cases, outside reviewers may be used or the development group ma
be called on to provide a review of the requirements before they accept tl
development task.

In addition to being correct, requirements must meet at least five oth
critical criteria: They must be necessary, complete, measurable, unambigu
ous, and consistent (both internally and with external interfaces).

10.2.1.1 Correct

Correctness of the requirements is of primary concern, both to the custome
and the producer. The description of what is wanted and the surroundir
needs and constraints must be stated correctly if the development is to resu
in an acceptable product. The use of an equation that is not correct for th
situation or addresses a government regulation incorrectly will result in
system that does not meet the needs of the customer, even though it migh
comply with the requirements as stated.

10.2.1.2   Traceable

Each requirement must be documented in such a way as to make clear its source or participation in the solution of the user's problem or the user need that it addresses. In addition, the requirements document should be constructed in a manner that will enhance the tracing of design and tests back to the requirements. Ultimately, each requirement has a genesis in the existing need, is supported by a solution in the software itself, and has been demonstrated to be satisfied in the testing of the software.

10.2.1.3   Necessary

A requirement that places unnecessary restrictions or demands on a software system also raises the cost in time and money at no advantage to the system. Such things as overly stringent timing, unnecessary precision in calculations, unjustifiably tight memory restrictions, excessive processing capability, and the like sometimes creep into requirements. They may sound nice or seem necessary at the outset but unnecessary requirements can cause poor development later on. The requirement for a check processing capability of 200,000 per day may sound fine, but if it is for a small bank that actually needs only to process 50,000 checks per day, it will add unnecessarily to the cost of the system and provide capability that will not be used.

10.2.1.4   Complete

Completeness may seem to be an obvious criterion for requirements, but it is no less important. When a requirements document is published that does not address the whole problem to be solved, the developer is usually in store for surprises. Either a situation will arise during design or coding that has no basis in the requirements, or the customer may ask where a desired a feature is after the producer thinks the job is done. At the very least, the producer may be put in the position of having to add or modify requirements, actions that rightfully are the responsibility of the customer. Completeness also means that nonuser requirements must be defined.

10.2.1.5   Measurable

Measurability is the key to testing. A requirement that cannot be measured cannot be demonstrated by the test program. For example, a requirement for rapid response time clearly is faulty. What exactly does rapid mean? Another example is a requirement to process multiple targets. Multiple is undefined and therefore cannot be measured or demonstrated. Requirements that cannot be measured introduce opportunities for conflict at all points within the SDLC, particularly at system demonstration and acceptance time.

A two-second response time that seems adequately rapid to the dev oper may be unacceptably slow in the eyes of the customer. Multiple n mean 20 to the developer but only 10 to the customer, who does not w to pay for the extra capability.

10.2.1.6 Unambiguous

Unambiguous requirements leave nothing to the imagination of the p ducer. There is no need to guess what the customer really meant or want A requirement for a response time of no more than two seconds sounds a good, measurable requirement. It is ambiguous, however, in that it d not state the point at which the measurement of two seconds is to begin to end. A major source of ambiguity is such familiarity with a subject t one forgets that others may not know all the jargon or have insider inform tion. Sometimes the requirements writer presumes that everybody kno that. Another source of ambiguity is weak wording. Requirements are to worded in terms of the imperative verb shall. Verbs such as should or m or even will might show desire, but they do not demonstrate intent. To that a system should compute the square root of 3 implies that it might no

10.2.1.7 Consistent

Finally, the criterion of consistency must be considered. Requirements m be consistent within themselves and also with the world outside themselv with which they must interface. For example, the requirement in one s tion to process 1,000 checks per hour is inconsistent with the requireme in another section that calls for 10,000 checks in an 8-hour day. Both the requirements may be inconsistent with the outside world if the che handling machinery to be used is only capable of processing only 900 chec per hour.

10.2.2 Design specifications

Preliminary and detailed design specifications depict how each requireme will be approached and satisfied by the software. Detailed design specific tions are of two types. The final design specification prior to coding can considered the build-to design. It presents what the designers believe to the correct solution and response to the approved requirements. The desi description, which reflects the software as it was actually completed, is oft referred to as the as-built design.

As was the requirements, the design must demonstrate the criteria correctness, necessity, completeness, measurability and testability, lack ambiguity, and consistency. Further, the design must be traceable back the requirements. Each element of the design must be able to be shown as satisfying some part of the requirements. In return, each requirement must be able to be traced forward into the design. In that way, there is confidence that the designers have not added or omitted anything during the design process.

Regular formal and informal reviews of the design as it progresses are held to ensure that the design is not straying from the requirements. The reviews are also intended to show that the design is sound and adheres to the various criteria. The software quality practitioner plays an instrumental role in these reviews by ensuring, first of all, that they are, in fact, held. Software quality practitioners do not necessarily have to attend informal reviews, such as peer reviews, but the practitioners must be sure that the reviews are taking place and are fruitful in the search for design defects. Formal reviews may be chaired by software quality management, although some organizations find it better to have someone from the project as the chair. Software quality practitioners are responsible for attending the formal reviews and reporting on their actions. The software quality practitioner is also responsible for making sure that any and all action items resulting from the reviews are fully addressed and closed and that full reports are filed with management for any managerial action that may be necessary.

10.2.2.1 Preliminary design specification

The preliminary design (sometimes called the functional, architectural, or external design) provides the initial breakdown of the requirements into functional groups for further design efforts. Each functional group repre-sents a major portion of the overall software system. The preliminary design must specify the approach to be taken in the performance of the function, the database requirements, and the interfaces with the other functional groups present in the system. It must also specify the interfaces with the external world, such as terminals, networks, other computers, other software systems, and so forth. Appendix E shows a sample preliminary design document format.

10.2.2.2 Build-to design

The detailed design is a specific statement of how each part of the preliminary design will be implemented in code. The detailed design is often called the build-to specification, since it is the input to the programming staff for translation into the compiler language for implementation on the target computer. This document must completely describe the design so that programmers are not in the position of having to make design decisions as they

make the translation into source code. An example of a format for a detai
design document is given in Appendix F.

10.2.2.3 As-built design

A final version of the detailed design document should be prepared after
completion of the coding and testing processes. This usually is called the
built design or design description and represents the statement of the des
that was actually translated into code. It is an important document for
future maintainers of the software system. It serves as the product baseli
from which all changes will be made for corrections of defects found
operation of the system and for the addition of enhancements to the sc
ware as they become necessary. Obviously, this document must be kept c
rent and configuration managed.

10.2.3   Other documentation

The larger the system, the more documentation is appropriate. Databe
design and interface design documents may be needed.

Some documents are not always required as separate entities. T
required content of the database design and interface design documer
may be incorporated into the preliminary and detailed design documents f
small or noncomplex systems.

The role of the software quality practitioner is much the same wheth
the database or interface discussions are part of larger documents or v
umes unto themselves. Software quality practitioners must still ascerta
that format and content standards are defined and met and that appropria
expression techniques are used. They also will ensure that the document
tion criteria are met and that the information is consistent with itself a
between documents.

There will be projects that have special documentation needs. Two th
arise most often are those projects that have many, or complex interface
and those involving the development of, or significant interaction with,
database. When the system's interfaces, either within the software syste
or with the external world, are many or complicated, the preparation
interface requirements and interface design specifications should be consi
ered. These specifications can eliminate misunderstandings of the interfac
that arise when each interface is described from one side in one docume
and other sides in other documents. By combining all aspects of each inte
face in a single place, all parties can see the full set of the interface
descriptions.

Database specifications are needed when the system being developed either creates or causes significant modification to the database(s). Even when a new or highly modified database is not the case, significant interaction with the existing database(s) may benefit from a specialized database document.

It should be remembered that the purpose of documentation is to describe how the user's or customer's requirements are being met and to ensure that the correct solution is being developed and implemented.

0.3 Test documentation

Test documentation includes all test program documents from the overall test plan through the final test report. Test documentation is a parallel effort, as shown in Figure 10.1. It starts with the original requirements statement, like the development documentation. On the basis of the requirements, test plans, cases, scenarios, procedures, data, and results documentation are generated as the SDLC progresses. (Chapter 4 addresses the topic of test documentation more fully.) Testing is documented through

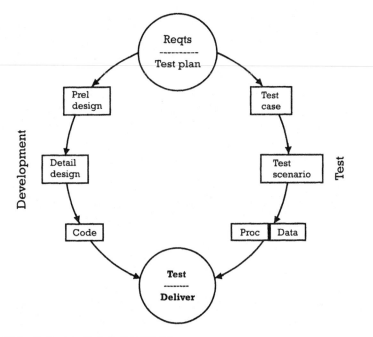

Figure 10.1 Software test development.

a series of increasingly specific documents, starting with the test plan a
including test cases, test scenarios, detailed test procedures, test data, a
test results. Test documentation spells out the sequence of events
which compliance of the software with its requirements is ultimate
demonstrated.

Software quality practitioners play a major role in the whole testi
process. They may, in fact, actually conduct the testing at the acceptan
level. Nonetheless, the software quality practitioner must carefully revie
the entire test program to make sure it is sufficient to exercise the softwa
in a manner that will maximize the defect-finding capability of the tes
Remember that the goal of testing is to find defects. Software quality prac
tioners must be sure that this goal is being met. The second goal is to der
onstrate that the software performs as the approved requirements demar
Software quality practitioners, together with the user or customer, mu
review the testing and ascertain whether the software does perform
required. When deficiencies are found, either in the tests or in the resu
the software quality practitioner is responsible for making sure that t
deficiencies are recognized by management so that appropriate action
taken.

10.3.1 Test plan

As shown in Figure 10.1 (and in Figure 4.3), test documentation begi
with the test plan (see Appendix G), which is based on the original requir
ments. In fact, the initial test planning is performed during the requiremen
phase. This not only gets the test activities off to an early start but helps
ensure the measurability and testability of the requirements themselve
The test plan will grow and evolve, just as the requirements grow ar
evolve, throughout the development life cycle, but it is important to begin
this point in order to keep pace with the development of the code. Plans a
made for the expected test tools, data generators, simulators, and so on th
are anticipated to be needed.

10.3.2 Test cases

As the design begins to mature and functions are identified, test cases (se
Appendix H) are correspondingly identified. These groups of individual tes
will be applied to major sections of the software. They are usually based o
logical groupings of requirements in much the same way as the function
design is approached. If Use Cases were used in the requirements, they ar
logical bases for the test cases. Test scenarios are optional subsets of the te

cases. They provide for the simplification of complicated or lengthy test cases.

10.3.3   Test data

Initial test data requirements are also identified at this time. Test data must be provided, not to show that the software works as it was written, but that it works as was intended by the requirements. This means that the test data must cover as wide a spectrum of both legal and illegal values as possible. Nominal values, as prescribed in the various design documentation, will only show that the software meets nominal conditions. The object of testing is to uncover defects in the software, so the test data must be carefully chosen to present abnormal and incorrect inputs as well as expected inputs to determine the response of the software to unexpected, borderline, and erroneous conditions.

10.3.4   Test procedures

As the design and coding progress, test procedures (see Figure 4.4) are prepared. Test procedures are the step-by-step actions to be taken during each test. Every operator action, every data entry, and every expected response is specified in a sequence of steps for the given test. In that way, the exact conditions of the test are controlled, and each actual output or response of the software can be compared against the expected result. Each difference between the expected and actual results is recorded as a probable defect and is analyzed to determine whether or not the software is performing as required.

10.3.5   Test reports

The test reports (see Appendix I) record the actual happenings during each test. They specify the expected and actual results and the conclusions drawn from the results. Anomalies and the final disposition of the anomalies are recorded. Test reports are the key factor in determining when testing has reached its beneficial conclusion.

0.4   User documentation

The best software is not useful if the end user does not know how to use it. User documentation may include not only the user manuals, but also maintenance, operator, training, and other project specific documents, such as the version description document. User documentation provides instr tions to the end user of the software system. It addresses proper preparat and presentation of inputs, operating instructions, and directions for interpretation of the output data. It may also present operating instructio training needs, descriptions of differences from one version to the next, maintenance information.

User documentation shows and tells the user how to make use of software system. It should discuss the system, specify the format and c tent of the inputs, and describe the outputs that are the result of the syst processing.

The software quality practitioner must take an active role in the revi and evaluation of the user documentation. If the software cannot be u properly, it matters little if it is a quality product. The user documentati must make proper use possible. Software quality practitioners should m a test run of the user manual to see if the instructions make it possible actually use the system as it was meant to be used. This can sometimes made a part of the final acceptance or demonstration testing or may be individually conducted exercise. The important thing to be accomplishe the verification that the user documentation does make proper operati and use of the software possible.

10.4.1   Input requirements

With respect to input, the user documentation will tell the user what inf mation is required by the system. It will present data formats, ranges of le values, schedules of input, and other information concerning the input da Such things as methods of input (e.g., hardware registers, keyboard entri data from other systems), where the data are to be submitted (e.g., dial- access, via a terminal), when the input is required (e.g., every Thursd when prompted), and other appropriate information specific to the partic lar system must be available to the user in the user manual.

10.4.2   Output description

Another important part of the user documentation is instructions on how interpret the results of the processing. Full descriptions of all outputs necessary. The documentation must, of course, contain instructions on h to understand the displays or printouts that are created. In addition, it m provide a complete and understandable description of all nonstandard o puts such as error messages, abnormal halts, loss of system sanity, and so Each of these situations or outputs will be described and the proper respon spelled out. If the system is running in a central or remote data center, instructions for the distribution of hard-copy output will be provided.

10.4.3 Operation instructions

The user documentation should include the operation instructions, as well as pure user information; that is, the details on how to actually make the system operate. Such information as how to load the system, what storage media are required, special peripherals such as high-speed printers or mass storage devices that are to be on-line, and how to bring the system down when processing is complete may be included in the operators' instructions. Whether this information is in the user manual or in a separate document is usually a function of the size of the system and where it is run (e.g., on a desktop computer or in the central data center). Some installations may have documentation standards that specify where this information is to be provided.

An operator manual or similar document is often needed for complicated systems that require the involvement of computer center personnel. This involvement may be the mounting of tapes and disk packs, handling of output forms or reports, sequencing of several systems into the proper executional order, and so on. Many systems are self-sufficient once they are initiated. In those cases, there may be few or no operator instructions. Larger systems may however, justify a separate operator manual to provide detailed information concerning the operation of the software system.

The software quality practitioner is responsible for reviewing operator documents for format and required content both at the initial release and during the operation and maintenance phases of the SLC.

10.4.4 Maintenance

Good maintenance documentation helps keep the software running and up-to-date. Whoever is responsible for the maintenance of the software should prepare a software maintenance plan. The primary tool of the software maintainers is the body of software documentation. Without clear and complete documentation of the software, the maintainers must recreate the data on which they will base enhancement and correction actions. Of course, the single most important document is the listing of the source and corresponding object code of the software. Without this, the maintainer must work backwards from the object code to recreate the source code or must work in object code itself.

The next most important document is the final design description (or as-built) document discussed in Section 10.2.2.3. This document, or its

equivalent, together with the up-to-date requirements and flowcharts
processing diagrams, explains to the maintainer exactly what the software
supposed to contain and how it is constructed. It is with these docume:
that maintainers study defect reports and requests for system enhan
ments. The flow diagrams (in whatever form is the standard for the spec:
installation) and the as-built design document present the software syst
design and implementation and describe what it does and how it does
The requirements describe the full environment into which the char
must fit.

The maintenance portion of the user documentation contains inforn
tion of importance to the persons who are to maintain the softw;
system. This portion usually contains the as-built design informati
(see Section 10.2.2.3), descriptions of phased implementation modificatio
made and pending (see Section 7.4.1.4), records of software changes ma
since implementation (see Section 6.4), and the like. Anything that v
make the work of the software maintainer easier is appropriate for inclusi
in the maintenance portion of the user documentation.

In the evaluation of maintenance documentation, software quality pr;
titioners must be sensitive to the environment of the maintainer and t
documentation needs involved. Reviews of the maintenance documen
tion should be attended by and heavily influenced by representatives of t
maintenance organization. Deficiencies noted in the maintenance doc
mentation will then be brought to the attention of management f
resolution.

10.5 Training documentation

Training documentation, when required, will address both developer a
user training. The more complicated and involved a system becomes, t
more likely it is that there will be people working on it who do not ha
prior experience in one or more aspects of their tasks. Languages, progra:
ming environments, and technical subjects are all areas in which develope
may need new or further education and training. Likewise, the customer
user may need to be trained.

Training documentation should be prepared anytime there is a need f
formal or extensive informal training. The format and content of the doc
ments will vary according to need and application.

Software quality practitioners should evaluate the developer and us
training needs and be sure that training documentation is appropriate, pr
vided, reviewed, compliant with existing standards, and applicable to t

project. Software quality practitioners probably will not perform the training or write the documents, but they must make management aware of any training needs.

10.6 Documentation standards

A wide variety of documentation standards is available. In many companies and organizations, the first thing that is standardized is documentation. This may be because documentation is the least favorite activity of most software developers. It is the only product produced by a large portion of the SLC and is usually the object of most of the complaints about a system. Or perhaps it is the easiest to standardize since there are so many standard examples from which to choose.

Industry organizations have published or are developing standards for documentation, not only in the software field but also, and for a longer time, in the hardware arena. For example, the IEEE has standards for several software development documents (Table 2.1). These standards represent the consensus of a large portion of the computing industry. The Department of Defense and various other government agencies, such as NIST, have promulgated documentation standards both for general applications and for use in particular situations or special computing environments.

In some cases, these externally prepared standards can be used directly. Otherwise, they can be modified to fit the needs of an individual organization. These standards often include very specific content and format instructions so that very little is left to the author except the information to be documented. Others provide generic requirements or guidelines on which an organization can build. Some companies are willing to share their documentation standards or at least give guidance in the area.

As in the case of standards in general (see Section 2.2), each company or organization must develop or adapt documentation standards to meet its own specific needs. Documentation standards, like anything else, must serve the users of those standards or they will be improperly followed or ignored all together. It is incumbent on the software quality practitioner to review documentation standards periodically to be sure that they are up-to-date and appropriate for the organization. When they become inadequate or obsolete, the practitioner should prompt the standards coordinator to take action to improve them.

10.7 Summary

Software documentation is composed of management, development, te and user documentation. It is intended to follow the evolution of the so ware as it progress through the SLC. Each SDLC phase has a product products, which are the statements of the increasingly complete solution the user's needs as development proceeds.

Documentation is like the markers along a highway. Looking ahead, provides a trail to follow toward the destination. Looking back, it provide record of the trip thus far. Each phase of the SDLC prepares the directio for the next phase in the form of some sort of documentation. These sar documents are the record of what has happened during the phase itself.

The SDP is the document that lays out the management approach to t software project. In its most basic form, it will include the schedule a resource needs for the project. The methods, requirements levied on t producers, contracted requirements, and tools to be used for software C should be defined and explained.

The SQSP addresses the activities to be performed on the project in su port of the quest for quality software. All activities to be accomplished in t software quality area should receive the same personnel, resource, a schedule discussion as in the overall SDP. Whatever the format of the SQS it is very important that this document (or its information if in anoth document) be complete and approved by management and the developers

The requirements document is the keystone of all software document tion. Preliminary and detailed design documents depict how each requir ment will be approached and satisfied by the software. The prelimina design provides the initial breakdown of the requirements into function groups for further design efforts. The detailed design is often called tr build-to specification. It is the input to the programming staff for translatic into the compiler language for implementation on the target computer. Tr final version of the detailed design is sometimes called the as-built docu ment, since it describes the software as it actually was delivered.

Test documentation includes all test program documents from the ove all test plan through the final test report.

User documentation tells the user how to make use of the software sy tem. The user documentation may include the operators' instructions well as strictly user-oriented information.

The larger the system, the more documentation is appropriate. Databa design and interface design documents may be needed. Maintenance ar training may deserve separate and extensive treatment. Finally, there ma be a need for a separate operations manual.

.8   The next step

There are few texts written about software documentation as a subject unto itself. However, since all software development, testing, and maintenance processes depend on the requirements, you can start with the following texts:

R. Dorfman et al. (eds). *Software Requirements Engineering, Second Edition,* Los Alamitos, CA: IEEE Computer Society Press, 1997.

Alan M. Davis, *Software Requirements: Analysis and Specification,* Englewood Cliffs, NJ: Prentice Hall, 1990.

Additional reading

Buckley, F. J., *Implementing Software Engineering Practices,* New York: John Wiley & Sons, 1989.

Guide International, *Quality Requirements—GPP 217,* Chicago, IL: Guide International, 1989.

Shumate, Ken, and Marilyn Keller, *Software Specification and Design: A Disciplined Approach for Real-Time Systems,* New York: John Wiley & Sons, 1992.

CHAPTER

11

Contents

Quality System Implementation

Chapters 1 through 10 described the individual elements of the SQS. Those elements must be assembled into a manageable whole that will become the SQS. Figure 11.1 shows that all the elements are connected and that the connections are formed through the overall SQS. As it begins to implement the individual elements into the SQS, each organization must select the method and order of implementation and ensure that sufficient support is present for a successful implementation and that the SQS will become part of the new quality culture.

The key concerns in the implementation of the SQS include the following:

▸ Planning;

▸ The quality charter;

▸ Organizational culture change;

▸ The roles of the organization;

▸ Implementation and improvement.

11.1   Planning the implementation

The planning of an SQS should involve consideration of all the elements discussed so far in this text. Many of the concerns of the SQS are depicted in Figure 11.2. Prior to beginning any actual implementation, careful consideration must be given to each step that will be taken. Those SQS elements that are already in place or that are partially implemented must be

227

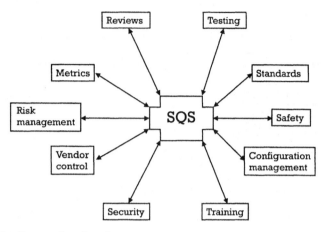

Figure 11.1 Connecting the elements.

Figure 11.2 Software quality system concerns.

recognized and built on to the maximum extent compatible with the over
system. Each activity must be assigned to the appropriate organizatior
entity for execution. A period of training must be planned both for ti
implementers of the various portions of the plan and for the data processi

organization as a whole. Inclusion of each group to be monitored in the planning process will benefit the overall system by instilling a sense of system ownership in the whole organization.

The actual implementation of the SQS plan requires careful planning and scheduling. Starting with the definition of the charter of the software quality practitioners and ending with the SQS implementation strategy and execution, each step must be laid out and accomplished with the maximum involvement of the affected groups. Even the best conceived system can fail if it is implemented in the wrong way.

1.2 The quality charter

Without clear direction and support from management, an SQS faces an uphill struggle.

Early in the planning stages of the SQS, a statement of what the system will accomplish is necessary. In other words, the requirements for the system must be established. Following that, the software quality group itself must be recognized with a specific charter of its role, responsibilities, authority, and organizational placement for the specific software development project.

The sample charter in Appendix J defines the limits of the software quality group's activities. It describes the expectations of and degree of support by management for the group and its efforts. In so doing, the charter formally demonstrates the commitment that management is making to the software quality group and its system. The charter can also be the instrument that describes the allocation of SQS functions and the organizational groups to which they are assigned, although that is often a part of the implementation plan, which comes later.

In summary, the charter is the written statement of management's intention to proceed with the SQS. With this document in hand, the software quality group can go forward with a clearly defined role in the total organization. Without it, there is no recourse when one or another of the SQS activities is challenged or ignored.

1.3 Changing the organizational culture

Implementing a successful SQS requires a change in the culture of the organization with respect to quality. The key component of any cul-

ture change is commitment, in this case, the commitment of the ent
organization.

11.3.1 Culture change

Changing a cultural is a four-step process:

> Step 1 is the realization that the current situation, whatever is to
> changed, is no longer satisfactory. This is the first step, because if t
> current situation is acceptable or desirable, there is no basic motiv
> tion to change at all. An example of an unsatisfactory situation mig
> be that all projects have excessive postimplementation defect rate

> Step 2 is the determination that there is a situation better that the cu
> rent one. If the current situation is undesirable but is the "least worst"
> all available situations, the motivation to change is still not prese
> Since the testing of the project prior to implementation is at the state
> the art of the organization's testers, a preferred situation in the examp
> might be full user testing prior to implementation.

> Step 3 is the determination that the preferred situation (found
> Step 2) is attainable. In some cases, there is a preferred situation, b
> "you can't get there from here." At this point, even thought the motiv
> tion to change is present, the change cannot be completed. Continui
> the example, it is noted that full user testing is not feasible if the us
> refuses, for whatever reason, to do it.

> Step 4 is taken when Steps 1 through 3 have been successful. There
> dissatisfaction with the current situation, and a better situation exis
> and is attainable. Step 4 is the application of the commitment
> attaining the preferred situation. In the case of implementing an SQ
> it is the combined commitment of management and the rest of tl
> organization to expend the required effort and aim for doing thin
> right the first time.

11.3.2 Management commitment

A management involved on the planning and implementation of a progra
is more likely to commit itself to that program. Management is going to t
asked to commit resources to the SQS. No matter who carries out the ind
vidual activities represented by the 10 basic elements of the system, there
a resource cost involved. Management is usually sensitive to those costs an
the payback that can be expected for them. If there has been little or n

management participation in the planning and development of the SQS, there will be little or no understanding of the value to be expected from the expenditures.

The costs involved in an SQS include not only the actual SQS resource costs for personnel and so on but also nontrivial costs to the project development as well. Software quality activities will have an impact on the time and resources required to develop the software product. In the experience of the author, these costs could range from as little as 5% for a minimum SQS application to as much as 20% for a fully applied SQS. Note that probably not all of the costs will be new costs. It is to be expected that at least some resources were being expended for testing, CM, and defect reporting and correction even before there was a formal SQS. In any case, the costs to be incurred must be explained to management. If they are a part of the planning for the system, they will have a much better understanding of where these costs come from and what they will accomplish. Management must be given the opportunity to have direct inputs into the SQS planning and must be recognized for those inputs.

Without management commitment, any program is unlikely to succeed. The charter is the demonstration of management's commitment to the SQS.

11.3.3   Organizational commitment

It is often observed that a quality program will not succeed without the commitment of management. While management commitment is necessary, it is not sufficient. Also required is the full commitment and support of the organization, which must change its work habits to enable the success of the SQS and the software quality program. The cultural orientation of the organization must become one of "do it right the first time." The software quality practitioner must remember that the full set of changes cannot be made in one fell swoop. "Do it right the first time" will take effect in smaller steps of "do it more correctly, sooner." As this habit becomes entrenched, the organizational culture will begin to change.

As Figure 11.3 shows, there can be involvement without much effort, but commitment requires much stronger support.

1.4   Organizational considerations

Software quality management is the discipline that maximizes the probability that a software system will conform to its requirements, as those requirements are perceived by the user on an ongoing basis.

Consider veal scallopini

The bull **participates**

The cow is **involved**

The calf is **COMMITTED**

Figure 11.3 True commitment.

Like a hardware quality system, the software quality system is a measing and monitoring function. It is a set of activities that is intended encourage and, to a degree, enable conformance of the software to requirements. Throughout this text, reference has been made to the role the software quality practitioner. In general, this role has been one of mo. toring the status of the software development or some aspect surroundi that development. The several aspects of the SQS—testing, education, sec rity, and the others—are all factors that influence the capability of the so ware to conform to its requirements. The software quality practitioner's rc is to monitor the status and progress of the organization with respect these factors. Its findings are reported to the level of management that h the authority to take any necessary corrective action.

Two points are important here. First, software quality practitioners ma but usually do not, perform all the various activities that the SQS compris or on which it reports. The software quality practitioner rarely writes t documentation, performs the testing, teaches the programming cours installs disaster recovery procedures, and so on. Those tasks should be pe formed by the part of the organization best capable of performing them. Tl role of the software quality practitioner is to ascertain that those activiti are being performed and whether that performance is sufficient to pern the software to conform to its requirements.

The second point is that software quality practitioners are not ¿ enforcement agency. A software quality practitioner reviews, inspec evaluates, measures, and then reports. The final report is usually a ship-c don't-ship recommendation. The organizational level at which software quality practitioners report can strongly affect the perceived value of the reports that a software quality practitioner generates and the influence the practitioner can exert over the software development process. The task of enforcement is the responsibility of management. Only management has the authority to take corrective action in the case of reported deficiencies.

While it is true that everyone should be responsible for the quality of his or her own work, in most organizations the overall accountability for software quality rests with one person. It is simplistic to say that the overall accountability for software quality lies with the president, chairman, or CEO of the organization. Obviously, final accountability for everything in the organization lies with that person. The question is, to what level has the day-to-day, effective accountability been delegated? In most cases, the manager of the data processing organization (whatever title that person might have) has the delegated accountability. That is the person who can make the enforcement decisions, weighing the inputs from the various concerned areas such as software quality, development, and the user. The manager, in turn, will delegate the quality tasks and their performance to those parts of the organization that are best suited to accomplish them. Management must weigh the severity of the deficiency, business factors, resource utilization, schedule considerations, political aspects, and other considerations surrounding the SLC and then make a decision as to the action that should be taken for each specific situation. The reports received from software quality practitioners are one form of input to this decision-making process. Certainly, software quality practitioners may offer recommendations with its reported findings, but the enforcement actions are management's to take.

11.4.1   SQS task performance

The best-qualified entity of the organization should perform the day-to-day quality system tasks. There are few activities within the purview of the SQS that must be specifically performed by software quality practitioners. For this reason, it could be argued that there is no need to have a group called software quality at all. The basis for this idea is that since everyone is responsible for the quality of the software product, a separate group is not needed for the SQS tasks. If all persons involved in the specification, design, coding, testing, and operations of the software were infallible, this might be a workable situation. Humans are not infallible, however; in spite of their best intentions and efforts, they make errors, which cause defects. The intent of the SQS is to help discover those defects and correct them as early as possible. In addition, the formation of a software quality group, or at least

the identification of a single accountable person, tends to focus attention
quality and efforts to attain it. And, just like in a software development pr
ect, it is a good idea to have a champion for the software quality system
that champion is a member of senior management, so much the better.

The software quality group is responsible for ensuring that the vari
SQS tasks are performed. That does not mean that software quality is alw
the proper group to actually perform the tasks. Remember, software qua
is a monitoring group. If there are tasks for which the software qua
group is qualified from a technical standpoint and there is no other m
logical group, software quality practitioners certainly may be assigned to
task. In some organizations, the practitioner does, in fact, perform all of
elements of the SQS. In most companies, however, the bulk of the tasks
handled outside the software quality organization. Each function should
assigned to the organizational entity that is in the business. Educatio
needs should be filled by the training and education entity, CM by the C
entity, and so forth. Each company must review its own needs, prioriti
and capabilities and then determine the proper distribution of softw
quality tasks for its own situation. It may even be advisable or necessary
bring outside consultants in for specific tasks, at times.

11.4.2 Reporting level

Software quality must be independent of the group(s) that it monitors a
thus should report at least the same organizational level. Reporting at low
managerial levels can dilute, or even negate, the influence of the softwa
quality practitioner on the software development or maintenance projects

Figure 11.4 shows the least-favorable structure and the one that shou
not be used. In this case, software quality reports to the very person who
group software quality is monitoring. It is unlikely that much useful repo
ing of noncompliance with standards, defect trends, or other insufficienci
will reach the ears of the portion of management that can take the necessa
corrective action. Organizational independence from the groups bei
monitored is the single most important consideration in the placement
software quality.

Figure 11.5 presents the best realistic compromise. It shows softwa
quality reporting at the same level as each of the other groups in the da
processing department. The manager of software quality is a peer with t
managers whose groups are being monitored. A common higher manager
available to mediate any issues that cannot be resolved directly between t
affected managers.

The advantages of this scheme are as follows:

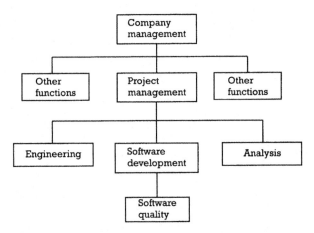

Figure 11.4 Least-favorable organization.

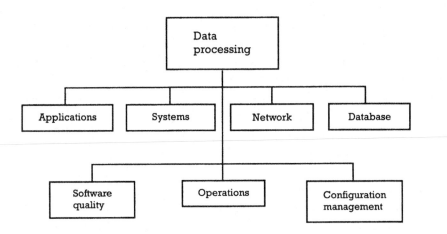

Figure 11.5 Acceptable organization.

- The software quality practitioner is reviewing the work of peer groups.
- A single superior is available to mediate questions or disputes.
- The software quality practitioner is independent of each of the groups it will monitor.
- The software quality practitioner is accessible to the other groups for assistance.

A very important aspect of the suggested reporting level is that the sc
ware quality practitioner is specifically not a part of any of the groups tha
must monitor. When a situation that may need correction is found, i
reported to the manager of the data processing organization directly, r
through an intermediate level.

Another arrangement is shown in Figure 11.6. This particular reporti
scheme is sometimes found in manufacturing companies that have a stro
and mature quality system. Software quality in these companies is a recc
nized extension of the overall quality system. In this case, the software qu
ity practitioners report completely outside the data processing departme
and have a direct reporting line to top company management. A potent
drawback is that, except in large organizations with experience in hardwa
product quality practices, this scheme may have the software quality prac
tioners too far removed from the development organization to be as effe
tive on a day-to-day basis as is desirable. The success of this type of reporti
structure depends on the interaction between the software quality gro
and data processing. If, in spite of the organizational separation, the so
ware quality practitioner maintains a high degree of communication a
rapport with the data processing groups, this can be a workable solution.
is also a candidate arrangement when there is a strong matrix organization
structure for project management.

There are probably many different reporting arrangements that can
envisioned. Most, though, if the software quality practitioner is at a low
level than the groups being reviewed, do not support a strong SQS effo

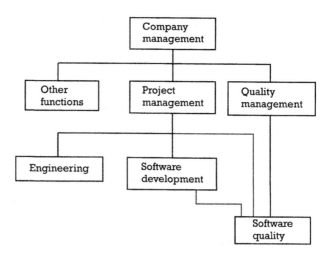

Figure 11.6 Alternative organization.

Some arrangements would place the software quality practitioner at a higher level than the other groups. This can sometimes lead to conflict because the software quality group is perceived as having inordinate power. Whatever the reporting structure chosen, software quality practitioners will be most effective when they report to at least the same organizational level as those groups whose activities they must monitor.

.5   Development organization participation

The development organizations that will be monitored by software quality practitioners must have some say in the criteria and methods to be used. Acceptance of the SQS by the rest of the organization is the critical factor is the success or failure of the SQS.

Openness by software quality practitioners in the beginning of the system will enhance openness by the developers later on. No one likes to feel as though someone is constantly looking over his or her shoulder. Yet that is exactly the impression that software quality practitioners can give if they have not requested and welcomed participation and involvement by the development groups in the preparation of the SQS. When the developers have been a part of the overall planning and development the system, there will be less resistance to the requests by software quality practitioners for information about progress and status, let alone data on defects being found.

Participation by the developers can also help create more meaningful measures of progress, trends, and areas in need of additional attention from the SQS. Most people know their skills and limitations. If they have the attitude that someone else is going to discover and tattle on their weaker capabilities, there is resistance to exposing those areas. On the other hand, if given the opportunity, most people will point out those areas in which they feel they can use assistance. If that assistance is provided, there is a growing trust built, and fear and suspicion are reduced. By maintaining close contact with and participation by the developers during the planning and implementation of the SQS, the software quality group can build a feeling of SQS ownership on the part of the developers.

1.6   Implementation strategies

There are several strategies for implementing an SQS. Probably the least effective methods are the ones that impose the SQS on the whole development organization without regard to which stage each project i in its SDLC.

First is the all-at-once approach. In this case, the whole SQS is imp mented at one time. Each project is expected to stop what it is doing and bring the project in line with the new SQS requirements, whether or every requirement is meaningful. The result is usually a period of confus and a corresponding antagonism toward the SQS and the software qua group. Faced with this negative attitude, the software quality group ha very difficult time establishing itself and often fails and is disbanded.

Another poor method is the one-element-at-a-time approach. In t case, a particular element is chosen for organizationwide implementati again without regard to the status of the various ongoing projects. Sir there is varied success based on the position of each project in its SLC, element tends to fade away due to decreasing application. When it is re ized that element is ineffective, the decision is made to try one of the othe It, too, eventually fails. As each element is tried in turn, each faces the sa fate. Finally, the decision is made to scrap the SQS because it is obviou not effective.

Both these implementation methods can work if consideration is giv to each project to which they will be applied. There must be recognition t each project will be in a different portion of its life cycle and thus will ha differing abilities, or needs, to comply with a new SQS. Provisions for dev tions from, or waivers of, specific requirements of the SQS based on t projects' needs must be allowed, which will make either method of imp mentation much more likely to succeed.

11.6.1 Single-project implementation

The all-at-once approach can be successful when the software quality sy tem is to be applied only to new projects.

One popular method of this type of implementation is to permit ongoi projects to complete on their own and to concentrate the software qual practitioners' efforts on new projects as they are begun. This has the dra back that some ongoing projects may be less successful since none of t system is formally applied to them. It has the advantage that no project h to change processes in the middle of its development. It is also likely th there are some portions of the SQS that will be adopted by the ongoing pr ects because they are seen to be of value and cause little disruption in t project's progress.

Another strong recommendation for this approach is in the data proces ing organization that experiences frequent project startup. Companies li defense contractors, which often have several dissimilar contracts starting and ending independently from one another, can use this method very successfully. It is often favored by software vendors as well because, again, there is wide project-to-project separation.

11.6.2 Single-element implementation

The one-element-at-a-time implementation picks one SQS element to impose on all projects, new and ongoing, but does so with careful consideration of each project's ability and need to conform to the element. This, too, can be a successful method of implementation, but it requires careful planning.

Two primary aspects of single element implementation must be considered: the order of implementation and the project benefit. Some SQS elements may add more value if implemented sooner, while some may actually have negative impact if implemented too soon.

Certainly, some elements are rather project-status independent. Portions of the education and security elements can be implemented irrespective of project status. Others, like documentation or CM, may require significant retrofitting of projects if implemented in the later phases of the SDLC.

An advantage of the single element approach is that each project has the opportunity to benefit from at least a portion of the overall SQS as early as possible. In this way, development personnel are able to see benefits of the system and tend to be more supportive of elements that are introduced later. A disadvantage is that new projects may not get the full benefit from the SQS because some of its elements are not yet in place.

The most likely type of organization to use the single element approach is that in which most of the development is closely related, for example, the more traditional in-house data processing for financial and business applications. Here, too, there is a rather steady flow of new projects, but they tend to be similar in nature. The single element approach allows each element to take root and become a routine part of the SDLC before another element is introduced.

11.6.3 Combined implementation

A combination of the two methods can be the best answer in most cases. As is the case in any discussion of methods or approaches, there is no single, always correct situation.

The single-project and single-element approaches are clearly the extremes of the implementation method spectrum. The single-project

approach would be successful in the information systems organization t
had no ongoing development projects to consider. The single-elem
approach could be the best answer if there is no new project activity. N
ther of these situations is likely to be the case in most organizations. 1
answer, obviously, is to fit the implementation method, or combination
implementation methods, to the actual experience of the particular orga
zation and to the specific projects being affected.

For new projects, it is almost always best to implement as much of 1
total system as possible. Only those elements that, in a given organizati
would conflict with ongoing projects should be delayed. An example mi;
be a new form of database security system that would seriously impact
ongoing development effort. In most cases, however, new projects can
started using the full SQS with little or no impact on the rest of the develc
ment activity.

Ongoing projects can be the subject of various subsets of the full S(
depending on their status and needs. Projects late in the SDLC proba
would be unaffected by the imposition of new programmer training 1
could benefit from increased user training requirements. A project early
the SDLC can be placed under more stringent CM procedures without mu
impact on completed work. Each project must be evaluated against the f
SQS, and those elements that are feasible should be implemented.

As the SQS is implemented and experience is gained with it, it should
evaluated and modified as appropriate. The experiences of each proj
should be considered and changes, additions, and deletions made. Pro
sions for deviations and waivers will make the actual implementation
each element to each project as smooth as possible. A study of the waive
and deviations will show the modifications that may be needed in the ov(
all system.

11.6.4 Adapting the SQS

It must be remembered that no one SQS is suited to all information syster
organizations. The elements presented in this text are the building block
but the organization itself is the architect of its specific SQS. Each eleme
will mean different things to different people. The various priorities, bu
ness considerations, political influences (both internal and external), a
many other factors will determine the provisions of the SQS for a speci
company.

In exactly the same manner, there will be adapting of the basic compar
SQS to meet the needs of each specific project. Contracts, visibility, offic

sponsorship, and other factors will affect the final contents of the project software quality plan and system.

It is desirable that each company develop a basic SQS. The SQS will present the minimum software quality requirements that must be met by all projects undertaken by the development groups. For each individual project, additional requirements may be added as the basic system is tailored to fit. The elimination of any portion or of the basic company SQS should be permitted only in the most justifiable of circumstances. All adaptation should be of an additive nature. The increase, not the reduction, of the potential for quality software should be the goal.

1.7   SQS improvement

One of the goals of the SQS is to find ways in which to improve the development and maintenance processes being applied to the software. Clearly, the SQS and its implementation are also a process. As a process, the SQS is open to review, assessment, and improvement. Several process investigation and evaluation avenues apply to the software quality process. Among the process evaluation approaches are as follows:

- Assessment of the process;
- Certification of the process;
- Recognition of process quality.

The goal of assessments, certifications, and awards should go beyond the single event. The results, winning or not, should serve as starting points for intentional improvement of the quality system or practitioner. It must be remembered that each of these events provides only a single snapshot of the situation at a specific time. Their real value is serving as a benchmark from which improvement can be addressed and measured.

11.7.1   Assessment

The most widely known of the process assessment approaches is that developed by the SEI. Founded to provide software development process evaluation for the DoD, the SEI has conceived the software CMMI. While the CMMI is specifically intended for the assessment of the software development process, it can be applied to the software quality process. By answering a series of questions about the process, an assignment of maturity level is accomplished.

The quality system is an integral part of the level determination, a
some of the questions are intended to assess its effectiveness. The answers
the quality system-oriented questions can give an idea of the maturity of t
quality process and indicate areas for its potential improvement.

11.7.2 Certification

Two types of certifications directed specifically at the quality system a
organizational and personal.

Organizational certification can be based on the ISO 9000 series of sta
dards (see Section 2.2.1). The standards can be used in-house as se
evaluation, or applied through assessments by third-party assessors. An i
house assessment cannot result in a recognized certification as can a thir
party assessment. The value of an in-house assessment is that it gives a p
ture of the effectiveness of the quality system within the needs a
resources of the organization. Third-party certification is of value when t
outside world needs to be considered or when absolute independence of t
assessors is desirable.

Personal certification of quality practitioners is available through t
American Society for Quality for most quality applications. The softwar
oriented Quality Assurance Institute administers certifications for both so
ware quality analysts and software testers. Personal certifications do n
guarantee that the SQS will succeed, but they do offer assurance that t
software quality practitioners are capable of their tasks.

11.7.3 Quality system awards

A number of awards for organizational quality system excellence are ava
able throughout the world. Many countries now have national quali
awards such as the Malcolm Baldrige Award in the United States. In add
tion, several individual states are also granting quality system excellen
awards. One such state award is the New York Excelsior Award. There a
also awards for individuals in the quality field such as the Japanese Demir
Award that can be presented to either organizations or individuals.

11.8 Summary

The software quality activities like hardware quality activities are a monito
ing and reporting function. The role of the SQS is to monitor the status an
progress of the software development and maintenance processes. It the

reports its findings to the level of management that has the authority to take any necessary corrective action.

Implementation of an SQS requires planning by the software quality group and the involvement of the affected groups.

Early in the planning stages, a statement of what the system will accomplish is necessary. A charter will describe the expectations and the authority of the SQS and group. Without management commitment, any quality system is unlikely to succeed. The charter demonstrates management's commitment to the SQS.

Involvement of the development groups is also necessary to the success of the SQS. Encouraging the groups to be monitored to have a say in what the monitoring will comprise ensures that the system will be met with reduced resistance when it is implemented.

Many system implementation schemes exist. No one approach is likely to be useful in all cases. Likewise, no one SQS will be appropriate in every case. Each system and its implementation must be tailored to the particular company needs and the project being addressed.

It is desirable in the case of the SQS itself that a minimum set of quality assurance functions be established. Each project may add to that minimum set, but none may do less. In that way, all software projects are monitored to some degree, and the likelihood of requirements compliance is raised.

Three important points should be made. First, software quality practitioners may, but usually do not, perform the various activities that constitute the SQS. The actual performance is carried out by those parts of the overall organization best qualified to perform them.

Second, the software quality practitioners are not an enforcement agency. Only decision-making management has the authority to enforce anything. Software quality practitioners only monitor and report.

Finally, software quality practitioners must be administratively and financially independent of the groups performing the functions that the practitioner is monitoring. Further, the software quality practitioner must report to at least the same organizational level as the monitored groups. That permits the software quality practitioner the freedom to report objectively to management.

1.9 The next step

For a discussion of the implementation of the software quality program, see the following:

Bernard J. Kramer, *Building Quality Software,* Upper Saddle River, NJ: Prentice H 1997.

David M. Wilson (ed.). *Implementing a Software Quality Management System,* Computational Mechanics (CD-ROM), 1998.

Additional reading

Bossert, James L., *Quality Function Deployment,* Milwaukee, WI: ASQC Press, 199

Florac, William A., and Anita D. Carlton, *Measuring the Software Process: Statistical Process Control for Process Improvement,* Reading, MA: Addison-Wesley, 1999.

Glass, Robert L., *Building Quality Software,* Upper Saddle River, NJ: Prentice Hall, 1997.

Hromi, John D. (ed.), *The Best on Quality,* Milwaukee, WI: ASQC Quality Press, 1995.

Schmidt, Warren H., and Jerome P. Finnigan, *TQManager: A Practical Guide for Managing a Total Quality Organization,* San Francisco: Jossey-Bass, 1993.

Thayer, R. H. (ed.), *Software Engineering Project Management,* Los Alamitos, CA: IEI Computer Society Press, 1988.

Vincent, James, et al., *Software Quality Assurance: Volume 1—Practice and Implementation,* Upper Saddle River, NJ: Prentice Hall, 1988.

Sample Outline of Software Development Plan*

Title Page
Revision Chart
Preface
Table of Contents
List of Figures
List of Tables

*Source: IEEE Standard 1958.1-1987; used with permission. Copyright 1987 IEEE. All rights reserved.

Sample Outline of SQS Plan*

*Based on IEEE Standard 730.1-1989; used with permission.

APPENDIX

C

Sample Outline of Configuration Management Plan*

*Based on IEEE Standard 828-1990; used with permission.

Sample Outline of Software Requirements Specification*

Sample Outline of Software Preliminary Design Specification*

*Adapted from IEEE Standard 1016-1987.

CHAPTER

F

Sample Outline of Software Detailed Design Specification*

*Adapted from IEEE Standard 1016-1987.

APPENDIX

Sample Outline of Test Plan (System)*

Sample Outline of Test Case*

1	Test Case Specification Identifier
2	Test Items
3	Input Specifications
4	Output Specifications
5	Environmental Needs
5.1	Hardware
5.2	Software
5.3	Other
6	Special Procedural Requirements
7	Intercase Dependencies

Sample Outline of Test Report*

*Based on IEEE Standard 829-1983; used with permission.

Sample Quality Management Charter

Scope:

It is the policy of the Management Information Service Organization to provide a SYSTEMS ASSURANCE function as an internal means of maintaining the quality and effectiveness of applications, facilities, and services provided by MIS.

A primary purpose of the Systems Assurance function is to assure that adequate MIS policies, standards, and guidelines exist and are followed in accordance with the company's strategic direction. The major emphasis is on the measuring and monitoring of the internal development and operational process at appropriate times ensuring quality systems and reduced business risk.

In defining the scope of Systems Assurance, the following should be highlighted:

1. The Systems Assurance function performs reviews from an internal MIS perspective primarily evaluating the installed systems development and methodology to assure through reviews that systems are being designed and implemented according to MIS policy, standards, and/or guidelines. Reviews of operational systems will determine the effectiveness of, and adherence to, policy and standards and design criteria related to overall controls and security features.

2. Systems Assurance reviews will frequently be conducted on N
    policies, procedures, standards, and/or operating guidelines with
    respect to a specific system. The internal coordination of these pro
    dures and standards from one MIS group to another (i.e., System
    D.P. Services) will be reviewed for effectiveness.

Responsibility:

The Systems Assurance function is responsible for the following functio

I. Systems Development Reviews

Conducts systems assurance phase reviews of MIS development projects
assure ADHERENCE TO established MIS policies, procedures, standar
and operating guidelines.

Systems Assurance reviews examining the adherence to established p
cedures and standards relative to specific projects will be conducted or
scheduled basis.

Selection of which systems will undergo an evaluation process will
primarily based on the significance of the application to business objectiv
operations, or strategic plans.

Selecting from the annual planned objectives of each group within M
Systems Assurance reviews objectives with the appropriate MIS develc
ment group's management and confirms the systems assurance schedu
On a quarterly basis, the schedule is reviewed with MIS management a
updated.

In conducting systems development reviews, a phased approach will
followed. A review will be conducted at the completion of each of the f
lowing phases: (See Sequence of Events)

▸ Systems Design Alternatives (SDA)

▸ Systems External Specifications (SES)

▸ Systems Internal Specifications (SIS)

▸ Implementation Phase (IMPL)

▸ Post Implementation (PIR)

Each review will, when applicable, evaluate the following criteria:

▸ design meets business/project/economic objective

- conformance to standards/guidelines
- clarity of material
- operating efficiency
- adequacy of controls/security considerations
- presence of restart and recovery consideration
- file/data retentions
- conversion procedures
- test procedures

The Systems Assurance staff will have reasonable access to all the information, records, and personnel of the project or activities under review. Certain sensitive information may require user approval for access during the review process. Systems will determine the need for user approval prior to the start of the review.

Formal reports, regarding accuracy of the findings and the achievability of recommendations will be agreed to by both Systems Assurance and the MIS area involved. (See Sequence of Events)

Systems Assurance will follow-up to ensure that all recommendations have a planned implementation date and are completed.

II. Standards Review

Systems Assurance develops and maintains program/plans for conducting systems assurance reviews to assure the ADEQUACY OF MIS policies, procedures, standards, and operating guidelines.

All MIS policies, procedures, standards, and operating guidelines in effect will be utilized by Systems Assurance as the base from which to conduct their reviews.

As well as using this information as a base, there is an inherent responsibility by Systems Assurance to recognize and report the need for change. Recommendations will be provided to the appropriate MIS group's management for approval and implementation. The MIS groups are as follows

- Data Processing Services
- Systems
- Office Information Services
- Planning & MIS Services

Policies, procedures, standards, and operating guidelines maintained utilized by these groups are subject to review and recommendations p vided by Systems Assurance.

III. Coordination-Audit

Upon notification by Internal Audit of EDP-related audit reports and fi ings relative to MIS, the Systems Assurance function will review the reco mendations as they relate to MIS policies, standards, and guidelines.

When applicable, Systems Assurance will review proposed chang improvements to policies and standards with MIS management. A fi report will be issued and the changes/improvements will be implemen by the responsible MIS area.

IV. Management Review

Annually, key operational systems will be selected by Systems Assurance review to determine adherence to standards, procedures, and operati guidelines.

One measure of selection would be based on the volume and frequen of incidence requiring corrective action. Also, Data Center or Systems ma agement can request a review based on their perspective of the syster condition.

Included in these operational reviews will be the examination of conti gency planning and file/data retention to guarantee adequate backu provisions.

Strategic planning responsibilities within MIS will necessitate invento type operational reviews to gain an insight into the current systems env ronment. Identification of the need to upgrade hardware and/or software be in line with future planning due to technology or standardization will recommended.

Acting in an MIS consultative capacity, selective reviews will be pe formed to evaluate the MIS procedures, standards, and guidelines bein followed.

V. Security Standards

Systems Assurance will interface with Data Services Security, Corpora Safety, and Corporate Security through periodic meetings to share in th establishment of uniform MIS safety and security standards and guidelines.

In response to MIS management requests, review of computer cente and/or systems development departments will be performed. The revie will cover existing safety and security operational and maintenance elements within the facility. Recommendations will be made to enhance protection and control through new or revised procedures or additional physical protection devices.

stems Assurance Review—Each Review Phase:

1. Systems presents a phase review of a given project to the user attended by Systems Assurance.
2. Documentation appropriate to the development phase is reviewed and additional input is provided by Systems when requested.
3. Findings and recommendations are drafted by Systems Assurance.
4. Draft is given to Systems for review.
5. Systems Assurance meets with Systems to discuss and correct report where required. Unresolved differences are brought to the attention of progressive levels of authority within MIS for resolution.
6. The report is formally issued to MIS management.
7. Systems drafts plans for implementation of recommendations and indicates recommendations that will be deferred or are considered impractical to implement as previously agreed.
8. Draft is given to Systems Assurance for review.
9. Systems Assurance meets with Systems to resolve differences and finalize report.
10. Report is issued with signatures from both parties.

Sample Software Safety Plan*

*Based on IEEE Standard 1228-1994; used with permission.

Sample Risk Management Plan*

*Based on IEEE Standard 1540-2001; used with permission.

271

(Describe the function or organization assigned responsibilit
for risk management within the organizational unit.)

10   Risk Management Orientation and Training
11   Risk Management Costs and Schedules
12   Risk Management Process Description
        (If there is an organizational risk management process that i
        being used for this project or situation, refer to it. If adaptatior
        the process is appropriate, describe the adaptations made.
        Describe the procedures that implement the risk manageme.
        process. If no organizational process exists, describe the risk,
        management process, and procedures to be used for the projec
        or situation.)
12.1   Risk Management Context
12.2   Risk Analysis
12.3   Risk Monitoring
12.4   Risk Treatment
        (Describe how risks are to be treated. If a standard
        management process exists for handling deviations or problem
        refer to this process. If risks require a separate risk treatmen
        activity due to specific circumstance, describe this activity.)
13   Risk Management Process Evaluation
        (Describe how this project or organization will gather and
        use measurement information to help improve the risk
        management process for the project and/or for the
        organization.)
13.1   Capturing Risk Information
13.2   Assessing the Risk Management Process
13.3   Generating Lessons Learned
14   Risk Communication
        (Describe how risk management information will be
        coordinated and communicated among stakeholders, such as
        what risks need reporting to which management level.)
14.1   Process Documentation and Reporting
14.2   Coordinating Risk Management with Stakeholders
14.3   Coordinating Risk Management with Interested Parties
15   Risk Management Plan Change Procedures and History

Acronyms

ANSI	American National Standards Institute
CA	configuration accounting
CC	configuration control
CCB	CCB
CDR	critical design review
CE	critical error
CI	configuration item
CID	configuration identification
CM	configuration management
CMM	Capability Maturity Model
CMMI	Capability Maturity Model Integrated
CMP	configuration management plan
COA	cost of achievement
COF	cost of failure
COQ	cost of quality
DoD	Department of Defense
EIA	Electronic Industries Association
FA	functional audit
FnPt	function point
I	involved
IEC	International Electrotechnical Commission
IEEE	Institute of Electrical and Electronics Engineers

ISO	International Organization for Standards
JTC1	Joint Technical Committee 1
KLOC	thousands of lines of code
LCL	lower control limit
LOC	lines of code
NIST	National Institute of Standards and Technology
P	primary
PA	physical audit
PDR	preliminary design review
PIR	postimplementation review
RTM	requirements traceability matrix
SC	standards committee
SDLC	software development life cycle
SDP	software development plan
SEI	Software Engineering Institute
SG	standards group
SLC	software life cycle
SQS	software quality system
SQSP	software quality system plan
SRR	software requirements review
Std	standard (IEEE designation)
STR	software trouble report
TTM	test traceability matrix
TRR	test readiness review
UCL	upper control limit
UDF	unit development folder

About the author

John W. Horch has an undergraduate degree in experimental statistics and an M.S. and a Ph.D. in information systems. He has been active in the software field for more than 45 years, of which some 40 years have been in software quality management. Dr. Horch has been granted professional certification as a software quality analyst, software test engineer, software quality examiner, and systems professional.

With extensive experience in the defense arena, Dr. Horch has worked on Army, Air Force, and Navy weapon systems in development, verification and validation, and quality management assignments. He designed systems for inventory control, configuration status accounting, secure data transmission, hardware test, and emulation of a military computer. He was responsible for documentation, standards, and software quality management on the Safeguard ABM system, and was manager of systems integrity for the International Systems Division of Sperry Univac. He also managed the Verification and Validation Section for Teledyne Brown Engineering and was director of quality for the COLSA Corporation.

In the commercial area, Dr. Horch developed and implemented formal software quality programs for large organizations, implemented and tested disaster recovery programs, performed detailed physical security risk analyses, and audited software quality and development programs for commercial enterprises.

Currently, in addition to international seminar and workshop presentations, Dr. Horch is active in verification and validation of documentation and software development programs. He reviews developers' software development, documentation, and quality programs on behalf of government and commercial clients.

Dr. Horch speaks regularly at conferences, symposia, and workshops worldwide. He is one of the authors of IEEE Standards 730-2002, 983-1985,

1074-1995, 1074.1-1995, and of ISO/IEC IS 12207 and Australian Stand
AS 3563-1988. He is the project editor for the revision of IEEE Stand
1074 and participates in the international work on ISO standards 15504 ä
9000-Part 3. He publishes on software quality management topics, refer
submitted papers for conferences and journals, and is a book reviewer
software-oriented technical magazines.

Active in several professional organizations, Dr. Horch is a former me
ber of the IEEE Standards Board, chaired its Procedures Audit Committ
and served on its New Standards Committee. He chaired the IEEE Compu
Society Software Engineering Standards Subcommittee for 7 years and v
the first IEEE CS representative to ISO/IEC JTC1/SC7.

Dr. Horch is a member of the board of advisors and has served as direc
of certification activities for the Quality Assurance Institute. He was
founding chairman of the Certification Board for Information Quality P
fessionals. He currently serves on the board of advisors for QAI (USA) a
QAI (India). Dr. Horch is a senior member of the IEEE and the ASQC an
member of the Quality Assurance Institute. Dr. Horch is the recipient of
IEEE Millennium Medal, the IEEE Computer Society's Golden Core awa
and the QAI Lifetime Achievement Award.

Index

Risk-Based E-Business Testing, Paul Gerrard and Neil Thompson

Secure Messaging with PGP and S/MIME, Rolf Oppliger

Software Fault Tolerance Techniques and Implementation, Laura L. Pullum

Software Verification and Validation for Practitioners and Managers, Second Edition, Steven R. Rakitin

Strategic Software Production with Domain-Oriented Reuse, Paolo Predonzani, Giancarlo Succi, and Tullio Vernazza

Successful Evolution of Software Systems, Hongji Yang and Martin Ward

Systems Modeling for Business Process Improvement, David Bustard, Peter Kawalek, and Mark Norris, editors

User-Centered Information Design for Improved Software Usability, Pradeep Henry

Workflow Modeling: Tools for Process Improvement and Application Development, Alec Sharp and Patrick McDermott

For further information on these and other Artech House titles, including previously considered out-of-print books now available through our In-Print-Forever® (IPF®) program, contact:

Artech House	Artech House
685 Canton Street	46 Gillingham Street
Norwood, MA 02062	London SW1V 1AH UK
Phone: 781-769-9750	Phone: +44 (0)20 7596-8750
Fax: 781-769-6334	Fax: +44 (0)20 7630-0166
e-mail: artech@artechhouse.com	e-mail: artech-uk@artechhouse.com

Find us on the World Wide Web at:
www.artechhouse.com

DATE DUE

SP
796.33
CLA

Clay, Kathryn
Datos geniales sobre futbol
(bilingual)

BC#32457121000081 $18.49

Morrill ES
Chicago Public Schools
6011 S. Rockwell St.
Chicago, IL 60629

W9-BBN-011

Datos geniales sobre deportes!/
Cool Sports Facts

Pebble®
Bilingüe/
Bilingual Plus

Datos geniales sobre
fútbol americano

Cool
Football
Facts

por/by Kathryn Clay

Editora consultora/Consulting Editor:
Gail Saunders-Smith, PhD

Consultor/Consultant: Craig Coenen, PhD
Profesor Adjunto de Historia/Associate Professor of History
Mercer County Community College
West Windsor, New Jersey

CAPSTONE PRESS
a capstone imprint

Pebble Plus is published by Capstone Press,
1710 Roe Crest Drive, North Mankato, Minnesota 56003.
www.capstonepub.com

Library of Congress Cataloging-in-Publication Data
Clay, Kathryn.
[Cool football facts. Spanish.]
Datos geniales sobre fútbol americano = Cool football facts / by Kathryn Clay.
p. cm. — (Pebble plus bilingüe/bilingual)
Includes index.
ISBN 978-1-4296-9214-4 (library binding)
ISBN 978-1-62065-338-8 (ebook PDF)
1. Football—Miscellanea—Juvenile literature. I. Title.
GV950.7.C59 2013
796.332—dc23   2011050105

Summary: Simple text and full-color photos illustrate facts about the rules, equipment, and records of football.

Editorial Credits
Erika L. Shores, editor; Strictly Spanish, translation services; Kyle Grenz, designer; Eric Manske, bilingual book designer and production specialist; Eric Gohl, media researcher

Photo Credits
AP Images/LM Otero, 21
Corbis/Bettmann, 19; Reuters/Tim Shaffer, 13
Dreamstime/Ken Durden, cover; Wisconsinart, 15
Getty Images Inc./George Gojkovich, 9; George Rose, 5; Michael Burr, 7; Nick Laham, 17
Landov LLC/Boston Globe/John Bohn, 11
Shutterstock/Trinacria Photo, cover (football), back cover, 1

Note to Parents and Teachers

The Datos geniales sobre deportes/Cool Sports Facts series supports national social studies standards related to people, places, and culture. This book describes and illustrates football. The images support early readers in understanding the text. The repetition of words and phrases helps early readers learn new words. This book also introduces early readers to subject-specific vocabulary words, which are defined in the Glossary section. Early readers may need assistance to read some words and to use the Table of Contents, Glossary, Internet Sites, and Index sections of the book.

Printed in the United States of America in North Mankato, Minnesota.
0620124   008228R

Table of Contents

Tabla de contenidos

Touchdown!

More than 90 million people watch the NFL Super Bowl on TV each year. In 1990, the San Francisco 49ers amazed fans with a record 55 points.

¡Touchdown!

Más de 90 millones de personas ven el Súper Tazón de la NFL por televisión cada año.

En 1990, los 49s de San Francisco asombraron a sus aficionados con un récord de 55 puntos.

NFL stands for National Football League.

NFL son las siglas en inglés de la Liga Nacional de Fútbol Americano.

5

Cool Equipment

Teams that play outside have 48 footballs ready for each game. Games played indoors use only 36 footballs.

Equipo genial

Los equipos que juegan en exteriores tienen 48 balones de fútbol listos para cada partido.

Los partidos que se juegan en interiores usan solo 36 balones de fútbol.

Quarterbacks started wearing radio headset helmets in 1994. Coaches talk to the quarterback from the sidelines.

Los mariscales de campo empezaron a usar cascos con radio en 1994. Los entrenadores hablan con los mariscales de campo desde las líneas laterales.

Cool Rules

Players can't celebrate too much
after a touchdown.
In 2008, Wes Welker
paid a $10,000 fine
for making a snow angel.

Reglas geniales

Los jugadores no pueden celebrar
demasiado después de un touchdown.
En 2008, Wes Welker pagó una
multa de $10,000 dólares por
hacer un ángel de nieve.

Players can't rough
the punter or kicker.
Breaking the rule is
a 15-yard penalty.

Los jugadores no pueden derribar
al despejador o pateador.
Romper esta regla tiene una
penalización de 15 yardas.

Cool Records

In 1894, deaf quarterback Paul Hubbard first used the huddle. He didn't want other teams to see his signs.

Récords geniales

En 1894, el mariscal de campo sordo Paul Hubbard fue el primero que usó la reunión en círculo o huddle. No quería que los otros equipos vieran sus señales.

As a starting quarterback,

Brett Favre has beaten

every team in the NFL.

He is the only player

to hold this record.

Como mariscal de campo iniciador,

Brett Favre ha derrotado a todos

los equipos de la NFL.

Él es el único jugador que

tiene este récord.

Kicker Tom Dempsey had
no toes on his right foot.
That didn't stop him from
kicking a 63-yard field goal.

El pateador Tom Dempsey no
tenía dedos en el pie derecho.
Esto no le impidió anotar un gol
de campo de 63 yardas.

Deion Sanders played
in both the NFL's Super Bowl
and Major League Baseball's
World Series.
No other athlete holds this record.

Deion Sanders jugó en el
Súper Tazón de la NFL y en la
Serie Mundial de las
Grandes Ligas de Béisbol.
Ningún otro atleta tiene este récord.

Glossary

deaf—being unable to hear

huddle—a group of football players planning the next move

penalty—a punishment for breaking the rules

rough—to tackle and knock down

sideline—the line that marks the edge of a football field

Super Bowl—the championship game of the National Football League

touchdown—a six-point score in a football game

Internet Sites

FactHound offers a safe, fun way to find Internet sites related to this book. All of the sites on FactHound have been researched by our staff.

Here's all you do:

Visit www.facthound.com

Type in this code: 9781429692144

Super-cool stuff!

Check out projects, games and lots more at
www.capstonekids.com

22

Glosario

derribar—taclear y tirar al suelo

el huddle—grupo de jugadores de fútbol americano que planean el siguiente movimiento

la línea lateral—la línea que marca la orilla del campo de fútbol americano

la penalización—castigo por romper las reglas

sordo—que no puede oír

el Súper Tazón—el partido de campeonato de la Liga Nacional de Fútbol Americano

el touchdown—un puntaje de seis puntos en un partido de fútbol americano

Sitios de Internet

FactHound brinda una forma segura y divertida de encontrar sitios de Internet relacionados con este libro. Todos los sitios en FactHound han sido investigados por nuestro personal.

Esto es todo lo que tienes que hacer:

Visita www.facthound.com

Ingresa este código: 9781429692144

Index

Índice